SMOLLETT'S REPUTATION
AS A NOVELIST

PRINCETON STUDIES IN ENGLISH

No. 27

SMOLLETT'S
REPUTATION
AS A NOVELIST

By Fred W. Boege

1969

OCTAGON BOOKS

New York

89864

Reprinted 1969
by special arrangement with Princeton University Press

OCTAGON BOOKS
A DIVISION OF FARRAR, STRAUS & GIROUX, INC.
19 Union Square West
New York, N. Y. 10003

LIBRARY OF CONGRESS CATALOG CARD NUMBER: 75-96150

Printed in U.S.A. by
NOBLE OFFSET PRINTERS, INC.
NEW YORK 3, N. Y.

PREFACE

Some writers settle easily and at once into their proper place
in the scale of literary values. As their merits were assessed
by their contemporaries, so they have been esteemed by succeeding
generations, and a survey of the even course of their fame leads
to the conclusion that there are as much certainty and continuity
in literary criticism as in most other departments of earthly affairs. The reputation of other authors has been subject to violent fluctuations, now being inflated by extravagant praise, now
depressed by unmerited contempt. As we examine the judgments
once passed on these men, we reap a goodly share of that amusement
which comes from observing the aberrations of our forefathers as
they groped toward the enlightenment of the present age.

Smollett unquestionably belongs in the second group. His reputation has suffered more vicissitudes in two centuries than Horace's
in two millenniums. His writings have been recommended to young
ladies, as tending to protect their chastity; they have been called
fit manuals for the courtesan. Competent critics have declared certain passages in his work to be the most pathetic in all literature;
other competent critics have found him the most brutal and unfeeling
of novelists. These antipodal attitudes are not so much the result
of individual temperament as the reflection of changing conventions
and tastes. There are personal eccentricities, to be sure; yet each
age seems to have its own dominant, almost semi-official attitude
toward Smollett. So with his popularity. At one time perhaps the
most widely read novelist in England, at another time he becomes so
esoteric that the ability to name one of his books is a mark of
learning.

There is interesting variety, then, in the story of Smollett's
reputation. There is instruction, too, for if in this welter of
conflicting opinions a critic may not enlighten us on Smollett, he
invariably does tell us something about himself and his age. There
is also satisfaction in piecing out the scanty literature about a
man whose work evoked the high praise of such giants as Johnson,
Burke, Burns, Wordsworth, Coleridge, Hazlitt, Lamb, Keats, Carlyle,
and Dickens.

Something should be said about the scope of the ensuing investigation. This is a study of Smollett's reputation, not of his
influence. Accordingly, even the most obvious examples of his
influence on later works have generally been ignored. As for the
material covered, for the years 1748 to 1800 (in America to 1820),

the volumes of every available literary periodical were examined, as well as the works of all authors not completely insignificant in literary history; and any other sources thought likely to yield useful material were investigated. From 1800 on, the treatment has been increasingly selective on the principle that a reverse perspective operating in these matters tends to make that which is most remote loom largest in our mind's eye. In the later chapters, then, I have tried to do only two things: to report the opinion of Smollett held by the major writers, and to give such additional evidence as seemed to reveal a general trend. The study has been confined to England and the United States for several reasons, among them the existence of Joliat's *Smollett et la France.*

My earnest thanks are due to Professor Emory Holloway and Professor George B. Parks of Queens College for their helpful suggestions; also to Professor Donald A. Stauffer of Princeton University for much valuable advice based on a reading of the entire manuscript. To Professor Gordon Hall Gerould of Princeton University I cannot adequately express my indebtedness, but I hope that the work which follows will bespeak to him some part of my obligation and gratitude.

CONTENTS

CHAPTER I

The Foundation of Smollett's Fame
1748-1751

*Those who now read the novels of Fielding,
Richardson, Smollett, or Scott, neither read
nor care to read what was written about them
by the reviewers of their own time.*
                    Edward Robert Bulwer Lytton

Not long ago we observed the two-hundredth birthday of the
English novel. Rich as the legacy of these two centuries has
been, it would be difficult to find a more fruitful year than
1748. Thousands of Richardson's devotees were at last being rewarded for their patience as Clarissa, in a series of monthly
curtsies, enraptured them with all the tearful enjoyment they
had anticipated. *Tom Jones*, well nigh finished, was being read
in manuscript by Fielding's many friends and was already well
known through the enthusiastic praises of Lord Lyttelton. The
one book was widely hailed then as the greatest of all novels;
the other has since often been honored by that title. This con-
junction of Venus and Jupiter in the fictional empyrean did not
mark an auspicious time for a young and unchampioned novelist to
light his candle, but Tobias Smollett had already formed the
habit of acting in his own worst interest.

Prior to the publication of *Roderick Random* in 1748,
Smollett had done nothing to cause his name to be inscribed on
those contemporary records which have come down to us. He had
written some verse, which his friend Alexander Carlyle referred
to, under the year 1746, as follows:

> I saw not Smollett again for some time after, when he
> showed Smith and me the manuscript of his *Tears of Scotland*,
> which was published not long after, and had such a run of
> approbation. Smollett, though a Tory, was not a Jacobite,
> but he had the feelings of a Scotch gentleman on the re-
> ported cruelties that were said to be exercised after the
> battle of Culloden.[1]

But there is no record of the publication of this poem until 1767, when it appeared anonymously.[2] The 'run of approba-

[1] A. Carlyle, pp. 155-156.
[2] John P. Anderson's bibliography appended to Hannay's *Life of Smollett*, p. vi.

tion' must have been confined to a small circle of Smollett's Scotch friends. Nor is there any evidence that *Advice* or *Reproof,* his poetic satires, brought the name of the young Scotch author before the public. But as a result of his activities on behalf of the *Regicide,* Smollett must have been known to several prominent people as a dramatist -- more persistent than talented. On this point we do have one bit of evidence in Garrick's letter to the Reverend John Hoadley of September 14, 1746.

> I have a Play now with Me, sent to me by My Lord Chesterfield & wrote by one Smollett. it is a Scotch Story, but it won't do, & yet recommended by his Lordship & patroniz'd by Ladies of Quality: what can I say or do? must I belye my Judgment or run the risque of being thought impertinent, & disobliging ye great Folks?[3]

> Beyond this we hear nothing of Smollett as a man of letters before 1748.

Despite the competition it encountered, there is no doubt that *Roderick Random* was an immediate success. Fortunately, we now have direct evidence to corroborate the statements of Smollett's biographers on this point. A few years ago Lewis M. Knapp was able to gain access to the printing records of the publisher Strahan, which show that the first edition of the novel numbered 2000 copies; the second edition, 3000 copies; and the third edition, 1500 copies, or a total of 6500 copies by November, 1749.[4] This is a huge number for the times, as we see by comparisons with other successful novels. *Joseph Andrews* sold just about an equal number of copies in thirteen months,[5] but Fielding was by no means an unknown author in 1742. *Tom Jones,* indeed, overshadowed all novels but those of Richardson: ten thousand copies were distributed in less than one year;[6] yet even in comparison with this almost unique record, Smollett's success appears very creditable. In the latter part of the century, when the number of novel-readers in Great Britain was no doubt far larger, the sale of *Roderick Random* would still have been remarkable: witness a letter from Fanny Burney to her father in October, 1786, stating that the first edition of *Evelina* numbered 800 copies, the second 500, the third, 1000. 'Of "Cecilia" the first edition was reckoned enormous at two thousand.'' And of her later work she wrote: 'The sale (of *Camilla*) is truly astonishing. Charles has just sent to me that five hundred only remain of four thousand, and it has appeared scarcely three months.'[7]

3 *Some Unpublished Correspondence of David Garrick,* p.37.
4 'Smollett's Works as Printed by William Strahan,' *Library,* XIII (1932), pp.283–284.
5 W.L.Cross, *Henry Fielding,* I, 357.
6 'Smollett's Works as Printed by William Strahan,' *Library,* XIII (1932), p.284.
7 F. D'Arblay, *Diary and Letters,* VI, 65–66.

Further evidence is supplied by the record of early editions of *Roderick Random*. A second edition was called for in about three months, or in April, 1748.[8] There is a Dublin 'third edition' of 1749, a London third in 1750, a fourth in 1754, and a fifth in 1760.[9] An account of later eighteenth century editions will be found on page 45.

It was not long before Smollett's success began to be reflected by references to him in contemporary documents of one sort or another. As early as February 15, 1748, we find Miss Talbot writing to Mrs. Carter:

> There is, to tempt me out, a new comedy, which I hear much commended, and which is well acted. Now I name acting, have you read that strange book Roderic Random! It is a very strange and a very low one, though not without some characters in it, and I believe some very just, though very wretched descriptions. Among others, there is the history of a poor tragedy author, ill used by actors and managers, that I think one cannot but be touched with, when one considers how many such kinds of scenes there are every day in real life.[10]

Thus at the very beginning we find two notes struck - Smollett's fidelity to life and his lowness - whose variations seem to have been inexhaustible. That the first point would necessarily lead to the second was a later discovery. A few weeks later Roderick's fame had reached Ireland. The Earl of Orrery wrote to Thomas Carew from Caledon on March 12th that *'Clarissa* kept us up till two in the morning. *Rhoderic* will keep us up all night, and he, I am told, is to be succeeded again by *Clarissa.*[11] Some time during the year a dramatic hack sought to profit from the popularity of the novel with a wretched play entitled *The Northern Heroes; or The Bloody Contest . . . With a Comic Interlude, call'd The Volunteers; Or, the Adventures of Roderick Random, And his Friend Strap.* 'As it is now acting by a Company of Comedians from both the Theatres, at the Great Booth in the George Yard, in West-Smithfield.' Beyond the similarity of names, and the common picaresque situation of master and servant on a battlefield, there is not even a remote connection between this piece and the novel. It is not impossible, therefore, that the names of Roderick and Strap were substituted for others in an already completed composition, when it was realized that the growing fame of these two characters would make such a change profitable.

An author's testimony as to the popularity of his own works is usually of debatable value, to be sure, but Smollett's letter

---

8 *Jacobite's Journal*, April 16, 1748.
9 The date for the fourth edition is taken from Knapp's article in *Library* cited above. Copies of the other editions are at Yale Library.
10 *A Series of Letters between Mrs. Elizabeth Carter and Miss Catherine Talbot*, I, 210.
11 *The Orrery Papers*, II, 23.

of June 7 to his friend Alexander Carlyle has a ring of sincerity that makes it worth inserting here. Moreover, what he says seems to be borne out by the number of people who in later years claimed the honor of being the original of Strap or of some other of his characters.

> I am not a little mortified to find the characters strangely misapplied to particular men whom I never had the least intention to ridicule,- by which means I have suffered very much in my moral capacity. Some persons, to whom I have been extremely obliged, being weak enough to take umbrage at many passages in the work on the supposition that I myself am the hero of the book, and they of consequence concerned in the history. I take the opportunity of declaring to you, in all the sincerity of the most unreserved friendship, that no person living is aimed at in all the first part of the book, that is, while the scene is laid in Scotland; and that (the account of the expedition to Carthagena excepted) the whole is not so much a representation of my life as that of many other needy Scotch surgeons whom I have known either personally or by report. The character of Strap (who I find is a favourite among the ladies) is partly taken from life, but the circumstances of his attachment are entirely feigned.[12]

It is early in the next year, 1749, that we find the *Gentleman's Magazine* printing the first periodical reference to Smollett. A reference in a footnote to a sermon on 'A Persuasive to Chastity' by Edw. Cobden, D.D., begins as follows:

> Of this wretched state, a most lively and striking picture is exhibited in *Roderick Random*, which we have copied as a warning to one sex, and a remonstrance against t'other.

> Miss *Williams*, who had been betray'd into a course of vice, by the fraud and cruelty of a man of pleasure, is introduced relating the story of her own misfortunes.[13]

And her story follows. In view of the treatment which the moralists later bestowed upon Smollett, it is ironical that this first reference to him in public print - under circumstances not altogether unlike Dr. Slocock's recommendation of *Pamela* from his pulpit - should praise him for his ethical value. And in the *Gentleman's Magazine*, of all places! The *Monthly Review* also noticed Smollett in 1749. Among other highly complimentary remarks on the *Regicide*, it spoke of the preface with its 'strokes of humour, and portraiture, peculiar to the author of *Roderick Random*.'[14]

It must have been at about this same time, 1749, that Laetitia Pilkington penned the following lines, *a propos de bottes*, in her *Memoirs:*

---

12 *The Letters of Tobias Smollett, M.D.*, pp. 7–8.
13 *Gentleman's Magazine*, XIX, (1749), 126.
14 *Monthly Review*, I (1749), 72.

Stand apart now, ye Roderick Randoms,
Foundlings, bastard sons of wit,
Hence ye profane, be far away,
All ye that bow to idol lusts, and altars raise,
Or to false heroes give fantastic praise.[15]

Further evidence of the popularity of the novel, and this from a
more respectable source, appears in a letter by Mrs. Delany addressed to Mrs. Dewes, dated about August, 1750, wherein she
stated that she had read *Roderick Random*.[16] Perhaps it is as
well that she did not make any comment; Richardsonian as she was
she probably would have liked this work no better than the next
two novels by Smollett.

What of Smollett's two great confreres? Neither had anything to say, at least for the time, although Fielding, it will
be remembered, in his announcement of the Court of Criticism in
the *Jacobite's Journal* (January 9, 1748) had written: 'In this
Court we intend, moreover, to recommend all Books and Writings,
which have the least Merit in them, to the Public.' Professor
Cross notes the 'glaring exception' of *Roderick Random* and offers
the explanation: 'Unfortunately Smollett was a Scotsman, and that
meant a probable Jacobite.'[17] Richardson's silence probably
needs no explanation; his opinion, if he read the book, must have
been unfavorable. That he at least knew of Smollett's existence
at this time is indicated by the fact that early in 1749 he sent
a copy of the *Regicide* to Jane Collier, the novelist.[18]

The number of early references to Smollett is not impressive;
it seems even more meagre when compared to the avalanche of notices and opinions which greeted *Clarissa* and *Tom Jones*. Why was
so little attention paid to Smollett? The first and most obvious
reason is that these two works were undoubtedly recognized then,
as they have been almost ever since, as clearly superior to
Roderick Random. Yet this recognition in itself hardly seems to
account for the great disparity in the reception of the three
novels. *Roderick Random*, selling about half as well as *Tom Jones*,
evoked scarcely a tithe of the notices.

Professor Cross, observing a similar situation after the appearance of *Joseph Andrews*, states that 'it takes time for a novel
to get into letters and memoirs outside an author's circle of
friends.'[19] *Joseph Andrews* received more attention after the success of *Tom Jones*; the phenomenon is common enough in literary
history. We must also keep in mind the situation mentioned at

15 Laetitia Pilkington, III, 350.
16 Mary G. Delany, II, 582.
17 W.L.Cross, *Henry Fielding*, II, 91.
18 Samuel Richardson, *Correspondence*, II, 65.
19 W.L.Cross, *Henry Fielding*, I, 357.

the beginning of this chapter. A young novelist could hardly
have chosen a worse time to make his bid for fame and fortune
than the early months of 1748. At least, if there is any exception to this statement, it would be that memorable year a century
later, when *Dombey and Son* and *Vanity Fair* were appearing in
monthly installments, and the three Bronte sisters made their
startling entrance into the lists. But in Smollett's lifetime
1748 was the year of great novels. Both Richardson and Fielding
had a name and a following before the appearance of their masterpieces; Smollett was unknown.

Conditions were different in 1751. Not only had Smollett
made himself known by that time, but the establishment of the
Monthly Review two years previously meant that any new work of
even moderate distinction would be greeted with critical notices –
for other periodicals were quick to imitate the review feature of
the *Monthly*. Among these was the *Gentleman's Magazine*, but
Peregrine Pickle was not one of the books favored with the notice of this oracle. The *Royal Magazine*, however, printed a
rather detailed summary of the novel, prefaced by these remarks:

> The author of these adventures, is the same gentleman
> who some years since published, those of Roderick Random,
> and it is probably owing to the reception of that work met
> with from its readers, that the author has again appeared
> as a writer in the romantic biographical way, and now
> offer'd the adventures of Mr. Pickle to the perusal of the
> public.[22]

The *Monthly Review* opened its notice by condemning fiction filled
with romantic impossibilities, and praising that which deals with
real life. After a reference to *Roderick Random,* 'which has
been so well received by the public, as to encourage his entering
on the present work,' the reviewer admits that Smollett has not
always observed the strict rules of propriety and quotes the incident of Mrs. Trunnion's perforated chamber-pot as evidence. But
no condemnation is implied by the reviewer himself, who merely
observes that some of the most humorous adventures in other works
deal with a similar topic. The whole account, indeed, is distinctly favorable.[23]

But what was the public reaction to the book? What sort of
comments were called forth from its readers? Howard S. Buck, in
his *A Study in Smollett*, states that Lady Vane's 'Memoirs' virtually monopolized the attention of the public. He quotes seven
or eight notices which appeared within a year, all of them ignor-
ing everything else in the novel to speak only of the 'Memoirs.'[24]

22 *Royal Magazine*, II (1751), 396–397.
23 *Monthly Review*, IV (1751), 355–364.
24 Pp. 48–52.

Further evidence only strengthens Buck's conclusion. If Smollett
inserted the 'Memoirs' in order to attract attention to his book,
he succeeded only too well; so well that perhaps before long he
regretted his action.

Early references to *Peregrine Pickle* among letter-writers,
for example, deal amost exclusively with the 'Memoirs.' Thus,
Samuel Richardson's sole reference to any of Smollett's novels is
the following, which occurs in a letter to Mrs. Chapone dated
January 11, 1751: 'I send to your worthy Son . . . that Part of a
bad Book which contains the very bad Story of a wicked woman. I
could be glad to see it animadverted upon by so admirable a Pen.'[25]
Horace Walpole had his inevitable comment on the latest bit of
gossip:

> There have been two events, not political, equal to any
> absurdities or follies of former years. My Lady Vane has
> literally published the Memoirs of her own life, only sup-
> pressing part of her lovers, no part of the success of the
> others with her: a degree of profligacy not to be accounted
> for; she does not want money, none of her stallions will
> raise her credit; and the number, all she had to brag of,
> concealed.[26]

Nor are we disappointed when we turn to the almost equally omniscient Lady Mary. Writing to her daughter, the Countess of Bute,
she acknowledged receipt of a case of books:

> . . . the entertainment they have already given me has
> recompensed me for the long time I expected them. I began
> by your direction with Peregrine Pickle. I think Lady V's
> Memoirs contain more truth and less malice than any I ever
> read in my life . . . . Her style is clear and concise, with
> some strokes of humour, which appear to me so much above her,
> I can't help being of opinion the whole has been modelled by
> the author of the book in which it is inserted, who is some
> subaltern admirer of hers. I may judge wrong, she being no
> acquaintance of mine, though she has married two of my rela-
> tions.[27]

And so on, with considerably more about Lady Vane, but no word for
Peregrine or his friends.

A few writers do acknowledge the existence of other portions
of *Peregrine Pickle* than the 'Memoirs,' but only to express their
disapproval. Gray (who also disapproved of Fielding) wrote to
Horace Walpole on March 3rd:

> Has that miracle of *tenderness and sensibility* (as she
> calls it) Lady Vane given you any amusement? *Peregrine,*
> whom she uses as a vehicle, iis very poor indeed, with a few
> exceptions. In the last volume is a character of Mr. Lyttel-
> ton, under the name of "Gosling Scrag," and a parody of part
> of his Monody, under the notion of a Pastoral on the death of
> of his grandmother.[28]

25 Quoted from the Forster MSS. in the Victoria and Albert Museum by McKillop, p. 180.
26 *Letters of Horace Walpole*, III, 37.
27 *Letters and Works of Lady Mary Montagu*, ed. W. May Thomas, II, 227-228.
28 *Letters of Thomas Gray*, I, 212.

Mrs. Delany, after writing to Mrs. Dewes on April 6, 1751: 'You *do not* recommend *Peregrine Pickle:* so I shall *not* buy it,'[29] later succumbed to the curiosity aroused by Smollett's much-bruited work. On October 7, 1759, she referred to *Peregrine* again, in terms much like those of Gray:

> At candlelight D.D., and I read by turns, and what do *you think* has been part of our study? - why truly Peregrine Pickle! We never undertook it before, but *it is wretched stuff;* only Lady V.'s history is a curiosity. What a wretch![30]

Lady Luxborough's letter to Shenstone of May 27, 1751, is of special interest because of her direct statement concerning the effect of the 'Memoirs' on the popularity of the book.

> Peregrine Pickle I do not admire: it is by the author of Roderick Random, who is a lawyer: but the thing which makes the book sell, is the History of Lady V---, which is introduced (in the last volume, I think) much to her Lady-ship's dishonour; but published by her *own* order, from her *own* Memoirs, given to the author for that purpose; and by the approbation of her *own* Lord. What was ever equal to this fact? and how can one account for it?[31]

Shenstone must have rebuked her taste in reading, for she excused herself in her letter of August 25th, and took the opportunity of condemning the work more explicitly.

> As to *Peregrine Pickle,* I hired it, and that merely for the sake of reading one of the volumes, wherein are in-serted the Memoirs of Lady V---; which, as I was well ac-quainted with her, gave me curiosity. The rest of the book is, I think, ill wrote, and not interesting.[32]

There is, finally, one favorable notice to record, though it is doubtful whether Smollett was included in the praise. Elizabeth Montagu wrote to her sister Sarah Scott early in 1752: 'I recom-mend to your perusal "The Adventures of Peregrine Pickle." Lady Vane's story is well told.'[33]

Like the letters, the verses and other periodical notices elicited by the occasion were also concerned exclusively with Lady Vane. Buck mentions only one of these, the following lines which he quotes from the *Ladies' Magazine* for June, 1751 (they had already appeared in the *British Magazine* for May):

To Lady V--e

As is your person without fault,
So should your conduct be,
For what avails a beauteous form,
When stampt with Infamy.

29 Mary G. Delany, III, 34.

30 *Ibid.,* III, 162.

31 *Letters written by . . . Lady Luxborough to William Shenstone,* pp. 265–266. Lady Lux-borough's mistake about Smollett's profession may be explained by the fact that she lived in the country.

32 *Ibid.,* 290–291.

33 Emily J. Climenson, II, 2.

> If you'd not give up worldly ease
>   For titles, wealth, and fame,
> Nor forfeit every hope of heav'n,
>   To gain contempt and shame:
>
> Hate vice, let virtue be your guide,
>   For all her paths are peace,
> And nobly toil to make your mind,
>   As beauteous as your face.[34]

But several other poems appeared at this time besides the one above cited by Buck. The following tribute appeared in both the *London Magazine* and the *Universal Magazine* for March, and was widely copied during the succeeding months.

The Heroines: or, Modern Memoirs

> In ancient times, some hundred winters past,
> When British dames for conscience sake were chaste,
> If some frail nymph, by youthful passion sway'd,
> From virtue's paths incontinent had stray'd;
> When banish'd reason re-assum'd her place,
> The conscious wretch bewail'd her foul disgrace;
> Fled from the world and pass'd her joyless years
> In decent solitude and pious tears:
> Veil'd in some convent made her peace with heav'n,
> And almost hop'd - by prudes to be forgiven.
> Not so of modern wh - s th' illustrious train,
> Renown'd Constantia, Pilkington, and -----,
> Grown old in sin, and dead to am'rous joy,
> No acts of pena(n)ce their great souls employ;
> Without a blush behold each nymph advance,
> The luscious horoine (sic) of her own romance;
> Each harlot triumphs in her loss of fame,
> And boldly prints and publishes her shame.[35]

In the *Magazine of Magazines* for April a correspondent dilates on the annoying habits of persistent authors. 'Go on, and the next beggar you shall meet is an author, who scarce says a word - - - 'Tis only, - - - *The history of a foundling* - - - *The adventures of Peregrine Pickle* - - - *The Scribleriad* - - -.'[36] In the same issue of this periodical appeared an extract from *Peregrine Pickle* - selected, of course, from the 'Memoirs.' The *London Magazine* for June contained a poem 'On the two celebrated Miss G---,' the third stanza of which is as follows:

> Of beauty let V--e with much arrogance boast,
> Yield, P--m, yield, you're no longer a toast;
> Attend all ye beaux and view maids form'd to please,
> Those Helens I own, but two Venus's these.[37]

By the end of the year the 'Memoirs' were still a live subject, if we may judge from lines in the *London Magazine* under the title 'On Miss Gunning's first Coming from Ireland,' which seem to be a variant of the above.

---

34 *British Magazine*, 1751, p. 256 (title page missing).
35 *London Magazine*, XX (1751), 135—136.
36 *Magazine of Magazines*, I (1751), 287.
37 *London Magazine*, XX (1751), 279.

<pre>
      Shall P--rf--m reign publick toast
         In country and in town?
      And V--ne with arrogance still boast
         That all the world's her own?
</pre>

Farther on in the same piece comes the following stanza:

<pre>
      Let me, mamma, now quit this chain,
         And but for this once try;
      I'll have my lords as well as V-ne,
         Or know the reason why.³⁸
</pre>

   Meanwhile, for reasons not always creditable to Smollett,
his name was getting into the publications of some of his fellow-
authors. John Hill in his *Inspector* satirized Smollett under the
name of Smallhead. The novelist was admonished by Genius that
'until he understood more of Human Nature, and could distinguish
better between Satire and Scurrility, he could not have the
leave of the Court to print again.'[39] In this same year, Hill
was also one of two writers to make the inevitable comparison between Smollett and Fielding, a comparison which runs through the
whole course of Smollett criticism up to the present time, and
which has done as much as any single circumstance, perhaps, to
prevent his fame from being greater than it is. Both comparisons
of 1751 were, prophetically, unfavorable to Smollett. Hill, in
his account in *The London Daily Advertiser* 'had given the palm to
the author of "Tom Jones" above all the "imitators" of that novel,
including Smollett.'[40] The other writer, the anonymous author of
the *Essay on the New Species of Writing founded by Mr. Fielding,*
complained that the sect of biographers founded by Fielding was
already so numerous that some attempt was necessary to put a stop
to them. He hoped that these sheets would 'hinder the weak, sickly Birth of a Joe Thompson, Charlotte Summers, or Peregrine Pickle
in Embrio.'[41] Fielding was praised for not giving away the story
in advance. 'Tis to be wish'd this Custom had been observ'd by
the Author of *Roderick Random,* who tells us in his Preface, his
Book is wrote in Imitation of the *Gil Blas* of Monsieur Le Sage.
But with very little Success in my humble opinion. As to the
Titles of his Chapters, he is particularly tedious in them.'[42]

   'Thus we see that Fielding's great achievement had so completely overshadowed all others that, in the eyes of some, Smollett was merely one undistinguished name among others now completely forgotten. More than that, he was set down as the imi-
tator of a book which had not appeared until a year after the
publication of his own first and most characteristic novel. This
error has not died easily. Smollett may very well have profited

38 *Ibid.,* 568.
39 John Hill, p. 75.
40 Quoted from Cross, *Henry Fielding,* II, 391.
41 *Essay on the New Species of Writing,* pp. i–ii.
42 *Ibid.,* p. 23.

by the reading of *Joseph Andrews,* but more than one later critic
implies, if he does not actually state, that the Smollettean novel
was in some way vastly indebted to *Tom Jones.*

It is interesting to notice that even Fielding's two references to *Peregrine Pickle* are confined to the 'Memoirs.' In the
first of these, although no names are mentioned, it can hardly be
doubted that he was thinking of Lady Vane. It occurs in *Amelia,*
where, after narrating that Booth and Miss Matthews were locked
up together by the governor of the jail where they were sojourn-
ing, Fielding continued:

> In imitation of him we will lock up likewise a scene
> which we do not think proper to expose to the eyes of the
> public. If any over-curious readers should be disappointed
> on this occasion, we will recommend such readers to the
> apologies with which certain gay ladies have lately been
> pleased to oblige the world, where they will possibly find
> everything recorded that past at this interval.[43]

As for the second reference, early in the next year, 1752, probably as a result of Smollett's unpleasant remarks about him in
Peregrine Pickle, under the name of Spondy, he made a more
direct attack through the *Covent-Garden Journal,* in his account
of the paper war.

> A little before our March, however, we sent a large
> Body of Forces, under the Command of General A. Millar, to
> take Possession of the most eminent Printing-Houses. The
> greater Part of these were garrisoned by Detachments from
> the Regiment of Grub-Street, who all retired at the Approach
> of our Forces. A small Body, indeed, under the Command of
> one Peeragrin Puckle, made a slight Show of Resistance; but
> his Hopes were soon found to be in *Vain;* and, at the first
> Report of the Approach of a younger Brother of General Thomas
> Jones, his whole Body immediately disappeared, and totally
> overthrew some of their own Friends, who were marching to
> their Assistance, under the Command of one Rodorick Random.
> This Rodorick, in a former Skirmish with the People called
> Critics, had owed some slight Success more to the Weakness.
> of the Critics, than to any Merit of his own.[44]

Another account of this war appeared in the *Have-at-you-all*
of Bonnell Thornton, which, as Cross says, attacked or parodied
almost everything in Fielding's periodical. Thornton introduces
his account thus:

> Sir Alexander Drawcansir having thought fit to publish
> a most partial and scandalous Account of his late Quixote
> Expedition, I have procur'd with vast pains and assiduity
> the proper authentic materials, and employ'd an old Veteran
> . . . to draw them up.

---

43 *Amelia,* Book IV, ch. i.
44 *Covent-Garden Journal,* No. 2, Jan. 7, 1752. Without dissenting in any essential from the
   verdict which has been passed on the merits of Fielding and Smollett in this
   controversy, one may wonder whether the tone of Professor Cross's comment is not,
   perhaps, a little too favorable to Fielding: 'Fielding's reference to Roderick
   Random and Peeragrin Puckle were merely in a spirit of fun, without satirical
   intent. Still, by giving these gentlemen commands in the army of the enemy, he
   really classed Smollett, if the author wished to take it that way, among the
   Grub Street writers.' Cross, *Henry Fielding,* II, 397.

11

The Champion takes the field,

> Then, meeting with one Pickle at the head of a troop
> of Novellists (with whom he had before an encounter, in
> which he was slightly wounded by a *Random* shot,) he left
> him to dispute the field with his noseless Amazon Amelia.

It is worth noticing that both Fielding and Thornton here
add their testimony concerning the success of *Roderick Random*.
Thornton's *Have-at-you-all* purports to be by Roxana Termagant.
Saying that all sorts of guesses have been made concerning her
identity, Thornton continues:

> I have also had the honour to be mistaken for some
> one of those Female Apologists, who have admitted us into
> the privacy of their most secret (I might say, most scan-
> dalous) intrigues. The ladies of quality will have it,
> that no one but the Right Honourable Memoir-Writer in P.
> Pickle's Adventures could have attack'd the *loose* part of
> Sir Alexander's (Fielding's) essays, as no woman, they
> are sure, could express herself so *feelingly* on those sub-
> jects as her Ladyship.[45]

Finally, at this time, we find Smollett's novels included
among the targets of Kenrick's satire in his play entitled *Fun*.
Among the characters is Sir Nackadil Trunnion, Kt., who, however,
bears no relation to Smollett's creation except in name. In the
first scene of the play, three witches make a potion wherein
they throw *Pasquin*, *Tom Thumb*, *Pamela*, *Clarissa*, *Random*, *Loveill*,
Pickle, and a noseless wench.

A discussion of the imitations of *Peregrine Pickle*, or
rather of the 'Memoirs,' does not fall within the limit of this
study, since this is an account of Smollett's reputation, not of
his influence. With but very few exceptions, no attention will
be paid to works which may well have been influenced by him, unless the indebtedness has been pointed out by the author himself
or by third parties who, through their statements concerning the
relationship, reveal something of their own attitude towards
Smollett.

In summarizing our evidence thus far, we note first that
Smollett had an undoubted popular success in *Roderick Random*. It
is this book above all others which has ever since been associated with his name. The Legend 'By the author of *Roderick Random*'
soon began to appear on the title-pages of his other novels:
first, apparently,[46] in the 1751 Dublin edition of *Peregrine
Pickle* (though not in the London editions), and then in the first
and subsequent editions of *Ferdinand Count Fathom*, *Sir Launcelot
Greaves*, and *Humphry Clinker*. And in references to Smollett in
many different places, it is as the author of this work that he

---

45 Thornton, *Have-at-you-all*, pp. 14, 17, 29.
46 The *Regicide* had already carried this inscription.

is identified, again and again. Furthermore, critical observations of *Roderick* and references to it soon become much more common, though the disparity between the number of the readers of
the novel and the amount of attention it drew from Critics seems
to have continued throughout the century, in somewhat lessening
degree.

The reception of *Peregrine Pickle* was very different. Smollett's growing fame might well have caused the penning of such a
number of notices as greeted the novel, but these notices, as we
have seen, had nothing to do with Smollett. None of the writers
we have quoted seems to have realized that he was reading a novel
of rare distinction, or of any distinction. In contrast to *Roderick Random*, again, the number of readers was probably rather
small, despite all the furore, for London got along without a
second edition for seven years. Not until the 'Memoirs' had been
pretty well forgotten, apparently, did the novel begin to attract
attention on its own merits. After 1758, editions followed at
intervals averaging about five years.

*Next Smollett came. What author dare resist
Historian, critic, bard, and novelist?*
                                    Cuthbert Shaw

When Horace Walpole, writing to the Reverend William Mason in
1772, was seeking a disparaging adjective for Smollett, he might
have found several appropriate ones. But the word he incredibly
fixed upon was indolent - 'indolent Smollett!'[1] The times aboun-
ded with more virulent epithets, but could we find any more
astonishing? Smollett's productive period extended over twenty-
three years, several of which must be counted out because of his
illness. Yet the Henley edition of his works runs to twelve
thick volumes, and another dozen, and perhaps two, could be
filled by those ephemeral writings which the various editors of
his collected works have generally omitted.

'Indolent Smollett!' We can only wish that it had been possible for Smollett to remain indolent; for though some of his
writings between *Peregrine Pickle* and *Humphry Clinker* helped to
make his name better known, and some of them still have a certain
interest for us, it is extremely doubtful whether the total effect of all this work was not to impair rather than enhance his
reputation.

Let us first consider Smollett's various literary activities
during these years and note the opinions which they called forth.
A few of them may be dismissed here by a mere mention, since
their effect on his reputation seems to have been almost negligible. Such works are the *Essay on the External Use of Water*,
the *Modern Part of an Universal History*, *A Compendium of Authentic and Entertaining Voyages*, *The Present State of All Nations*,
and the various translations. But it is difficult to trace his
reputation as a novelist through this period without considering
certain of his other writings which were commented upon by his
contemporaries, people who usually made no sharp distinction between the novelist and the man of letters. It will be necessary,
therefore, to pay some attention to these works as we come to them.

---

1 *Letters of Horace Walpole*, VIII, 184. The context of the phrase is as follows: 'What a
figure will this our Augustan age make . . . What a library of poetry, taste,
good sense, veracity, and vivacity! ungrateful Shebbear! indolent Smollett!
trifling Johnson! piddling Goldsmith!'

The series of quarrels in which Smollett was involved for most of his literary life had their beginning even before the writing of *Peregrine Pickle*, in connection with the unhappy fate of the *Regicide*, recounted at length, and under a transparent disguise, in *Roderick Random*; more openly in the preface to the play printed in the next year; and with greater bitterness in the first edition of *Peregrine Pickle*. Since the story has been told in considerable detail elsewhere,[2] it need not detain us here, except as we note that we seem to hear the last echoes of the episode (saving the handsome but tardy praises of his opponents which Smollett inserted in some of his later writings) with the publication of *Habbakkuk Hilding* in 1752, which, Blanchard says, did more harm to Fielding's reputation 'than most of the anony- mous pamphlets of the Newspaper War; for his reputation as a novelist (Smollett's) was now so well established that a word from him was eagerly read.'[3]

Smollett's next publication was his third novel, *Ferdinand Count Fathom*. It was not a success. Although a Dublin edition appeared in the year of its issue, 1753, a second London edition was not called for until 1771 - the poorest record of any of his novels. The only critical notice appeared in the *Monthly Review*, which opened with the conventional remark, 'As the public is al- ready very well acquainted with the genius and talents of this writer, for works of imagination, there is little occasion for our saying much of his present performance.' A discussion fol- lows on the advisability of having such a rogue as Fathom for the principal character, which the reviewer questions. The story of Monimia and Melville is praised, and Don Diego de Zelos is noticed as an admirably drawn character. 'On the whole, the history of count *Fathom* is a work of mixed character, compounded of various and unequal parts.' There are indications of 'the performance being hastily, nay and carelessly composed. Yet, with whatever crudities it may be chargeable, - with all its im- perfections, we may venture to pronounce that the work has still merit enough to compensate with the discerning reader for its defects: it carries with it strong marks of genius in the author, and demonstrations of his great proficiency in the study of man- kind.'[4] To sum up, the tone of the whole notice would scarcely distinguish this novel from dozens of others which received equal praise and which have now long been forgotten.

Again, with the appearance of *Ferdinand Fathom*, we find Mrs. Delany reading Smollett, and keeping her friend Mrs. Dewes in- formed of the progress of her reading. On March 24, 1753, she wrote, 'We are reading "Count Fathom," a very indifferent affair,

2 H. S. Buck, *A Study in Smollett*, pp. 53 ff.
3 F. T. Blanchard, p. 87.
4 *Monthly Review*, VIII (1753), 203-214.

as far as we have gone: they say it mends in the second volume, and so it had need.' On April 7 (this letter and the preceding are dated 1754, but the editor says they were evidently written in 1753) she continued, 'Have you read "Count Fathom?" Though a great deal bad, there are some things very interesting, and the whole well-intended.' Finally, by April 21, she evidently had finished the book. 'I think "Count Fathom" (though a bad, affected style) written with a better intention (than *Jemmy and Jenny Jessamy*), and Melvin's character a good one, but they none of them are to be named in a day with our good friend Richardson.'[5]

Lady Mary did not think much of the novel. In that well known passage on Fielding wherein she called Tom Jones and Booth sorry scoundrels, it will be remembered that she attributed *Roderick Random* to his pen. And then she added, 'I cannot think Fadom wrote by the same hand, it is every way so much below it.' In another letter, Jan. 1, 1755, her reference was again to *Fathom*, evidently, when she said, 'I am sorry my friend Smollett loses his time in translations: he has certainly a talent for invention, though I think it flags a little in his last work.'[6]

As we shall see, *Ferdinand Count Fathom* came to have its admirers; its Gothic effects especially were praised by many later readers; but for the time being it did little to gain for Smollett a higher place in the general estimation, nor has it ever enjoyed the acclaim or the popularity of his three greater novels.

If this work did little for Smollett's reputation, what shall we say of his next venture, his connection with the *Critical Review?* It was - thus far, at least - his most unfortunate literary undertaking. The story of all the quarrels ensuing therefrom is in the biographies; it does not need to be repeated here, especially since references to the novels seem very uncommon. Perhaps this can be explained by the fact that Smollett was not given to praise of his own works, only to their defence when they were under attack, and the other side had nothing to gain by calling attention to their opponent's finest achievements, especially when much better game offered itself in the shape of the *Regicide*. It was this poor corpse, for example, which drew the ridicule of Churchill in the *Apology*.[7] Churchill returned to the attack in *The Ghost*, 1762, and *The Author*, 1763. In the latter poem, he accused Smollett on different grounds.

> Is there an Author, search the Kingdom round,
> In whom true worth, and real Spirit's found?
> The slaves of Booksellers, or (doom'd by Fate
> To baser chains) vile pensioners of State;
> Some, dead to shame, and of those shackles proud
> Which Honour scorns, for slav'ry roar aloud,
> Others, *half-palsied* only, mutes become,
> And what makes SMOLLETT write, makes JOHNSON dumb.[8]

5 Mary G. Delany, III, 216, 220, 223.
6 Lady Mary Montagu, *Works*, ed. J. Dallaway, IV, 261, 283.
7 L. Melville, *Tobias Smollett*, p. 188.
8 Charles Churchill, *The Author*, p. 12.

This same suggestion that Smollett was drawing a pension was stated more definitely in the following year in a *Memorial to Mr. Grenville in favour of Dr. Shebbeare,* signed by fourteen members of Parliament, in which the following sentence occurs: "We should not have taken this liberty if we had not been informed that the late Dr. Thomson, Pemberton, Johnson, Smollett, Hume, Hill, Mallet, and others have had either pensions or places granted them as Men of Letters.' The editor of the Grenville Papers states than an examination of the Pension List of the time reveals that only Johnson of those named appeared on it.[9]

Cuthbert Shaw also centered his attack on the *Regicide* in the poem (*The Race*) from which the lines at the head of this chapter are taken. Joseph Reed, in his *A Sop in the Pan for a Physical Critick,* 1759, had a special reason for mentioning the play, for he had already made fun of it, in the manner employed by Fielding in *Tom Thumb,* in his mock-tragedy *Madrigal and Truletta,* the unfavorable review of which called forth this reply. For us, the most interesting point about Reed's rather competent and not ill-natured pamphlet is that he praised Smollett's *Roderick Random:* 'The best (I was going to add the only tolerable) piece you have yet published.' In view of the well-established rules for the conduct of a literary quarrel, this statement must have seemed nothing short of unethical.

Such was Smollett's stature by this time that he and the *Critical* were thought of as one and the same thing. An attack on the *Critical* was almost always an attack on Smollett; he was blamed for reviews he did not write; and even several years after he had severed all ties with the review, as announced in his letter of Nov. 13, 1765, to Moore,[10] he was held responsible. Thus in 1767 George Canning, smarting under an unfavorable notice, addressed his reply to Smollett,[11] and in the following year, when Philip Thicknesse made the same error, this explanation was printed by the then editor of the periodical:

> We have already paid our compliments to this author as a traveller, and we now return him thanks for informing the public of a notorious untruth . . . by asserting that Dr. Smollett has within these few years written part of the Critical Review. In this allegation, however, we hope Mr. Thicknesse will be favoured with the preferable credit, because we think no circumstance can prove of more effectual service to our undertaking.[12]

Besides the attacks which fell upon Smollett from many quarters because of his editorship of the *Critical,* only the more relevant of which have been mentioned here, we find another unfortunate result of his reviewing activities: the changing atti-

9 W. J. Smith, II, 270-272.
10 *The Letters of Tobias Smollett, M.D.,* p. 96.
11 *Ibid.,* p. 216.
12 *Critical Review,* XXV (1768), 277.

tude assumed by the *Monthly Review* toward his works. Hitherto, it had been kindly disposed; *Peregrine Pickle* was warmly received and *Ferdinand Fathom* accorded as much praise as could reasonably be expected. But from 1756 on, the *Monthly's* treatment of Smollett was often hostile and sometimes deliberately insulting, not only during the years of his association with the *Critical*, but for the rest of his life. The first sign of this change might have been seen in 1757, when Smollett finally succeeded in gaining a place in theatrical history with Garrick's production of the *Reprisal*. The entire notice in the *Monthly* was as follows: 'Calculated for the Meridian of Bartholomew-Fair; but, by some unnatural accident, (as jarring elements are sometimes made to unite) exhibited eight nights at the Theatre-Royal in Drury-Lane.'[13] In contrast, the *Critical* gave a summary of the story, praised the character of the sailor as 'masterly, and perhaps as good as any now on the stage,' pointed out that the author's knowledge of dramatic technique was in some respects deficient, but concluded that the close imitation of nature in the play 'will always please the judicious, though it may not set the galleries in a roar.'[14]

In 1764, Baker included a notice of Smollett in his *Companion to the Play-House*. Part of the article, referring to the popularity of the three novels we have mentioned thus far, needs to be quoted here.

> A well-known Writer of the present Age, is a Native of *North Briton*, and was bred a Sea Surgeon . . . Having then no farther Employment at Sea, he betook himself to his Pen; and, being happy in a lively Genius, he soon produced his celebrated Novel, entitled *Roderick Random;* which met with great success. - This encouraged him to pursue the same Path, and he afterwards gave the Town another Novel, entitled *Peregrine Pickle;* in which he luckily introduced the History of the celebrated Lady *Vane*. - This Episode gave the Book a great Run; but it had likewise no inconsiderable Merit, independent of that Lady's entertaining Story; the Materials of which, it is said, she herself furnished. - He likewise wrote a third Novel, entitled *Ferdinand Count Fathom*, which was judged greatly inferior to the two former.[15]

In the same year that the *Reprisal* was produced, Smollett began what was to be one of the outstanding financial successes of his life, the *Complete History of England*. His dedication of the work to Sir William Pitt brought forth a handsome acknowledgment, including the promise of an early perusal of 'a work, which I doubt not will fully answer, with all good judges, the great expectations which the known talents of the author have so justly raised.'[16]

13 *Monthly Review*, XVI (1757), 179.
14 *Critical Review*, III (1757), 160.
15 D. E. Baker, *The Companion to the Play-House*, Vol. II, article 'Smollett.'
16 *Portfolio*, I (1801), 2.

Even the *Monthly* dealt gently with Smollett's *History*: perhaps
because it was so popular, perhaps because the review was written
by Goldsmith,[17] to whom Smollett gave a position not long after on
a new periodical. The article did not praise Smollett's work
without discrimination, for the failure to present evidence was
pointed out as a defect, and the character sketches at the end of
each reign were unfavorably criticized. On the other hand, the
author's unbiased position and his clear, pleasing style were commended, and the amount of space given to the notice, six pages,
was many times larger than that allotted to any of Smollett's
other works after 1756.[18]

The popularity of the *History*, especially its favorable reception among some circles in Scotland, exceeded Smollett's own expectations.[19] Yet, despite its huge sales of over 10,000 copies
in the weekly edition, favorable comments on the work seem to have
been almost completely lacking. An exception occurs in Samuel
Richardson's postscript to his letter of July 19, 1757, to Edward
Young: 'I am glad to hear you like Dr. Smollett's History of
England.'[20] Against this there were several disparaging notices.
Perhaps Hume's comments might be included here, though their tone
can hardly be called hostile. On April 6, 1758, he wrote Millar:
'I am afraid, this extraordinary Run upon Dr. Smollett has a little hurt your Sales: But these things are only temporary.' Nearly
a year later he wrote to Robertson, the other famous historian of
this time, 'A plague take you! Here I sat near the historical
summit of Parnassus, immediately under Dr. Smollett; and you have
the impudence to squeeze yourself by me, and place yourself directly under his feet.'[21] A much more unpleasant reference came
from the pen of William Warburton. In a letter to Richard Hurd
dated Jan. 30, 1759, he wrote that 'when Clarendon and Temple
wrote History, they little thought the time was so near when a
vagabond Scot should write nonsense ten thousand strong.'[22]

In the first volume of the *Imperial Magazine*, 1760, appeared
an article 'On the present State of Literature in England,' which
noticed Richardson and Sterne, both very favorably, but omitted
any mention of Fielding. Concerning Smollett, the writer said:

> Dr. Smollett is certainly an ingenious writer on some
> subjects, but he strangely misapplies his talents when he
> writes history; his history of England, which has had so
> great a run amongst the vulgar (a set of people whose appro-
> bation would give me but an indifferent opinion of a book
> before I read it) is an instance of this. Novel-writing
> seems more adapted to his genius; his flowery style (?),
> which disgusts us in history, pleases in Roderick Random;

17 B. C. Nangle, p. 200.
18 *Monthly Review*, XVI (1757), 530–536.
19 *Letters of Tobias Smollett, M.D.*, pp. 50, 54.
20 *Monthly Magazine*, XLIII (1817), 328.
21 *The Letters of David Hume*, ed. J.Y.T. Greig, I, 273–274, 302.
22 *Letters from a late eminent prelate*, p. 207.

a novel, which though faulty in some respects, has certainly some merit; and is much superior to the common run of
those works, which reflect so great a disgrace on the polite
literature of this nation. I cannot help regretting the unhappy fate of many writers, whose abilities, were they possessed of independent fortunes, would do honour to themselves and country, obliged by want to subject themselves
to the imperious dictates of ignorant booksellers. This
it is that cramps the fire and genius of authors, and re-
duces a man of ingenuity to be a dirty writer of a critical
review.[23]

Lady Mary Montagu voiced a similar complaint in her letter to her
daughter on Oct. 3, 1758, when, after retailing a bit of gossip,
she commented, 'The story deserves the pen of my dear Smollett,
who, I am sorry, disgraces his talent by writing those stupid romances commonly called history.'[24] Fanny Burney also depreciated
Smollett's historical talents, saying that she was entertained,
in reading his work again, by the many familiar names, 'in spight
of the dislike I have to Smollett's language and style of writing.'[25] Goldsmith, it will be remembered, had praised the style
of the *History* in his review in the *Monthly*.

Walpole's unfriendly attitude toward Smollett was suggested
at the beginning of this chapter. Noyes advances as the reason
for this hostility that in his *History* Smollett had been at
pains to expose the venality of Sir Robert's administration.[26]
This is likely enough, since Horace condemned Fielding's works
for a similar reason. But another cause may be found in Walpole's
letter to John Chute of Feb. 2, 1758, in which he voiced his
suspicion that Smollett was one of the hostile reviewers of his
Catalogue of Royal and Noble Authors.[27] Be that as it may, his
attitude is expressed plainly enough, and in more than one place.
In a letter to Horace Mann in 1765 he sneered at Smollett's
sense thus: 'Times of party have their great outlines, which
even such historians as Hollingshed or Smollett can seize.'[28]
And in another letter to Mann five years later he referred to
Smollett as 'a most worthless and dangerous fellow, and capable
of any mischief.'[29]

But the best example of Horatian temperance and restraint is
found in his *Memoirs of George II*. The passage deserves to be
quoted in full.

Smollett was a worthless man, and only mentioned here
because author of a History of England, of the errors in
which posterity ought to be warned. Smollett was bred a
sea-surgeon, and turned author. He wrote a tragedy, and

23 *Imperial Magazine*, I (1760), 519.
24 Lady Mary Montagu, *Works*, ed. W. May Thomas, II, 349.
25 Fanny Burney, *Early Diary*, I, 94-95.
26 *Letters of Tobias Smollett, M.D.*, pp. 166-167.
27 *Letters of Horace Walpole*, IV, 236.
28 *Ibid.*, VI, 257.
29 *Ibid.*, VII, 372.

sent it to Lord Lyttelton, with whom he was not acquainted
. . . (Lyttelton advised comedy, but excused himself from
recommending the play Smollett wrote.) Smollett's return
was drawing an abusive portrait of Lord Lyttelton in Roderick Random, a novel; of which sort he published two or three.
His next attempt was on the History of England; a work in
which he engaged for booksellers, and finished, though four
volumes in quarto, in two years; yet an easy task, as being
pilfered from other histories. Accordingly it was little
noticed till it came down to the present times: then, though
compiled from the libels of the age and the most paltry materials, yet being heightened by personal invectives, strong
Jacobitism, and the worst representation of the Duke of Cumberland's conduct in Scotland, the sale was prodigious.[30]

The only saving factor is that this work was not published until
1822, when Walpole's opinion was not likely to bear much weight
with either critics or the reading public.

While we are on the subject of the *History*, it may be as well
to go beyond the chronological limits of this chapter and complete what there is to say of that work. Occasionally, in brief
notices of Smollett, the *History* was given remarkable prominence.
Thus the *Scots Magazine's* obituary notice read 'author of the
Complete History of England, and many other books.'[31] Again, in
the *London Magazine*, two years later, a list of the most eminent
writers has this entry for Smollett: 'History of England, novels,
and transl.'[32] This, by the way, is another place from which the
name of Fielding is strangely absent. Despite such anomalies,
the *History* was evidently recognized as an ephemeral best seller;
it was never accepted in serious circles, and before the end of
the century its vogue had long passed, though it was still not
forgotten or unread. A writer in the *Yorkshire Magazine* for 1786
asked: 'Had we not been better pleased to have viewed the ingenious author of *Roderick Random* dancing in the airy circles of romance, though on the brink of futurity, than amid the barren
deserts of chronology, toiling after the drudgery of unsuccess-
ful historians?'[33]

Discussions of English historians in the periodicals by this
time were generally confined to Robertson and Hume, with the
occasional inclusion (if the writer were unusually liberal) of
Gibbon. Smollett was rarely considered. Lord Gardenstone, one
of his staunch admirers, did include his favorite Smollett in his
'Critical Remarks on some of the eminent Historians of England,'
and his attitude shows as well as anything how Smollett's historical efforts were being regarded about this time.

> The immense bulk of his writings proves that he com-
> posed with greater facility than ordinary men are able to
> converse. By his own account, in the admirable expedition

30 H. Walpole, *Memoirs of George II*, pp. 419–420.
31 *Scots Magazine*, XXXIII (1771),558.
32 *London Magazine*, XLII (1773), pp. 643–644.
33 *Yorkshire Magazine*, I (1786), 33.

of Humphry Clinker, it appears that he very often wrote merely for wages; and on such occasions, nothing above mediocrity can with reason be demanded. The continuation of his English history, from 1748 to 1764, is a mere catchpenny chaos, without even a spark of merit. There is great reason to believe that he, or rather his journeymen, copied at random from somebody else, most of the quotations and references arranged with so much parade on the margin of his text.[34]

General Andreossi, in his 'Observations of the Writings of Historians of all ages and countries,' dismissed Smollett more cavalierly with these words: 'Smollett, a party writer, knew nothing of military affairs; but having been at sea, his descriptions of naval actions are free from gross blunders.'[35]

Yet, though no one had a kind word for the *History*, it continued to be read well into the nineteenth century, largely, we may suppose, by the less scholarly and discriminating sort of readers. One calls to mind the incident in *Vanity Fair* telling how Becky lightened the labors of being a governess at Queen's Crawley by reading with her charge 'many delightful French and English works, among which may be mentioned those of the learned Dr. Smollett. . . . Once, when Mr. Crawley asked what the young people were reading, the governess replied, "Smollett." "Oh, Smollett," said Mr. Crawley, quite satisfied. "His history is more dull, but by no means so dangerous as that of Mr. Hume. It is history you are reading?" "Yes," said Miss Rose; without, however, adding that it was the history of Mr. Humphrey Clinker.'[36]

Archibald Alison, writing toward the middle of the century, apparently was annoyed that the *History* was still in evidence.

> Smollett, whose continuation of Hume is to be seen in every bookseller's window beside its great predecessor, is wholly unworthy of the honourable place which chance, and the neglect of others, have hitherto assigned it. Admirable as a novelist - at least as that character was understood in those days - graphic, entertaining, humorous - Smollett had none of the qualities necessary for a historian. He was neither a soldier nor an orator, a poet nor a philosopher. . . . As to philosophic views of the progress of society, or the social and political effects of the Revolution of 1688 and the Reformation, the thing was out of the question: it belonged neither to his age nor character to dream of anything of the kind.[37]

The remarkable thing is not that histories written by such outstanding authors as Smollett and Goldsmith should now be complete-

---

34 *The Bee, or Literary Weekly Intelligencer*, III (1791), 90–91.

35 *Monthly Magazine*, XXII (1806), 443.

36 W. M. Thackeray, *Vanity Fair*, Ch. X. Only a short time before these happenings, the *Quarterly Review* had remarked (IX (1813), 444) that 'every day teems with new impressions of Hume and Smollett.' Hume long continued to enjoy a remarkably high reputation. Nineteen years later the same periodical stated (XLIV (1832), 6) that nothing could ever drive his history out of the market; it could no more be supplanted by another book on the same subject than could *Macbeth*, *Paradise Lost*, or the *Dunciad*; future historians should confine themselves to incorporating any results of their research in footnotes to Hume's work.

37 A. Alison, *Essays Political, Historical, and Miscellaneous*, III, 322.

ly forgotten, but that they should have enjoyed as long a life as
they did. Needless to say, Smollett's historical work has long
lost any importance it might ever have had. One exception to
this statement must, however, be noted. The part of the *Continuation* covering years within his own knowledge is still rather frequently referred to by historians and biographers of the period;
apparently it has value as a primary source. But when historians
use Smollett as an authority on the times, they are much more
likely to refer to his novels. His best history was written in
Roderick Random and *Humphry Clinker.*

Of Smollett's next literary undertakings, the editing of the
British Magazine and the *Briton,* little needs to be said. The
first seems to have gained him a firm friend in Goldsmith, of
whom more later; the second cost him a good friend, John Wilkes,
and his affiliation with Bute's administration was surely not de-
signed to make him more popular. But his unhappy venture into
political journalism had no direct effect on the fortunes of his
novels.

Launcelot Greaves, which was published in the first numbers of
the *British Magazine,* attracted a moderate amount of attention.
The *Monthly Review,* in fact, dismissed it with one of those sin-
gle-sentence reviews of which eighteenth-century critics seem to
have been fond: 'Better than the common Novels, but unworthy the
pen of Dr. Smollett.'[38] The *Critical Review,* naturally, was more
courteous. A few excerpts, typical of the whole, will suffice.
The writer begins by lamenting the rarity of the *vis comica in*
modern literature. Characters are distinguished merely by their
opposition to other characters.

> How different from this is the ridiculous simplicity
> of Adams, the absurd vehemence of Western, the boisterous
> generosity of Bowling, the native humour of Trunnion, and
> the laughable solemnity of Uncle Toby.

It may be said here that although Smollett's connection with the
Critical vitiates its opinions on his works, and it is cited only
for the sake of completeness, there was no prejudice manifested
against Fielding, as one might think likely in view of their
squabbles. Complimentary references to Fielding similar to the
one just quoted were common, and Murphy's edition of Fielding's
works was reviewed at length in the opening article of volume XVI
(1762), which spared no praise in favor of Smollett's great rival.

Here are two other comments from the *Critical's* review of *Sir
Launcelot Greaves.*

> The two principal characters, unless we except that of
> Miss Darnley, in this little ingenious piece, seem to be
> formed on those of the admirable Cervantes, the grave knight
> of la Mancha and his facetious squire. They resemble with-

38 *Monthly Review,* XXVI (1762), 391.

out imitating, and remind us of what imparted exquisite enjoyment, without diminishing their own novelty.

That admirable faculty of describing sea characters with propriety, so conspicuous in his other productions, is here displayed with renovated vigour. Captain Crowe is a tar of as extraordinary a cast as either Bowling, Trunnion, Pipes, or Hatchway.[39]

A shorter but almost equally commendatory notice appeared in the *Library* for May, 1762.

Such of our readers as are fond of novels, will receive ample gratification from two which the last month has produced. The first is Sir Launcelot Greaves, by Dr. Smollett, whose excellent talent at this species of writing hath been fully experienced in some former works, and particularly in his Roderick Random. Sir Launcelot Greaves is a kind of English Quixote, and his adventures are conducted with much humour. There are many characters well drawn, many diverting incidents, and many fine strokes of genius, nature, and passion. The author has introduced certain persons too often, and especially captain Crowe, whose appearance is sometimes disgusting, and whose sea jargon is absolutely unintelligible to a land reader; but, on the whole, the performance has considerable merit. The language in general, is such as might be expected from Dr. Smollett, who has, perhaps, as much facility and variety of expression, as most writers of the age.[40]

It has been remarked that Smollett's novel seems to have set a brief fashion for Quixotes in English literature, since at least four of them appeared in the succeeding years;[41] but the relationship is at least doubtful, for these works appeared over a span of twenty-six years, and for two of them, Graves' *Spiritual Quixote* and *The Amicable Quixote*, Blanchard has shown the probable influence of Fielding.[42] There is also to be considered Mrs. Lennox's *The Female Quixote*, which was published in 1752.

Beattie noticed Smollett's novel in his 'Essay on Laughter and Ludicrous Composition,' written in 1764, and seems to have approved it. He points out the similarity to *Don Quixote* and the differences between the two works, shows how the character of the hero is drawn consistently with the purpose Smollett had in mind, and remarks how a comic air is obtained by the contrast between Sir Launcelot and other people of very dissimilar tempers.[43]

As far as I know, there was no second London edition of this novel during Smollett's lifetime. There was, however, a 'fourth edition' in Cork in 1767, and after 1771 editions were fairly frequent, as will be shown in the next chapter.

39 *Critical Review*, XIII (1762), 427–429.
40 *Library*, II (1762), 262.
41 A. Whitridge, p. 52.
42 F. T. Blanchard, pp. 179, 247.
43 James Beattie, *Essays*, pp. 323, 324.

Of all Smollett's non-fictional works, the one which is in highest esteem today is his *Travels through France and Italy*. As Whitridge says, it is 'one of those curious books that excite considerable attention when first published, then disappear completely underground, only to emerge a hundred and fifty years later as a classic.'[44] The book was, as he indicates, popular in its early years. The *Critical* praised it extravagantly, alluding to its 'ethic plan,' saying that 'no painter ever drew a more lively or a more just groupe of figures,' and concluding, 'In short, we hazard nothing in saying, that a work of this kind does more service to Great Britain than fifty acts of parliament for prohibiting French fripperies and foreign commodities, or even forbidding the exportation of fools, fops, and coxcombs.'[45] But other favorable comments were not lacking. Thus, the *London Magazine*, which had had nothing to say about any of Smollett's novels, though *Tom Jones, Amelia,* and *Tristram Shandy* received considerable attention, printed seven extracts from the *Travels,* and in its introduction, which is here quoted, acknowledged Smollett's high reputation as an author.

> We are sure our readers will reap equal satisfaction with ourselves in the perusal of Dr. Smollett's travels through France and Italy; on which account we shall give them, now and hereafter, some extracts from that performance, which bespeaks the scholar and the gentleman. Here no affected, pert journalist presents his crude observations; every thing is the product of learning and experience, and that thorough knowledge of mankind which the Dr. is well known to have acquired. The whole is wrote in a very familiar and agreeable stile, in the form of letters.[46]

The review in the *Monthly* followed very similar lines, even to saying that the author's abilities as a writer "are universally known." After several quotations from the letters, this comment was added:

> We cannot take leave of the Doctor without thanking him for the entertainment we have received in the perusal of his travels.[47]

The *Royal Magazine* also introduced a selection in complimentary terms, saying that 'From a writer of Dr. Smollett's genius, judgment, and taste, the reader will naturally expect to meet with a fund of instructive and entertaining particulars in these Travels; and we will venture to assure him that he will not be disappointed.'[48]

The reception of the *Travels* on the other side of the Channel was, of course, less favorable. Mme. Riccoboni probably

44 A. Whitridge, p. 80.
45 *Critical Review,* XXI (1766), 322, 328, 406.
46 *London Magazine,* XXXV (1766), 243.
47 *Monthly Review,* XXXIV (1766), 419–429.
48 *Royal Magazine,* XIV (1766), 233.

expressed the feeling of many of her countrymen when she wrote
to Garrick in Nov., 1767, and called Smollett a 'vil gredin,
qui ne connoit pas mieux les moeurs de son pays que ceux de la
France, et donc tous les ouvrages sont detestables: oui, detestables.'[49] This transference of her spleen to Smollett's other
works was paralleled by that of many other people; his reputation in France, which in any event probably would not have been
very high, was blasted by the *Travels,* as Joliat has shown in
his *Smollett et la France.*

At home, though a Dublin edition appeared at once, another
in 1772, and another London edition in 1778, there were also
some exceptions taken to the *Travels.* Of these, the best known -
perhaps one should say the most famous of all comments ever made
about Smollett - was Sterne's passage in his *Sentimental Journey* on Smelfungus, which, for the sake of completeness, may be
reproduced once again here. It occurs in the section headed
'In the Street. Calais.'

> I pity the man who can travel from Dan to Beersheba,
> and cry, 'Tis all barren - and so it is; and so is all
> the world to him, who will not cultivate the fruits it
> offers. . . .

> The learned Smelfungus travelled from Boulogne to
> Paris - from Paris to Rome - and so on - but he set out
> with the spleen and the jaundice, and every object he
> pass'd by was discoloured or distorted - He wrote an
> account of them, but 'twas nothing but the account of
> his miserable feelings.

> I met Smelfungus in the grand portico of the pantheon -
> he was just coming out of it - *'Tis nothing but a huge cock-
> pit,* said he - I wish you had said nothing worse of the Venus
> of Medicis replied I - for in passing through Florence, I
> had heard he had fallen foul upon the goddess, and used her
> worse than a common strumpet, without the least provocation
> in nature.

> I popp'd upon Smelfungus again at Turin, in his return
> home; and a sad tale of sorrowful adventures he had to tell,
> 'wherein he spoke of moving accidents by flood and field,
> and of the cannibals which each other eat; the Anthropoph-
> agi' - he had been flay'd alive, and bedevil'd, and used
> worse than St. Bartholomew, at every stage he had come at.-

> I'll tell it, cried Smelfungus, to the world. You had
> better tell it said I, to your physician.[50]

Considering the tremendous popularity of Sterne, a popularity
so great that for the rest of the century one can hardly run
through a volume of a periodical without finding an imitation of
his style, who can estimate what this *locus classicus* did to
shape the popular opinion of Smollett, and what effect this
opinion of the man may have had on his novels? Smollett was
never the favorite of fortune. Here for once he was entirely

---

49 *Private Correspondence of David Garrick,* II, 524.
50 L. Sterne, *A Sentimental Journey,* p. 32.

blameless, and with the tide of sentimentalism still rising to
its flood, it was surely unkind that his lack of sentimentality
should thus be flaunted before the world. Sterne's works rolled
along on the crest of the wave; Smollett's had to struggle for
popularity against the adverse current of the times. A periodical essayist some years later remarked that it was difficult to
define sentimental writing 'unless we rest satisfied with what
a female writer once replied to this question, rather in a
peevish way, "It means to write like Sterne."'[51] In the following century, an anonymous writer on 'Art in fiction' remarked:
'Of all writers of great genius, Shakspeare has the most sentiment, and, perhaps, Smollett and Defoe the least.'[52] Probably
many novel readers put Sterne and Smollett at opposite ends of
the scale and rated their worth according to their degree of
sentimentality.

There was another writer who criticized Smollett's *Travels*,
at far greater length than Sterne and with proportionately
less weight. This was Philip Thicknesse. Displeased at an unfavorable notice of one of his works in the *Critical*, which he
suspected Smollett of writing despite the asseveration in the
Critical to the contrary, he relieved his hurt feelings by
spilling them out in print at great length. He called Smollett
the 'arch critic himself,' 'Toby, the martinet in literature,'[53]
referred to Smollett's imprisonment for 'perfidious calumnies,
and atrocious abuse . . . of a gentleman of rank,'[54] accused
the *Critical* of pro-Scotch bias,[55] and professed scorn for
Smollett's observations on standards of living and on the arts
abroad.[56] Perhaps the most interesting feature about Thicknesse's strictures of Smollett is that some years later, like
Smollett, he made amends by an apology. In the first letter of
his *Year's Journey* he referred to his earlier works, confessed
his fault of writing when his temper was disturbed, and added
this rather patronizing comment:

> Could Dr. Smollett rise from the dead, and sit down
> in perfect health, and good temper, and read his travels
> through France and Italy, he would probably find most of
> his anger turned upon himself. But, poor man! he was ill;
> and meeting with, what every stranger must expect to meet,
> at most French inns, want of cleanliness, imposition, and
> incivility; he was so much disturbed by those incidents,
> that to say no more of the writings of an ingenious and
> deceased author, his travels into France, and Italy, are
> the least entertaining, in my humble opinion, of all his
> works.[57]

51 J. W. Newman, III, 234.
52 *Monthly Chronicle*, I (1838), 50.
53 P. Thicknesse, *Useful Hints*, p. 2.
54 *Ibid.*, p. 15.
55 *Ibid.*, p. 19.
56 *Ibid.*, pp. 29-30, also his *Observations on Customs and Manners*, pp. 90-91.
57 P. Thickness, *A Year's Journey*, I, 2-3.

Here we may leave Smollett's *Travels*. They will not claim our attention again until we come to consider a much later period. Though popular for some time after their appearance, as stated above, they seem to have become lost among the excessive number of travel books of the time and to have been completely overshadowed by Sterne's *Sentimental Journey* and accounts of voyages to more exotic regions than France and Italy, until a later generation discovered that the passing of time had mellowed their spleen into rugged honesty, and their philistinism into refreshing originality.

No such length of time is needed to cover the fortunes of Smollett's next work, the bitter *Adventures of an Atom*. It was by no means the least successful of his productions. Two editions were called for in the year of publication, 1769; the 1778 edition was described as the 'tenth'; others are recorded for 1784, 1786, and 1799. Contemporary notices were much more favorable than later criticisms. The *Town and Country Magazine* praised its 'genuine wit, and original humour,' noting that it was written in imitation of Rabelais and Swift;[58] while the *Critical* puffed the work by saying that it united the 'happy extravagance' of the first of these authors to the 'splendid humour' of the second, and concluded that 'the man who does not love and relish this performance, has no wit in his own composition.'[59] The *London Magazine* called it a 'very shrewd and entertaining history.' The *Monthly Review* and the *Gentleman's Magazine*, however, though they both praised its 'spirit' and 'humour,' found it necessary to qualify their approval in view of its indecency and obscenity.[60]

Purely topical in nature, and having no qualities of style sufficient to prolong its appeal, the *Adventures of an Atom* has long ceased to attract any attention beyond a short notice in Smollett's biographies, except, perchance, in some work which happens to touch upon one of the figures whom Smollett satirized.[61]

It has long been recognized that Smollett's life forms a peculiarly satisfactory pattern, a pattern wherein the sinner repents and atones for his misdeeds; the rich promise of youth, obscured through many years of mediocrity, is redeemed at the last possible moment by one brilliant achievement; and the accumulation of misfortunes and catastrophes, coming from within and without, is made as nought by a last-act victory of the hero, as dramatically effective and nearly as mysterious as any *deus ex machina*. It is pleasant to note that the ending is equally satisfactory as we follow the reception of his works, one by one, and

58 *Town and Country Magazine,* I (1769), 269.
59 *Critical Review,* XXVII (1769), 362, 369.
60 *Monthly Review,* XL (1769), 454; *Gentleman's Magazine,* XXXIX (1769), 205.
61 Such a reference occurs in the recent best seller *Northwest Passage* by Kenneth Roberts.

come at last to *Humphry Clinker*. Indeed, it seems to have created something of a sensation upon its appearance, and this time, a sensation caused solely by Smollett's talent, unaided by any adventitious circumstances. Although there were two thousand copies printed of the first London edition of 1771 (dated 1671),[62] a 'second edition' appeared in 1771 and another 'second edition' (all three from different plates) in the following year. There was also a Dublin edition of 1771, followed by another in 1774. Moreover, the periodicals not only bestowed more attention and more favorable attention upon it than upon any of Smollett's previous works, but several of them departed from their usual practices to notice the book in unusual ways.

That the *Critical Review* honored *Humphry* with a full-length notice instead of the usual short account in its Monthly Catalog which was the fate of virtually all novels is not so remarkable, nor should we expect anything different from the enthusiastic commendations which it printed.[63] But the *Hibernian Magazine*, which printed extracts from very few books in its early years, honored *Humphry Clinker* in this way, and with the following introduction:

> The singular merit of the Expedition of Humphry Clinker just published in Dublin, (by the author of Roderick Random) hath induced us to present our Readers with the following extracts, being satirical Descriptions of London and Bath, which, we doubt not, will be agreeable and entertaining.[64]

The *Court and City Magazine*, which also was noticing very few books, printed extracts in three different parts of its second volume. Of criticism it offered nothing but this: 'The characters are strongly marked in point of spirit and humour, and supported with great propriety. Old Bramble is a curious original, and does honour even to the pen of Dr. Smollett.'[65] The *Town and Country Magazine* admitted that it was making an exception to its practice in favor of Smollett's last work, saying, 'We seldom make Extracts from printed Books, as our Intention is to furnish our Readers with original Matter, a Plan never before attempted; but the singular merit of Humphry Clinker . . . has made us . . . deviate from our general plan.' Farther on it tells us, 'The author of this production has so compleatly established his reputation as a novel writer, that to say this performance is not inferior to any of his former pieces, will be a sufficient recommendation of the work.'[66] Another periodical which noticed very few books, the *Universal Magazine of Knowledge and Pleasure*, was also led to take notice of the latest success in some 'Critical Remarks upon Humphry Clinker.' The 'Remarks' begin as follows:

62 Grolier Club, pp. 130–131.
63 *Critical Review*, XXXII (1771), 81–88.
64 *Hibernian Magazine*, I (1771), 324.
65 *Court and City Magazine*, II (1771), 310.
66 *Town and Country Magazine*, III (1771), 317, 323.

The Captain finding Mr. Crab in the library reading, according to custom, asked him if he had got any thing new. Yes, says Mr. Crab, it is The Expedition of Humphry Clinker. And how do you like it, says the Captain? I am sorry to say, replied Mr. Crab, that I am greatly disappointed - I expected something better from the author of Roderick Random. It seems to me to be exceptionable in everything but the style and language - Humphry Clinker is a lusus naturae a kind of human animal that never existed but in the brain of the author. Indeed he figures so seldom in the business of the drama, and furnishes so little entertainment to his guest the reader, that the book might as well have been intitled The Feast of Duke Humphry. Mr. Bramble, who, it must be confessed, has some originality about him is represented as a man of sense and erudition; and, he is the principle conduit-pipe, through which our author conveys his own real sentiments of men and things.

There follows a brief resumé of Bramble's travels and opinions, and Smollett's intention of contrasting Scotland and England to the great disadvantage of the latter is pointed out. The author fears this partiality will widen rather than heal the existing breach between South and North Briton.

Setting aside this objection, I think the book abounds in many masterly strokes, and has a great deal of merit; though I hate that Hottentot, Captain Lismahago; and the ridiculous letters of Mrs. Tabitha Bramble to her maid Jenkins are too childish to amuse the meanest capacity.[67]

For the first time, a novel by Smollett was noticed in the *Gentleman's Magazine;* as in the preceding citation, its praise was not unmixed, and yet to gain five pages in that periodical was a distinct achievement. The reviewer described it as not principally a narrative of events,

but rather a miscellany containing dissertations on various subjects, exhibitions of character, and descriptions of places. Many of the characters are drawn with a free but a masterly hand; in some particulars perhaps they are exaggerated, but are not therefore the less entertaining or instructive. . . .

In this part of the work consist its principal excellence, and its principal defect is the want of events. The whole story might be told in a few pages, and the author has been so parsimonious of his invention, that he has twice overturned a coach, and twice introduced a fire, to exhibit a scene of ridiculous distress, by setting women on their heads, and making some of his dramatic characters descend from a window by a ladder, as they rose out of bed.

It is by no means deficient in sentiment, and it abounds with satire that is equally sprightly and just. It has, however, blemishes, which would be less regretted where there was less to commend.

The blemishes, the account goes on, are that the book is often stercoraceous and often prurient.[68] The *London Magazine* made

[67] *Universal Magazine of Knowledge and Pleasure*, XLIX (1771), 256–257.
[68] *Gentleman's Magazine*, XLI (1771), 317.

the same criticism as the *Universal Magazine* that the title did
not fit the story, but otherwise its comments were favorable, as
when it remarked that the reader was continually being entertained or instructed with 'some original remarks upon men and
things, that do honour to the good-sense and humanity of the
author '[69]

By far the worst notice was in the *Monthly Review,* which
praised Smollett enough to avoid the charge of gross bigotry, but
made sure that nothing in its pages would instil into anyone a
desire to buy the book. It no longer mattered to Smollett whether
anyone did. The complete notice, a not incompetent piece of mali-
cious insinuation, was as follows:

> Some modern wits appear to have entertained a notion
> that there is but one kind of *indecency* in writing; and that,
> provided they exhibit nothing of a lascivious nature, they
> may freely paint, with their pencils dipt in the most odious
> materials that can possibly be raked together for the most
> filthy and disgusting colouring. - These nasty geniuses seem
> to follow their great leader, Swift, only in his obscene and
> dirty walks. The present Writer, nevertheless, has humour
> and wit, as well as grossness and ill nature. - But we need
> not enlarge on his literary character, which is well known
> to the public. Roderick Random and Peregrine Pickle have
> long been numbered with the best of our English romances.
> His present work, however, is not equal to these; but it is
> superior to his Ferdinand Fathom, and perhaps equal to the
> Adventures of an Atom.[70]

Further evidence that the novel was creating an unusual stir
in London is afforded by one of Smollett's correspondents, John
Gray, who wrote him on July 8, 1771, as follows:

> I have read the 'Adventures of Humphry Clinker' (like
> Thackeray, Gray seems to have had trouble in recalling the
> exact title) with great delight, and think it calculated
> to give a very great run, and to add to the reputation of
> the author, who has, by the magic of his pen, turned the
> banks of Loch Lomond into classic ground. . . . shallow
> judges, I find, are not so well satisfied with the perfor-
> mance as the best judges, who are lavish in its praises.
> Your half-animated sots say they don't see the humour.
> Cleland gives it the stamp of excellence, with the enthusi-
> astic emphasis of voice and fist; and puts it before any-
> thing you ever wrote. With many, I find, it has the effect
> of exciting inquiries about your other works, which they
> had not heard of before.[71]

A more famous letter-writer also noticed *Humphry Clinker,* not
in his correspondence, but in his *Memoirs of George III,* which
were completed by 1772. In that work Walpole remarked, referring to this novel, that 'offence was taken at a party novel,
written by the profligate hireling Smollett, to vindicate the
Scots and cry down juries.' The editor was moved to comment in

69 *London Magazine,* XL (1771), 317.
70 *Monthly Review,* XLV (1771), 152.
71 L. Melville, *Tobias Smollett,* pp. 249-250.

a footnote that 'Walpole here yields to the miserable party prejudices of his day, which pursued poor Smollett even beyond the tomb.'[72]

The same volume of the *Town and Country Magazine* which honored *Humphry Clinker* carried the news of the author's death. Among the list of deaths, we find, for October 21, 'Dr. Smollett, at Leghorn, after a long and painful illness, which he bore with great fortitude and resignation. The character this gentleman held in the republic of letters, has rendered it unnecessary to expatiate here upon his merit and abilities; and we learn that some works he has entrusted with a literary friend, will probably add to his reputation as a writer.' Two correspondents also noted the passing of Smollett in the same volume of this periodical. One sent in a letter from an Englishman in Italy to his friend in London, which read in part, 'You no doubt, long before this time, have heard of the death of Dr. Smollett. I sincerely regret the loss of this ingenious gentleman. I was in hopes of being honoured with his friendship during my residence in Italy, which would have been a valuable acquisition. He was much caressed by the princes and literati of this country, and whose death is no less generally lamented (sic).' Another writer remarked, 'How few inventions have been made in any of the sciences within these ten years to give birth to a new treatise upon any branch belonging to them? What works of fancy that can be ranked with Fielding or Richardson, Smollett excepted, who was certainly the best novel writer within this period; but he is no more!'[73] Aside from these notices, the only other immediate reference to Smollett's death seems to have been a few lines in the *Royal Magazine*, 'On the Report of the Death of Dr. Smollett,' as follows:

> Death's *random* darts too certainly transfix,
> And souls unwilling Charon's sure to land 'em;
> Ah! take some gloomier soul to gloomy Styx,
> And give us back facetious *Roderick Random*.[74]

2.

What was happening to Smollett's reputation during the twenty years after *Peregrine Pickle* is not revealed entirely by the reception given to his publications in that period. There is other evidence that his fame was growing, that he was acquiring that kind of recognition which might some day make him a classic. Thus we very early find his name associated with that of the other masters of the novel, especially Fielding. It is true that Richardson and Fielding stood apart from all others; as McKillop says, 'It was not Richardson against Fielding, but Richardson

72 H. Walpole, *Memoirs of the Reign of King George the Third*, IV, 328 and n.
73 *Town and Country Magazine* III (1771), 560, 651, 548.
74 *Royal Magazine*, XXV (1771), 656.

and Fielding against all comers.[75] Even the partial *Critical Review* began the notice of a novel in 1763 by remarking that 'The great and deserved success of Richardson and Fielding has spread the taste of novel-writing and novel-reading throughout the kingdom.'[76] But elsewhere McKillop says: 'Booksellers' records of sales of copyrights seem to show that in the sixties Smollett's novels were commercially about as valuable as Richardson's, and that in the next decade the copyrights of the major novels of Richardson, Smollett, and Fielding (with the exception of *Amelia)* were valued at about 70 pounds a volume for the standard editions in duodecimo.'[77] Perhaps McKillop had in mind the sale of Mrs. Mary Richardson's copyrights in 1766, at which the following prices were realized:

					VALUE FOR WHOLE		
1/16th share	Peregrine Pickle	12	pounds		192	pounds	
1/16th "	Roderick Random	13	"	13	218	"	8
1/24th "	Clarissa	25	"		600	"	
1/16th "	Pamela	18	"		288	"	
1/24th "	Grandison	20	"		480	"	78

These figures, it will be seen, do not bear out his statement that Smollett's novels were 'about as commercially valuable as Richardson's,' although if we figure the value per volume, the difference is much less. However, this is not a comparative study of the popularity of the eighteenth century novelists, although at times such comparisons have to be made before meaningful conclusions can be reached. Suffice it to say that at this time Smollett was third in public favor, but by no means a bad third; in critical and literary circles he trailed the two great masters by a noticeably wider margin.

In the periodicals, references to Smollett as a criterion by which to judge novels began to appear at an early date, and it is in such a connection that we often find his name associated with Fielding's and occasionally with Richardson's, as mentioned above. These references first began to be made in 1751. In the *Monthly Review* for that year (to return to the time when it was still friendly to Smollett), a review of *The history of a woman of quality* includes a reference to the memoirs which a lady has given to 'the author of a famous novel, entitled, "The adventures of Roderick Random."' The work being reviewed is judged unfavorably. The author 'has introduced no *Abraham Adams,* no Parson *Trullibers,* no *Thwackums, Westerns,* or *Straps;* so that the reader who takes up this book with any expectation of finding in it that fund of laughter and merry entertainment, that the works of *Fielding,* and the author of *Roderick Random,* afford, will find

75 Alan D. McKillop, p. 231.
76 *Critical Review*, XVI (1763), 449.
77 Alan D. McKillop, p. 227.
78 *Notes and Queries*, Seventh Series, IX (1890), 301.

himself utterly disappointed.'[79] In another review in the
Monthly for that year we are told that *The History of Miss Betsy
Thoughtless* is 'without any of those entertaining introductory
chapters, and digressive essays, which distinguish the works of
a *Fielding*, a *Smollett*, or the author of *Pompey* the little.'[80] In the following year, another novel which was found
wanting would, nevertheless, we are told, 'have its admirers,
especially among such as can dispense with, or would not perceive, the want of those beauties which have recommended the
novels of *Fielding, Smollett, Coventry*, etc.'[81] In the *Court
Magazine* for 1761 the writer of an 'Essay upon the most remarkable periods of English Literature' stated:

> Dramatic poetry seems indeed to have been too much
> neglected of late years, in its room has succeeded the
> Comic Romance, a species of writing near a-kin to Comedy,
> and which has been carried to its highest perfection by
> the late Mr. Fielding, and Dr. Smollett, who have admir-
> ably imitated the manner of Cervantes and Mons. Le Sage.[82]

Roderick Random is again found in noble company in the *Monthly*
for 1763, which said that the authors of a certain 'sober, moral
tale' 'have not yet eclipsed the merit of Clarissa, Roderick
Random, or Tom Jones.'[83] An interesting article in the *Royal
Magazine* for 1766, 'A Critical Examination of the respective
Merits of Voltaire, Rousseau, Richardson, Smollett, and Fielding,'
clearly places Richardson and Fielding in a class by themselves.
After discussing all those named in the title except Smollett, the
writer continued:

> Such are the modern writers that figure in the higher
> walks of fiction; but in both countries, there are many
> others that move in a subordinate station, and though with
> but half the praise of any of the former, are not yet with-
> out just applause. When we mention Marivaux in France, and
> Smollett in England, we are of opinion, that our readers who
> understand both languages will find a likeness. (?) In fact,
> both have written but one novel of any reputation; the Pay-
> san Parvenue of France, and Roderick Random here, being what
> has formed their respective fame. Marivaux is natural, so
> is the other, but with this difference, that the French wri-
> ter dives more deeply into the human mind, and exhibits its
> operations with profounder skill.[84]

As previously observed, Smollett was known above all as the
author of *Roderick Random*. The stress put on that novel by the
writer of the above article is significant - and very typical.

---

79 *Monthly Review*, IV (1751), 308.
80 *Ibid.*, V (1751), 394.
81 *Ibid.*, VII (1752), 470. Another example occurs in Vol. XXXVII (1767), 394.
82 *Court Magazine*, I (1761), 16.
83 *Monthly Review*, XXIX (1763), 160.
84 *Royal Magazine*, XV (1766), 148.

Another type of recognition that came to Smollett during these years was mention in several novels. The first example I have found is in *The Adventures of Capt. Greenland*, 1752, which referred to those heroes who 'have been the best received by the Public; as Madam Pamela, Mr. David Simple, Mr. Joseph Andrews, Mr. Roderick Random, Tom Jones, Esq.'[85] Moreover, there is a character in this novel called Captain Log-Line whose sea dialect represents an obvious attempt to imitate Smollett's sailors; e.g., in Book V, Chapter i, we find him applying nautical terms such as course, sail, wind, and knot, to a stagecoach in a manner strongly reminiscent of Commodore Trunnion's famous ride. In Kidgell's novel *The Card* the guests at an elegant entertainment at a Venetian palace included:

> Roderick Random Esq.; with Mrs. Booby, late Miss Pamela Andrews

and four other couples of famous fictional characters, such as Joseph Andrews, Tom Jones, Clarissa Harlowe, and Sir. Charles Grandison.[86] But not many of the writers made this kind of obvious attempt to bask in the light reflected from the best sellers. More often what they give us is a testimonial to the excellence or popularity of our author. The anonymous writer of the *Life and Adventures of Hamilton Murray* observed, truly enough, that 'had he the merits of Cervantes, Fielding, or Smollett, which he professes not to have a tythe of, it would not secure him from the censure of a set of men so influenced and so assuming.'[87] It is only natural that we should find *Roderick Random*, *Peregrine Pickle*, and *Ferdinand Count Fathom* among the novels which Colman listed in the preface to his *Polly Honeycombe*, and which he professed to have taken from the catalog of a circulating library.[88] His list runs to about two hundred titles, including, it would seem, all the good novels of the period, and many of the bad ones. In the course of the play, Polly refers to Narcissa as one of the heroines whom she has "out-topped" by her treatment of a lover.[89]

A much more significant reference occurs in the *Peregrinations of Jeremiah Grant, Esq.*, 1763. This seems to be the first time that anyone placed Smollett, even with reservations, at the head of English novelists. Although we may regard it as a custom more honored in the breach, it becomes, as we shall see, a not uncommon practice among later critics to make a similar appraisal, critics of incomparably greater distinction than the author of this forgotten novel, who wrote:

85 W. Goodall (?), *The Adventures of Capt. Greenland*, I, 6.
86 John Kidgell, II, 294–295.
87 *Life and Adventures of Hamilton Murray*, I, 4.
88 Geo. Colman, *Dramatick Works*, IV, Preface.
89 *Ibid.*, IV, 34.

Now, by way of drawing breath, and to divert the reader, I will give him three specimens of my genius for imitation, the first shall be in the Shandean style; the second in the Fieldean; and the third in the Smollettean, which I look upon to be the three originals of English Romance-writing. The order I have placed them (sic) in, should by no means be regarded as a mark of precedency; for the last is generally allowed to be at least equal, if not superior, to the two former; Sed quaere de hoc.[90]

In Cumberland's play *The Brothers,* produced in 1769, though there is no direct reference to Smollett, the author's biographer, Mudford, said of Captain Ironsides that 'we shall be forced to allow that much may be referred to the recollection of Smollett's *Lieutenant Bowling* and *Commodore Trunnion,*' and of another character that 'Skiff is only *Pipes* transferred from the novel to the play.'[91] In the following year, Charles Jenner, in his *Memoirs of Charles Beville,* expressed the hope of gaining ten times the number of readers that some of the historians could pretend to, 'even Dr. Smollett, now he has forsaken the flowery paths of imagination, for the barren ones of matter of fact.'[92] Presumably he had no hope of rivaling the popularity of Smollett the novelist.

4.

There remains one other angle from which to consider Smollett's position during these years, the question of how he stood with his distinguished contemporaries. The complete story belongs in his biography, to be sure; only that part of it may be included here which seems to throw light on his literary reputation.

So much emphasis has been placed on Smollett's quarrels that it would seem he must have been at loggerheads with almost everybody, and must have had such a petulant and unpleasant nature that no one would have cared to associate with him. As a matter of fact, he had no quarrels with any of the important writers of his time except during the course of the Regicide affair, and we should keep in mind as extenuating circumstances that his troubles with that play began when he was a very young man, and that when he reached years of greater discretion, he took a very different stand. On the other hand, Smollett was not a member of any of the important literary coteries of his day, nor does he seem to have been closely associated with people prominent in other walks of life. His letter to Moore of Dec. 11, 1765 is interesting on this point:

I have neither interest nor acquaintance with any person whose Countenance or Favour could be of advantage to myself

90 *Peregrinations of Jeremiah Grant, Esq.,* pp. 64-65.
91 William Mudford, *Writings of Richard Cumberland,* I, 171.
92 Chas. Jenner, I, 2.

or my friends. I live in the shade of obscurity, neglecting & neglected, and spend my vacant hours, among a set of honest phlegmatic Englishmen, whom I cultivate for their Integrity of heart and simplicity of manners. I have not spoke to a nobleman for some years; & those I once had the Honour of knowing were either such as had little interest of their own, or very little Consideration for me.[93]

Yet Smollett enjoyed the friendship or esteem or both of many of the prominent authors of his age. Each of these relationships seems to have been separate and distinct, rather than forming part of a social group, and very few of them seem to have developed into close intimacy: perhaps because he did not have enough time (even his moments of relaxation with his family had to be stolen from his work, apparently),[94] perhaps because intimacy with any number of people was not compatible with Smollett's well developed bump of proud independence. Yet some of the references to him are cordial enough. For example, Alexander Carlyle relates how Robertson, the historian, sought out Smollett on coming to London, and how they had dinner together.

> We passed a very pleasant and joyful evening. When we broke up, Robertson expressed great surprise at the polished and agreeable manners and the great urbanity of his conversation. He had imagined that a man's manners must bear a likeness to his books, and as Smollett had described so well the characters of ruffians and profligates, that he must, of course, resemble them.[95]

Smollett's fame has never lost the tarnish put upon it by people who made the same error as Robertson, but who lacked his opportunity of correcting it.

The Scotch have generally taken kindly to Smollett, both during his lifetime and since. John Home, author of the famous *Douglas*, expressed himself even more warmly than Robertson is reported to have done. He wrote to Alexander Carlyle in 1767 or 1768, 'I have seen nobody yet but Smollett, whom I like very well.' In his next letter to Carlyle, he was more emphatic. 'Your friend Smollett, who has a thousand good, nay, the best qualities, and whom I love much more than he thinks I do. . .'[96]

One of Hume's biographers sums up his relations with Smollett thus: 'David Hume was only just acquainted with Tobias Smollett, did not think much of him as a historian, never mentions any of his novels, but apparently had no real animosity against him.'[97] Although the statements here, with the possible exception of the first, are factually correct, they do not give us the truth. Boswell reported Hume as saying of Smollett in 1762, with reference to the latter's historical and periodical work, 'What a pity it

93 *Letters of Tobias Smollett, M.D.*, pp. 33–34.
94 *Ibid.*, p. 110.
95 A. Carlyle, pp. 275–276.
96 H. Mackenzie, pp. 134, 137.
97 J. Y. T. Greig, *David Hume*, p. 246.

is that he must write for Bread.[98] Noyes cites evidence to show
'that the friendship between the two men, so different in temperament and in fortune, was of long standing,'[99] and Smollett's only
letter to Hume, dated August 31, 1768, seems to bear out this conclusion. Toward the close of it, he said, 'In whatever part of
the earth it may be my fate to reside, I shall always remember
with pleasure and recapitulate with pride, the friendly inter-
course I have maintained with one of the best men, and undoubtedly
the best writer of the age.'[100] Smollett, I believe, has never
been accused of being a flatterer, but this letter shows that he
was not stinting in praise of real merit, even in a rival historian.

With Samuel Richardson, again, Smollett seems to have been on
uniformly cordial terms.[101] Both men showed herein a better
side of their characters than in their unfortunate dealings with
Fielding - though Smollett's belated apology in that affair
leaves the credit side of his ledger not entirely blank. But
Richardson does not seem to have expressed an opinion on Smollett's novels, although, as Poetzsche says, 'Ist es doch auch
höchst unwahrscheinlich, dass ihm die zu seiner Zeit erscheinen-
den Romane Smolletts: *Roderick Random* und *Peregrine Pickle,*
völlig unbekannt geblieben seien.'[102]

Goldsmith, of all the great names associated with Smollett,
has left the pleasantest references to him. Unfortunately,
there is a nigger in the woodpile. When the *British Magazine*
was launched in January, 1760, Smollett, as editor, got Goldsmith a job writing for it, and all of Goldsmith's friendly allusions bear suspicious dates - between November, 1759, and the
end of 1760. But any doubts of the motives behind them cannot
detract from their intrinsic interest. The first appeared in
the *Bee* for November 3, 1759. After having described how Hill
and Murphy had been denied admittance to the 'Fame Machine,'
and Johnson and Hume admitted, Goldsmith continued:

> My attention was now diverted to a crowd who were
> pushing forward a person that seemed more inclined to the
> *stage-coach of riches*; but by their means he was driven
> forward to the same machine, which he nevertheless seemed
> heartily to despise. Impelled, however, by their solici-
> tations, he steps up, flourishing a voluminous History,
> and demanding admittance. 'Sir, I have formerly heard
> your name mentioned,' says the coachman, 'but never as a
> historian. Is there no other work upon which you may
> claim a place?' 'None,' replied the other, 'except a
> romance; but this is a work of too trifling a nature to
> claim future attention.' 'You mistake,' says the inqui-

---

98 J. Boswell, *Private Papers,* I, 127.
99 *Letters of Tobias Smollett, M.D.,* p. 223.
100 *Ibid.,* p. 104.
101 See especially Smollett's letter to Richardson in *Letters of Tobias Smollett, M.D.,*
    pp. 40-41, and Richardson's reply in Melville, *Tobias Smollett,* pp. 133-134.
102 E. Poetzsche, p. 80.

sitor; 'a well-written romance is no such easy task as is generally imagined. I remember formerly to have carried Cervantes and Segrais; and, if you think fit, you may enter.'[103]

These are the only three people admitted, and it is honorable company indeed in which Smollett was placed, although as the account continues, he is not shown as thinking so; on the contrary, they all begin to grumble at one another, each discontented with his company. Again, in the *Citizen of the World*, Lien Chi Altangi remarks that the English are not 'so destitute of poetical merit as they seem to imagine. . . . their Johnsons and Smolletts are truly poets; though for aught I know they never made a single verse in their whole lives.'[104] Shortly after he had begun to write for the *British Magazine*, Goldsmith wrote for the daily *Public Ledger*, with which he had also just made a connection, a puff for the *British* in an article called 'Description of a Wow-wow.' The Wow-wow, which has emptied the town, is 'a confused heap of people of all denominations assembled at a public-house to read the newspapers, and to hear the tittle-tattle of the day.' A quarrel starts, whereupon –

> we should certainly have had a war at the Wow-wow had not an Oxford scholar, led there by curiosity, pulled a new magazine out of his pocket; in which he said there were some pieces extremely curious and that deserved their attention. He then read the 'Adventures of 'Sir Launcelot Greaves,' to the entire satisfaction of the audience, which being finished, he threw the pamphlet on the table: 'That piece, gentlemen,' says he, 'is written in the very spirit and manner of Cervantes; there is great knowledge of human nature, and evident marks of the master in almost every sentence; and from the plan, the humor, and the execution, I can venture to say that it dropped from the pen of the ingenious Dr. --------.' Everyone was pleased with the performance, and I was particularly gratified in hearing all the sensible part of the company give orders for the *British Magazine*.[105]

It would be pleasant to record that Goldsmith had written something so complimentary to Smollett at another period of his life, when we could be sure that he was disinterested, but apparently he did not. At any rate, he made no disparaging comments, as he did about Fielding and Sterne.[106]

An interesting side-light on Smollett's popularity about this time is afforded by the wife of the poet David Malloch or Mallet, who (the poet) died in 1765. We are told that she 'once lamented to a lady, how much the reputation of her husband suffered by his name being so frequently confounded with that of Dr. Smollett.'[107]

103 O. Goldsmith, *Works*, V, 89.
104 *Ibid.*, III, 231–232.
105 *Ibid.*, VI, 91.
106 See Blanchard, pp. 149–152.
107 *Correspondence of the late John Wilkes*, I, 78, n.

From Lady Mary's references, already cited (pages   and
above) to 'my friend Smollett' and 'my dear Smollet,' it may
seem that she and Smollett were intimately acquainted. As a
matter of fact, in a letter written in 1759, she referred to the
life of Lady Vane, 'writ by Dr. Smollett, whom I never saw.'[108]

But though Smollett had been ever so intimately acquainted
with these and many other luminaries of his time, his position
would still be highly equivocal until his relations could be
determined with the 'great Cham of literature,' to use the
phrase he himself coined. In the same letter to Wilkes wherein
that phrase occurred, he said that Johnson 'was humble enough to
desire my assistance on this occasion, though he and I were never
catercousins.'[109] Yet they seem to have been on rather friendly
terms, if we may judge from a remark in Hawkins' life of Johnson.
Hawkins tells us that once Johnson had admitted that his parlia-
mentary debates in the *Gentleman's Magazine* were fictitious, and
composed by himself, he was free in the communication of the se-
cret, 'for being informed that Dr. Smollett was writing a history
of England, and had brought it down to the last reign, he cautioned
him not to rely on the debates as given in the Magazine, for that
they were not authentic, but, excepting as to their general import,
the work of his own imagination.'[110]

Concerning Johnson's opinion of Smollett's talent we have two
rather surprising pieces of evidence. Beattie gives as one of
several examples of Johnson's violent prejudices that he preferred Smollett to Fielding.[111] We should be glad to have a
more detailed exposition of Johnson's views on the relative
merits of these two men. Our other information, of course, is
that supplied by Boswell in his account of the visit of Johnson
and himself to Bonhill in 1773. James Smollett, Boswell tells
us,

> had erected a pillar to the memory of his ingenious kins-
> man, Dr. Smollett; and he consulted Dr. Johnson as to an
> inscription for it. Lord Kames, who, though he had a great
> store of knowledge . . . was no profound scholar, had, it
> seems, recommended an English inscription. Dr. Johnson
> treated this with great contempt, saying, 'An English in-
> scription would be a disgrace to Dr. Smollett'; and in
> answer to what Lord Kames had urged as to the advantage
> of its being in English, because it would be generally
> understood, I observed that all to whom Dr. Smollett's
> merit could be an object of respect and imitation would
> understand it as well in Latin; and that surely it was
> not meant for the Highland drovers, or other such people
> who pass and repass that way.
> We were then shown a Latin inscription proposed for
> this monument. Dr. Johnson sat down with an ardent and

108 Lady Mary Montagu, *Works*, ed. W. May Thomas, II, 375.
109 *Letters of Tobias Smollett, M.D.*, p. 56.
110 Sir John Hawkins, p. 129.
111 Sir William Forbes, II, 165.

liberal earnestness to revise it, and greatly improved
it by several additions and variations.[112]

What was it in Smollett that won Johnson's esteem: his histories, his translations, his criticisms, his sound classical
learning, - or his novels? No explanation has been passed down
to us. But it is gratifying to know that his opinion was favorable, and that the evidence is not in the form of one of his
conversational verdicts, which were often given off carelessly
in contradiction of his more reasoned views.

With regard to what Johnson and Boswell said concerning the
proper language for the inscription, it is interesting to read
a passage from the memoirs of Bewick, the well known engraver:

> I kept passing onward, up the Leven, till Smol-
> lett's monument, near the side of it, arrested my atten-
> tion. There I stopped, for I had read Smollett's works,
> and almost adored him as an author. On the pedestal of
> the monument, was a long Latin inscription; which I was
> endeavouring to translate, but was puzzled to make out;
> having never looked into a Latin book since I had left
> school; and, for the first time, I felt mortified at not
> having done so. While I was thus employed, up came a
> 'lish,' clever young man, a Highlander, smartly dressed
> in the garb of the country. He jumped down beside me,
> and we together made out the translation.[113]

As for Boswell's attitude toward Smollett we have some further information besides his remark in the passage quoted above,
where he is obviously only parroting Johnson's opinion. One
dull morning in 1768, while he was on a jaunt, he amused himself by writing some nonsense verses in which Smollett and Hume
figure.[114] On March 14, 1768, having heard that Smollett was
piqued by one or two references in his account of Corsica, he
wrote expressing his regret for giving offence where none had
been intended, and assuring Smollett of his esteem in rather cordial terms.[115] But in the first edition of the *Life*, Boswell
could not resist making a gibe at Smollett's expense when he
thought he had detected an error in diction. Smollett's letter
to Wilkes reached Boswell in a version wherein the word 'Cham'
was incorrectly printed 'Chum,' and Boswell remarked that 'Had
Dr. Smollett been bred at an English University, he would have
known that a *chum* is a student who lives with another in a chamber common to them both. A chum of literature is nonsense.'[116]

112 *Boswell's Journal of a Tour to the Hebrides*, pp. 362–363.
113 T. Bewick, p. 74. Several interesting examples of Smollett's popularity with the general
public will be found in later chapters. We also hear of one Thomas Turner, a
general shopkeeper, reading *Peregrine Pickle* about 1754. *Sussex Archaeological
Collections*, XI, 185.
114 J. Boswell, *Private Papers*, I, 102–103.
115 L. Melville, *Tobias Smollett*, pp. 229–230. While the Hume-Rousseau controversy was waging,
a letter appeared in the *St. James Chronicle* which poked fun at several people,
including Smollett, referred to as 'that Roderick Random genius.' Hume's biographer says: 'It is not certain, but extremely probable, that Boswell wrote this
letter.' J. Y. T. Greig, p. 348, n.
116 J. Boswell, *Life of Samuel Johnson*, Dublin, 1792, I, 289, n.

Later, when Boswell discovered his error, this sarcastic comment was replaced by the following *amende honorable:*

> In my first edition this word was printed *Chum*, as it appears in one of Mr. Wilkes's *Miscellanies*, and I animadverted on Dr. Smollett's ignorance; for which let me propitiate the *manes* of that ingenious and benevolent gentleman. CHUM was certainly a mistaken reading for *Cham*, the title of the Sovereign of Tartary, which is well applied to Johnson, the Monarch of Literature; and was an epithet familiar to Smollett. See *Roderick Random*, chapter 56.[117]

One other member of Johnson's circle should be mentioned here. There is no evidence that he ever met Smollett, but his remarks were made during this period. George Birkbeck Hill tells us that 'Baretti has this curious note on Smollett: - "A Scotch wit, who had some name in his day."'[118] The note is curious and puzzling as it stands, but it would have been readily comprehensible had Hill quoted the context. Baretti continues, after the phrase given by Hill, 'He wrote a multitude of books, and among the rest, his travels through Italy, of which he gives such an account, as one would think it to be near as good a country as Scotland.'[119] Baretti's offended national pride will also explain the nature of some other remarks on Smollett. In number 9 of *La Frusta Letteraria*, his best known work, there is a criticism of a fictitious Denina's 'Essay on Scotch Literature,' wherein Baretti says, 'Smollet *(sic)*, or Smolett, as Signor Denina spells it, the translator of "Don Quixote" and author of "Roderick Random" and some other novels, has been much praised, though I cannot remember whether in the *Monthly* or the *Critical Review*, but has written nothing whatever to bring him real fame.' Continuing, Baretti advised Denina to study Johnson and Warburton, and abandon 'the Humes, the Smollets, the Tomsons, and the others he mentions.'[120]

As we know, Garrick's relations with Smollett, after a most unpromising start, became cordial and remained so until the end. Garrick's generosity in connection with the *Reprisal* was an act of kindness, to be sure, but presumably there was something in Smollett that led him to believe kindness would be justified. Indeed, it does not seem that Smollett had a single ill-wisher in his later years, except (and then most often for reasons creditable to himself) for several small fry - and Horace Walpole.[121]

---

117 J. Boswell, *Life of Samuel Johnson*, ed. G. B. Hill, I, 348-349.
118 *Letters of Samuel Johnson, LL.D.*, I, 286.
119 Lacy Collison-Morley, p. 165.
120 *Ibid.*, p. 164.
121 The latter's good friend, Sir Horace Mann, by the way, evidently did not share Walpole's feeling toward Smollett. Referring to *The False Alarm*, Mann said: 'I was at Pisa when that paper came in. I sent to Smollett, the author, who is settled there for his health. He approved much of both the stile and the method of treating the subject. He seemed persuaded that Johnson was the author of it.' Dr. Doran, II, 218.

In summary, we have found Smollett producing an incredible
amount of work for twenty years after *Peregrine Pickle,* and doing
virtually all of it with a high degree of competence, Only Goldsmith, of this period, could rival him in the number and variety
of literary jobs well done. It cannot be denied that Smollett's
incessant and generally successful literary labors must have been
very impressive to his contemporaries, and have done much to sus-
tain and spread his fame. Their effect should not be minimized.
And yet, as we have seen, nothing between *Peregrine Pickle* (or
Roderick Random, for that matter) and *Humphry Clinker* aroused
much enthusiasm in critical circles. When Smollett was to be
praised, it was invariably his earliest work that was mentioned,
above all, *Roderick Random.* It was the cumulative effects of
that book's lasting fame, as much as anything, that raised Smollett to the place he occupied in 1771. Having written one or two
masterpieces, he acquired added lustre by his versatile and by no
means despicable achievements in other directions, perhaps somewhat as today a president gains prestige by addressing a foreign
audience in their native tongue. But take away the one great
fact of the man's life, and the rest is much less significant
than it was before. Without *Roderick Random* and *Peregrine Pickle,*
Smollett's work would not have seemed very important either. But
having those great novels to his credit, he had the benefit of a
spotlight to illuminate whatever he might accomplish. So we see
his reputation constantly rising until he begins to approach the
exclusive domain of Richardson and Fielding, who, however, like
infinite numbers, can never quite be reached. Finally, with the
publication of *Humphry Clinker*, he received the immediate critical acclaim that had been denied to his earlier works. It might
be added that in the same year all his quarrels were forever ter-
minated. Consequently, for a time at least, the voices of praise
were to be more nearly unanimous than they had been heretofore.

What did Smollett stand for in the eyes of his contemporaries?
What sort of art was he thought to have created? What were regarded as his chief contributions to English literature? We get
scarcely any answer to these questions. As we well know, criticism of fiction in the eighteenth century was not regarded seriously. The great novelists, especially Fielding, laid down some
good principles, but the critics were not interested in the subject. They could separate the good from the bad, distinguishing
clearly not only among writers good, bad and indifferent, but also
among the works of the same writer. Two centuries have done
astonishingly little to revise their principal verdicts. But
since they lacked the critical theories and vocabulary that we are
used to in considering fiction, they seldom made accurate and detailed observations to support their judgment. As a result, we

notice the absence of any attempt at an extended criticism of Smollett's work as a whole, or of any part of it.

A few ideas can, however, be collected from the criticisms cited thus far. There were some charges of grossness, but very few;[122] on the other hand, Smollett's moral effect was twice praised.[123] His knowledge of life and his realistic characterizations were often commended.[124] Only two people denied his knowledge of life, and both criticisms are of very doubtful validity.[125] The originality of Smollett's sea characters received little attention aside from a few very general references to the excellence of his sailors, although something may be inferred from the imitations of this portion of his work. There were, of course, many references to Smollett's humor, wit, and entertainment value, but all in general terms. The structure of his novels was not noticed except on one occasion by the *Gentleman's Magazine*, which, seemingly misunderstanding the purpose of *Humphry Clinker*, complained there were so few events that the whole story might be told in a few pages. Smollett's vivid narrative style seems to have made little impression on his early readers, for those who spoke unfavorably[126] were as numerous as those on the other side.[127]

All in all, it is a very confused picture that we get from this cento of early criticisms. Later on, ideas about Smollett crystallized into well defined patterns. His reputation was not the gainer by the process.

---

122 Miss Talbot, page 3; Mrs. Pilkington, page 5; *Monthly Review* – a mere observation rather than a criticism – page 6; and the later and prejudiced *Monthly*, page 31.

123 *Gentleman's Magazine*, page 4; Mrs. Delany, who said *Ferdinand Count Fathom* was well intended, page 16.

124 Miss Talbot, page 3; *Monthly Review*, pages 6, 15; *Court Magazine*, which said he was natural, but did not go so deeply into the human mind as Marivaux, page 34.

125 John Hill, page 10; Mme. Riccoboni, page 26.

126 Lady Luxborough, who said *Peregrine Pickle* was 'ill wrote' page 8; Mrs. Delany, who alluded to the bad, affected style of *Ferdinand Count Fathom*, page 16; and Fanny Burney, who disliked the style of the *History*, page 20.

127 Goldsmith, who praised the clear, flowing style of the *History*, page 19; *Imperial Magazine*, which said the flowery style of *Roderick Random* pleases, page 19; and the *Universal Magazine*, which said *Humphry Clinker* was exceptionable in all but style and language, page 30.

CHAPTER III
The Rest of the Century
1772-1800

There are few, if any, who have not been amused
and delighted by some or all of his compositions.

British Critic

The three decades after Smollett's death witnessed a steady
rise in his literary reputation. References to his less creditable productions and activities soon decreased as the attention
of critics and the public naturally gravitated toward his best
work. Moreover, for the first time in history reviewers were
deluged with a great torrent of bad novels, and although some of
the writers were less bad, and a few received and deserved high
praise, no one appeared on the scene who seemed, in the opinion
of critics, to rival Smollett. Thus he and his three great contemporaries came to loom like promontories of ever-increasing
height out of the muddy waters of sensibility, Gothicism, and indecency, which receded at times to a very low ebb indeed. Reviewers looked back longingly on the good old days and often rewarded talent, when it appeared, by pointing to a character or a
scene as being not unworthy of the pen of a Fielding or a Smollett. Amidst this praise there were few dissenting voices - we
shall find little adverse criticism of Smollett's novels during
these thirty years. At the same time, he continued to be a
strong favorite with the reading public, now rapidly increasing
it numbers.[1]

Among the evidences of Smollett's popularity we may first
consider the editions of his novels. With the exception of
Ferdinand Count Fathom, there were at least eight or nine editions of each title during the years 1772-1799. All five novels
appeared in the *Novelist's Magazine* between 1781 and 1785, and
also in Cooke's editions from 1793 to 1795. Besides the individual editions there were the first collected editions in 1780,
1796, and 1797, the two latter with the biographies of Anderson
and Moore respectively. Thus we see that there was a call for a
new edition of Smollett's novels at intervals of little more
than two years during this period.[2] A student of late eighteenth-

1 The *Monthly Magazine* observed in 1801 that circulating libraries were only fifty or sixty
      years old. 'The number of circulating libraries in Great Britain was, in the
      year 1800, not less than one thousand.' *Monthly Magazine,* XI (1801), 238.
2 I have, for two reasons, made only a very superficial study of early editions of Smollett.
      (1) It is impossible to do much more without consulting the British libraries.
      (2) A bibliography of Smollett has been in preparation for some years by Miss
      Luella Norwood, who informs me it is to be published shortly.

century fiction comments on this point: 'Of the two thousand novels written in the period (1760-1800), it is safe to say that seventy-five per cent never got beyond a first printing, while such important ones as *Humphry Clinker* were constantly reprinted. Two editions indicate considerable attention, three positive popularity.'[3]

Further evidence of Smollett's popularity is seen in the printing of the minor works, authentic or spurious. It is quite likely that the publication of the *Plays and Poems* in 1777 was undertaken as a result of his wide fame quite as much as for the intrinsic merit of the pieces included in that volume. At any rate, although the *London Review* allowed him to be 'no mean versifier,'[4] the *Westminster Magazine* and the *Monthly Review* both took the occasion to state that it was as a novelist, not as a dramatist or poet, that he excelled. The *Monthly Review* said that for humor and the 'description of life and manners' he had 'no cotemporary equal, except Harry Fielding,' but when he tried drama, 'his genius, or, at least, his judgment, failed him.'[5] In 1785, a play called *The Israelite, or, The Pampered Nabob* was produced at Covent Garden Theatre and attributed to Smollett,[6] and two years later the *New Novelist's Magazine* printed a short piece called 'The Unfortunate Lovers,' with the ascription 'By Dr. Smollett.'[7] Again, in 1798 a Dutch translation of *The Spiritual Quixote* attributed the English original to Smollett.[8]

As with other successful novelists, especially Scott and Dickens, there has been some discussion concerning the originals of various characters portrayed by Smollett. Strap seems to have been the favorite; although Smollett himself indicated that he did have a certain individual in mind in drawing this character, a bookbinder by the name of John Lewis,[9] several other claimants appeared in later years. In the list of deaths in the *Gentleman's Magazine* for 1771 is this item: 'Mr. Duncan Rivers, Bailiff of Glasgow; the person, it is said, from whom Dr. Smollett took his character of Strap, in Roderick Random.'[10] Anderson records two other aspirants for the title.[11] The supposed originals of other Smollettean characters also were mentioned by several writers. Wraxall spoke of a Lord Harry Powlett, 'commonly supposed' to be Captain Whiffle, concerning whom Mrs. Piozzi made a marginal comment in her copy of Wraxall.[12] In Pegge's *Anonymia*, identification

3 R. B. Heilman, p. 84.
4 *London Review*, V (1777), 206.
5 *Westminster Magazine*, V (1777), 435; *Monthly Review*, LVII (1777), 77.
6 Charles Dibdin, V, 181-182; L. Melville, *Tobias Smollett*, pp. 265-266.
7 *New Novelist's Magazine*, I (1787), 24-27.
8 *Notes and Queries*, 10th Series, IX (1908), 88.
9 *The Letters of Tobias Smollett*, M.D., p. 45.
10 *Gentleman's Magazine*, XLI (1771), 571.
11 *Miscellaneous Works of Tobias Smollett, M.D.*, ed. R. Anderson, I, 26.
12 H. L. Piozzi, I, 354.

is made of several people in *Ferdinand Count Fathom* and *Peregrine Pickle*.[13] Another favorite was Matthew Bramble. The original, of course, has often been thought to have been Smollett himself, but the name appears several times in one way or another. In a sketch entitled 'The Misanthrope' in the *Perth Magazine*, we find this remark: 'Being frequently in company with *Friendly*, I endeavoured to form some consistent idea of his character, and was particularly struck with the likeness between him and old Bramble, in *Humphry Clinker.*'[14] In a similar way the author of the *Letters from the Mountains* met some one who reminded her of Matthew.[15] The name of Matthew Bramble was also used as a pseudonym by a young Scotchman, Andrew Macdonald, who left the ministry to pursue a literary career in London, and died of disappointments and a hard life at the age of thirty-three.[16]

A pleasing bit of evidence concerning Smollett's popularity among his own countrymen, toward whom he always felt such warm sympathy in spite of his almost continuous residence in England and other countries, is afforded by the account of a performance of *Venice Preserved* given for the benefit of his widow, then destitute, in 1784.

> On Wednesday Houston Stewart Nicholson, Esq. performed the character of Pierre in the tragedy of Venice Preserved for the benefit of the widow of the celebrated Dr. Smollett. The very brilliant and numerous assembly did the greatest credit to the feelings of the public. The price of seats in the pit was raised to five shillings, which was paid with the greatest cheerfulness. Every place in the theatre was filled, and so great an overflow that many hundreds could not get admittance.[17]

In view of the evidence in the preceding section, we should expect to find Smollett's name turning up frequently in the literary periodicals during these years. And indeed it does. Some of the references reveal affection; many of them, deep respect; a few, distaste, or at least some suspicion; but the prevailing tone through all of them, favorable or unfavorable, is one of intimacy which could only come from the writer's assurance that his readers were thoroughly conversant with the novels and the lesser writings. The affection, respect, and dislike can be found in later periods; but the tone of intimate acquaintance with his works, though persisting in certain quarters for a time after the end of the century, was never quite so noticeable again, and has long vanished altogether.

13 S. Pegge,. pp. 287–288.
14 *Perth Magazine*, I (1772), 5.
15 Mrs. Anne Grant, II, 217.
16 A brief biography of Macdonald appeared in the *General Magazine*, IV (1790), 397–398.
17 Lewis M. Knapp, 'Ann Smollett, Wife of Tobias Smollett,' *PMLA*, XLV (1930), 1035–1049.
    Quoted from the *Edinburgh Advertiser* for March 5, 1784.

The notices in the periodicals are of very diverse nature, but a certain number may be sorted into related groups. It is axiomatic that a popular and respected writer should be widely imitated. What happened to Smollett in this respect? I get the impression that Sterne, of the four great novelists of the age, was by a wide margin the most often imitated.[18] If this is so, it would be rash to conclude that he was necessarily, therefore, the most popular. It is rather that his style was the most easily copied - in certain superficial features. Fielding, with his half-playful introductory chapters and his passages of mock-epic prose, also seemed to many a later writer to have left guide-posts pointing the way to the realms of genius, and Richardson's epistolary minutiae of chastity in distress afforded a well de-fined pattern of proved worth. There is nothing so easily recognizable about Smollett's work. He contributed little to the form or technique of the novel except in *Humphry Clinker*, but the peculiar twist he gave to the epistolary form in that work does not seem to have been recognized until some time later. His style was not remarkable except for its vigor and narrative effect, qualities no more to be imitated by an inferior pen than the real excellences of Richardson, Fielding, or Sterne. His naval language, perhaps the most strikingly individualistic fea-ture of his work, could hardly be copied successfuly by anyone ignorant of life on board ship. It was perhaps intentionally, then, that Smollett's name was omitted from the following sen-tence in the *Monthly Review:* 'Paper-makers and printers certainly owe some public monument of gratitude to the memories of Fielding, Richardson, and Sterne, for the amazing consumption of paper and print which the numerous imitations of their patterns have occasioned within the last twenty years.[19]

Yet if, comparatively speaking, Smollett was but seldom imi-tated, reviewers did not fail to detect plunder from his stores in a number of later novels. One of these reviewers was Garrick,[20] who, in a notice of Mrs. Brooke's *Excursion*, alluded to 'the dull and hackneyed jest of the awful monarch of the theatre giving haughty audience to a levee of hungry poets - a jest which has been imitated from *Smollett*, which, by the way, he was afterward very sorry for.'[21]

Another review is interesting because it implies that Smol-lett was considered suitable reading for women. Having said that the book, the *Adventures of Jonathan Corncob, Loyal American*

18 In the *Monthly Review* alone, e.g., imitations of Sterne are pointed out in the following places: XXII (1760), 436, 548, 549; XXIII (1760), 83, 84, 327, 522, 527; XXIV (1761), 275, 276; XXV (1761), 320, 503; XXVIII (1763), 328; XXXIII (1763), 86; XXXIV (1766), 168; XXXVIII (1768), 323; XXXIX (1768), 83; XL (1769), 428; XLII (1770), 72, 360; XLVIII (1773), 71; LVII (1777), 406; LXIV (1781), 468; LXV (1781), 350.
19 *Monthly Review*, XLVIII (1773), 155.
20 B. C. Nangle, p. 67.
21 *Monthly Review*, LVII (1777), 142.

Refugee, was 'no bad imitation of Smollett,' the reviewer continued: 'It would have been well if the author had been as atten-
tive to Smollett's decency, for Jonathan Corncob abounds so much
in that broad humour, nearly bordering on obscenity, that we can
by no means recommend his Adventures to the perusal of *female*
readers.'[22] Although we have seen that *Ferdinand, Count Fathom*
was not reprinted as often as the other novels of Smollett, it is
not surprising, in view of the prevailing taste, that it was
drawn upon as often as any. Two of the reviews which pointed out
its inspiration specifically alluded to its Gothic elements,[23]
and, indeed, in a thumb-nail sketch of Smollett in the *European
Magazine,* the only specific reference to his works is this: 'What
power of description can exceed that of the adventure of Count
Fathom in the Black Forest?'[24]

Another group of references in the periodicals made use of
Smollett as a criterion for the judgment of other writers. We
saw this practice beginning during his lifetime, but now it becomes more common, as though his high rank as a master of fiction
were generally acknowledged. Six different literary periodicals
name him in this way, coupling him with such novelists as Richardson, Le Sage, Cervantes, and, most commonly, Fielding.[25] Smollett,
of course, was sometimes relegated to a place below the highest,
but it is probably indicative of the changing taste that four
times within the last fifteen years of the century the names of
Fielding and Smollett appear without that of Richardson,[26] while
twice the works of the same two were praised at the direct expense
of Richardson and the Richardsonian novel.[27]

Often the mention of these great names served only to remind
the writer of the low estate of fiction in his own day,[28] but
occasionally the comparison was more cheerful. Thus, one reviewer
in 1795 said that some of Charlotte Smith's characters were drawn
with a 'strength and truth which would not have disgraced a Fielding or a Smollett,'[29] and the year before, *Caleb Williams* had been
ranked 'greatly above the whole mass of publications which bear
the name of novels, if we except the productions of Fielding,
Smollett, or Burney.'[30] Thus, we see, Fanny Burney had not taken
long to get herself placed in the most exclusive company. Indeed,

22 *General Magazine and Impartial Review,* II (1788), 39.
23 *Critical Review,* LXIX (1790), 118; 2nd Series, X (1794), 349.
24 *European Magazine,* XIX (1791), 94. Other statements of Smollettean imitations will be
      found in the *Critical Review,* LXV (1788),130; LXVII (1789), 76; 2nd Series, II
      (1791), 233; 356; I (1791), 470; XXII (1798), 357-8; XXIII (1798), 472; XXX (1800),
      230; *Monthly Mirror,* II (1796), 85; *General Magazine,* III (1789), 362.
25 Besides the other references to this and the succeeding paragraph, see the *Critical Review,*
      XXXI (1771), 479; *Monthly Review,* LI (1774), 322.
26 *Critical Review,* LXVII (1789), 475; *Monthly Mirror,* I (1795), 36; *English Review,* I (1783),
      16; *Town and Country Magazine,* XVII (1785), 31.
27 *European Magazine,* XXXIII (1798), 309; *English Review,* XVII (1791), 310.
28 *Critical Review,* XLIII (1777), 473; *Monthly Review,* LXXVI (1787), 325.
29 *Monthly Mirror,* I (1795), 36.
30 *Critical Review,* 2nd Series, XL (1794), 290.

a few years previously the same journal had observed that 'The period of Evelina and Cecilia may be considered as a new aera in the age of novels. The more laboured and intricate plots of Fielding, the eccentric, and sometimes exaggerated characters of Smollett, are rendered smoother by the polish of fashionable life, and the modern novel consists of scenes more loosely connected, which seldom rise so high in comic humour, or sink so low.'[31] Although this extreme opinion was probably not typical, Fanny's father would not have been considered far wrong by some of his contemporaries when he said of *Evelina:* 'I wish I may die if I do not believe it to be the best novel in the language Fielding's excepted - for Smollett's are so d---d gross that they are not fit reading for women with all their wit.'[32]

Although there are still differences of opinion about Smollett today, he is by no means a subject of controversy. But in these years we are considering, discussion of his merits was common. Lamb and Hazlitt, Campbell and Crabbe are among the pairs we know to have indulged in friendly combat over his place in literature, and we can see from the periodicals that these were only two of many such occurrences. The expression of an opinion about him often brought forth a quick and lively retort. Thus, a writer in the *Monthly Ledger* in 1773 praised the moral effect of the novels, saying:

> Many novels are justly censured, as turning the brains of weak readers with idle romantic notions, fitted for some fairy land, but not current in that we inhabit... The novels of Le Sage, Fielding, and Smollett, are not liable to this objection; in them, the pencil of nature and dictates of prudence are united.[33]

This passage drew a vigorous reply from 'Caution,' who condemned Smollett for his 'excessive profanity' and for his failure to give us 'virtuous examples to follow.'[34] But the realization that Smollett was dangerous reading seems to have escaped most of the contemporaries of 'Caution'; it took another two or three generations for the world to catch up with his ideas. The more common attitude of this period is represented by a letter to the *Monthly Magazine*, written to oppose Dr. Johnson's dictum that in fiction only the most perfect models of virtue ought to be exhibited. In *Clarissa* the 'magic powers of a sovereign genius' cause us almost to 'lose sight of the false and pernicious principles, the violations of truth and nature, the absurd superstitions and ludicrous prejudices with which, notwithstanding the author's rectitude of intention, it abounds.' And the writer concludes: 'A good novel ought to be subservient to the purposes

31 *Critical Review*, LXV (1788), 485.
32 F. Burney, *Early Diary*, II, 231.
33 *Monthly Ledger*, I (1773), 311.
34 *Ibid.*, 461.

of truth and philosophy: such are the novels of Fielding and
Smollett.[35]

On this question of the relative merits of Richardson as
against Fielding and Smollett there was, of course, many a contest waged. A correspondent of the *Westminster Magazine* denied
Richardson a place in the ranks of the greatest novelists on the
same grounds as those just cited from the *Monthly Magazine*, that
his people are too good and that he is untrue to life. Fielding
is placed first and Smollett is preferred to Sterne for second
place. Another writer in the same volume of *Westminster* also
dismissed Richardson with a few words, but for the reason that he
was too well known and liked to need any praise! Yet he lauded
Smollett enthusiastically for his humor and characterizations and
promised to compare him in a future essay (which does not seem to
have appeared) with 'an Author no less celebrated than himself,
namely, Mr. Fielding.'[36] Another writer in the periodicals took
up the cudgels for Smollett against the censures of Blair and
Beattie. Having asserted that things would be different were
Smollett still alive to vindicate himself, the champion closed
his vigorously worded defence with these words:

> The variety of his abilities, his natural discernment,
> his knowledge of the world, the fertility of his imagina-
> tion, his wit, and his humour, drew to him the attention,
> which the more confined abilities of Dr. Beattie and Dr.
> Blair can never hope to command. And it is probable that
> his name will be remembered with respect and gratitude by
> the public, at a period when those of his detractors will
> be utterly forgotten.[37]

For one more example, when 'Trifler,' member of that vast progeny
spawned by Addison, remarked concerning the notorious Stephen
Duck, 'The works of this once-so-much celebrated writer are now
to be found only in the closets of peasants, or in the corner-
shelf of a pot-house, in the honourable association of Tom Brown
and Roderick Random,' the editor of the magazine, unwilling to
let even such a trivial comment go unheeded, appended this footnote: 'Roderick Random deserves and possesses a place in better
company.'[38]

Since Smollett was, then, being so widely talked about, it
is natural enough that occasional articles on the literature of
Scotland should have something to say about him. At least four
different periodicals mention him in this connection, all most
favorably.[39] There were also brief biographical notices, one in
1794 and another in 1796, both accompanied by short but highly

35 *Monthly Magazine*, IV (1797), 180–181.
36 *Westminster Magazine*, IV (1776), 522, 129.
37 *English Review*, II (1783), 92. It is to be noted that Smollett's friend and biographer, Dr.
    Moore, wrote for this review.
38 *Yorkshire Magazine*, I (1786), 303 and note.
39 *The Mirror*, No. 83, Feb. 22, 1780; *The Bee*, VIII (1792), 316; *Edinburgh Magazine; or Literary
    Miscellany*, IV (1786), 424; *Monthly Magazine*, IV (1797), 360.

laudatory comments on this work.[40] But the most important article of this kind was one which seems to have been first published
in the *Westminster Magazine* for 1775, along with an engraving of
Smollett. Though not long, it was the most extended commentary
on Smollett's novels yet to appear, and it was unusually popular,
appearing again in the *Annual Register* for the same year, the
1777 edition of Smollett's *Plays and Poems*, the *Encyclopedia
Britannica*, and other places. Moreover, Anderson quoted from it
freely in his life of Smollett, as will be shown later in this
chapter.

The writer did not say much about Smollett's life, observing
that the author wrought up the incidents of his own life in *Roderick Random*, 'which still continues to have a most extensive sale.'
But he seems to have been the first to emphasize Smollett's success with nautical characters.

> His *Trunnion*, *Hatchway*, and *Pipes*, are highly finished
> originals: but what exceeds them all, and perhaps equals
> any character that has yet been painted by the happiest
> genius of ancient or modern times, is his *Lieutenant
> Bowling*. This is indeed Nature itself; original, *unique*,
> and *sui generis* . . . his very name has long become prover-
> bial for an honest blunt seaman, unacquainted with mankind
> and the ways of the world.

Peregrine Pickle was held inferior to *Roderick Random* in 'naivete,'
but yet was highly praised. Concerning the feast of the ancients,
it was said that 'it would be difficult to determine whether profound learning or genuine humor predominate most in this episode.
Butler and Smollett seem to be the only two who have united things
seemingly so discordant, happily together.' We are told that
Ferdinand, Count Fathom and *Launcelot Greaves* are still on the
list of reading novels, though they should be placed far below
the two preceding works. In *Humphry Clinker*, Smollett avoided
the faults charged to his first productions; this novel contains
'no extravagant characters or unnatural situations'! A close resemblance was seen among the heroes of the three chief novels.
'*Roderick Random, Peregrine Pickle,* and *Matthew Bramble*, are all
brothers of the same family.' In these three persons 'the Doctor
seems to have described his own character at the different stages
and situations of his life.'[41]

The periodicals afford one of the best indexes to contemporary opinion, and they reveal that throughout these latter years
of the century Smollett had considerable 'news value,' that many
subscribers liked to write in about him, and that he was held in
high and growing esteem both by the learned reviews and the lighter

40 *Biographical Magazine*, I (1794) (pages unnumbered); *Scots Magazine*, LVIII (1796), 725-726.
41 *Westminster Magazine*, III (1775), 225 ff.

vehicles of entertainment. But if the periodicals are revealing, they are also ephemeral. There is no reason to suppose that many of the citations herein made from them had any currency beyond their own day. The tradition of Smollettean criticism, so far as it was being established in these years, no doubt owed more to the opinions of known authors. Many of these opinions would equally have passed into oblivion without delay, but others would continue to circulate for some years, while a certain residuum from this material has trickled down to our own day.

The first person to engage our attention is Sheridan, who is not only first in time but who stands out as the only major author of the period to express a dislike for Smollett. We have a letter from him dated 1772, when he was twenty-one years old, stating that he prefers romances, showing people as he wishes they were, to novels, showing people as they are. He says that the praise of the best novels, 'their being *natural*, as it is called, is to me their greatest demerit. Thus it is with Fielding's, Smollett's, etc. Why should men have a satisfaction in viewing only the mean and distorted figures of Nature?'[42] Despite his tastes, Sheridan paid tribute to Smollett's wide popularity three years after this. In Act I, Scene ii of *The Rivals*, Lucy, the maid, having canvassed the circulating libraries of Bath, is unable to get copies of *The Reward of Constancy*, *The Fatal Connexion*, *The Mistakes of the Heart*, or *The Delicate Distress*, but she does find *Peregrine Pickle* and *Humphry Clinker*, and presumably *Roderick Random* too, since it is among the works Lydia orders Lucy to hide when Sir Anthony is announced.[43]

But the statements which have come down from the other leading authors of this period are all favorable. It is pleasing to find Burke among his warm admirers. Concerning his reading at college, an early biographer tells us: 'Shakespeare, Addison, LeSage, Fielding, and Smollett, then a new writer, were his constant companions in every interval from graver studies.'[44] Anderson, Smollett's biographer, has added further testimony: 'I have it on the authority of Mr. Kemble, that Mr. Burke, one of the best of the English writers, was particularly delighted with *Pipes*, and thought it the most humorous and highly finished character that ever was invented.'[45]

Better known is Fanny Burney's reference to some of her predecessors in the preface to *Evelina*, wherein Smollett appears, and in most exclusive company.

> Yet, while in the annals of those few of our predecessors, to whom this species of writing is indebted for being

42 W. Fraser Rae, I, 235.
43 R. B. Sheridan, *Works*, pp. 97, 100.
44 James Prior, p. 17.
45 *Miscellaneous Works of Tobias Smollett, M.D.*, ed. R. Anderson, I, 129, n.

saved from contempt, and rescued from depravity, we can
trace such names as Rousseau, Johnson, Marivaux, Fielding,
Richardson, and Smollett, no man need blush at starting from
the same post, though many, nay, most men, may sigh at finding themselves distanced.[46]

Was Fanny speaking from her own knowledge or merely repeating the
general opinion of the times? Her father's assertion that Smollett's novels are not fit reading for women has already been cited.
Unfortunately, there does not seem to be anything in her novels or
elsewhere in her diaries to throw light on this point, unless we
wish to assume that her 'character-mongering' bespeaks an acquaintance with the eccentrics of Smollett; but the discussion of such
a debatable though interesting conjecture does not fall within
the limits of this study.

Of all the major eighteenth-century writers, it would not be
easy to think of one whose character and writings were more unlike those of Smollett than William Cowper's. Nevertheless, his
letters prove that he knew and liked Smollett's writings. In a
letter of 1779 he referred to Smollett's experiences with sea-
bathing.[47]   In 1788, he wrote to Lady Hesketh:

> *Don Quixcte* by any hand must needs be welcome, and by
> Smollett's especially, because I have never seen it. He
> had a drollery of his own, which for aught I know, may
> suit an English taste as well as that of Cervantes, per-
> haps better, because to us somewhat more intelligible.[48]

A few months later, asked by Lady Hesketh for his opinion of Smollett's translation, he gave it his approval.[49]

On the other hand, it is not in the least astonishing to find
that Burns was a steady reader and warm admirer of Smollett. Aside
from the fact that he was a Scotchman, and Scotch writers, as has
been said, have generally been enthusiastic about Smollett, there
were probably stronger bonds of sympathy resulting from Burns's
rich vein of not over-delicate fun, his detestation of sham, and
his more eloquently preached but not more ardently felt love of
freedom. His first reference to Smollett is found in a letter of
August, 1787, to John Moore (the 'autobiographical letter'), wherein, speaking of his reading in his twenty-third year, he wrote:
'My reading was only increased by two stray volumes of Pamela,
and one of Ferdinand Count Fathom, which gave me some idea of
Novels.'[50] The next reference, from a letter to his bookseller in
1788, is more explicit. Among the commissions for various books
we find this:

46 F. Burney, *Evelina*, p. xxi.
47 *Correspondence of William Cowper*, ed. Thomas Wright, I, 157.
48 *Letters of William Cowper*, ed. J. G. Frazer, II, 159.
49 *Correspondence of William Cowper*, ed. Thomas Wright, III, 262.
50 *Letters of Robert Burns*, I, 113.

I want Smollett's works, for the sake of his incomparable humor.--I have already Roderick Random and Humphry Clinker. - Peregrine Pickle, Launcelot Greaves, & Ferdinand Count Fathom, I still want; but, as I said the veriest ordinary copies will serve me. - I am nice only in the appearance of my Poets.[51]

Smollett's poems were often highly praised in his own day, but it is doubtful whether there were any words of commendation that he would have treasured more highly, had he known of them, than those of Burns included in another letter from this same year. After quoting the four lines beginning 'Thy spirit, Independance,' Burns said, 'Are not these glorious verses? They are the introduction of Smolllett's Ode to Independance: if you have not seen the Poem I will send it to you.'[52] It seems likely that Burns's high opinion of Smollett grew out of a fairly wide knowledge of fiction. Answering Dr. Moore's request for an opinion on *Zeluco*, he wrote in 1790, 'In fact, I have gravely planned a Comparative view of You, Fielding, Richardson, & Smollett, in your different qualities & merits as Novel-Writers.'[53] He adds that he will probably never write it. In 1791, we find Burns again ordering a copy of *Roderick Random*, although he had expressly said, three years before, that he already had the book.[54] Perhaps it had gone the same way his *Humphry Clinker* was destined to go; the latter, we are told, was one of four books he presented to Dumfries Library on September 30, 1793.[55]

To conclude our discussion of the bigger names of this period, we shall turn to Godwin. In an essay on prose style in the *Enquirer* he discussed four writers as representatives of the preceding reign, Middleton, Sherlock, Fielding, and Smollett. *Tom Jones* is adequately praised on other counts, but the style, Godwin finds, is 'glaringly inferior to the constituent parts of the work. It is feeble, costive, and slow. It cannot boast of periods elegantly turned or delicately *painted*.'[56] The discussion of Smollett is introduced with handsome compliments, in the following terms:

(Smollett) has published more volumes, upon more subjects, than perhaps any other author of modern date; and, in all, he has left marks of his genius. The greater part of his novels are peculiarly excellent. He is nevertheless a hasty writer; when he affects us most, we are aware that he might have done more. In all his works of invention, we find the stamp of a mighty mind. In his lightest sketches, there is nothing frivolous, trifling and effeminate. In his most glowing portraits, we acknowledge a mind at ease, rather essaying its powers, than tasking them. We applaud

51 *Ibid.*, I, 236.
52 *Ibid.*, I, 244.
53 *Ibid.*, II, 29.
54 *Ibid.*, II, 52.
55 F. B. Snyder, pp. 365, 438.
56 William Godwin, *The Enquirer*, p. 462.

his works; but it is with a profounder sentiment that we meditate his capacity.[57]

But Smollett's style, like Fielding's, is censured, though in less definite terms. 'The style of Smollett has never been greatly admired, and it is brought forward here merely to show in what manner men of the highest talents, and of great eminence in the *belles lettres*, could write forty or fifty years ago.' And Godwin adds that 'his most considerable production is Roderick Random.[58]

Thus we find Smollett standing in high favor with most of the important authors of the time, among whom might be included Johnson and Boswell, who, though discussed in the previous chapter because of their personal relations with Smollett, testified to their esteem for him chiefly in the years after his death. Popularity had come quickly, and now, somewhat more tardily, he was receiving the acclaim of responsible critics. But it is not until the next century that we meet his most famous and most enthusiastic admirers.

Before we come to that, however, we must see what other authors, not in the first rank, were saying about Smollett. It is noteworthy that we do not find here that almost complete agreement in Smollett's favor that we observed among the major figures, although there is little strong disapproval, and that from men now utterly forgotten.

It will be remembered that Lord Kames had suggested an English inscription for Smollett's tomb and that Johnson had treated this idea with 'great contempt.' In fact, Kames had composed an inscription, evidently in response to a request by James Smollett, which contrasted the novelist, 'destin'd by nature to banish spleen, and to promote cheerfulness,' with 'an Alexander or a Louis, men destin'd by nature for depressing the spirits of their fellow-creatures, and for desolating the earth.' Kames remarked that the inscription was no more than a just return for the praise which Smollett, in his review, had bestowed on the *Elements of Criticism*.[59] In that work, however, neither Smollett nor any other novelist was mentioned. Even at its best, fiction was long looked upon as a light form of entertainment which had no part in a discussion of serious literature.

Eventually of course the situation improved; another thousand years may put the novel on speaking terms with the epic, especially if novels have ceased meanwhile to be written. But though in the period we are discussing a second-rate poet could count on more attention from polite circles than a great novelist,

57 *Ibid.*, p. 467.
58 *Ibid.*, pp. 467–468.
59 J. Irving, p. 22, n.

we find occasional evidences of relaxation. Thus John Ogilvie found a few pages for the novel in his *Philosophical and Critical Observations on . . . Composition* (1774). In one place he spoke of Richardson and Fielding as 'our two most celebrated novelists, but he also spoke of *Gil Blas, Tom Jones, Amelia, Roderick Random,* 'and a few other English novels which appear to stand in the same rank of excellence.'[60] The Rev. Vicesimus Knox also had some thoughts 'On novel Reading' in his *Essays* (1778), and his comments give us a good idea of the change in taste which took place in the nineteenth century. From this conservative source we learn that Smollett 'undoubtedly possessed great merit.' His humor is coarse and his *Peregrine Pickle* has 'done much mischief'; yet the outcome is nothing more severe than that 'It is adviseable to defer the perusal of his works, till the judgment is mature.' The writings of such men as Richardson, Fielding, and Smollett 'display the beauties of that genius, which allures and rewards the attention of the discreet reader.'[61] The novels of the first two were even allowed a place in a lady's library, 'yet not without reluctance.'[62] Presumably Smollett, despite his 'great merit,' was to have no place in such a sanctum, though, as we shall see, he often got there.

It has already been pointed out that Beattie cited Johnson's preference for Smollett over Fielding as one example of the Doctor's violent prejudices.[63] The inference we might draw therefrom is confirmed by Beattie's remarks elsewhere. He was a strong admirer of Fielding, but his opinion of Smollett, as expressed in his *Dissertations* (1783), is neither flattering nor revealing of ability to appreciate Smollett's best work.

> Smollett follows the same historical arrangement (as LeSage) in Roderick Random and Peregrine Pickle: two performances, of which I am sorry to say, that I can hardly allow them any other praise, than that they are humorous and entertaining. He excels, however, in drawing the characters of seamen; with whom in his younger days he had the best opportunities of being acquainted. He seems to have collected a vast number of merry stories; and he tells them with much vivacity and energy of expression. But his style often approaches to bombast; and many of his humorous pictures are exaggerated beyond all bounds of probability. And it does not appear that he knew how to contrive a regular fable, by making his events mutually dependent, and all co-operating to one and the same final purpose. On the morality of these novels I cannot compliment him at all. He is often inexcusably licentious. Profligates, bullies, and misanthropes, are among his favourite characters. A duel he seems to have thought one of the highest efforts of human virtue; and playing dextrously at billiards a very genteel accomplishment. Two of his pieces, however, deserve to be mentioned with more respect. Count Fathom,

60 John Ogilvie, I, 342, n; 343–344.
61 Vicesimus Knox, I, 69.
62 *Ibid.*, II, 370.
63 *Supra*, p. 40.

though an improbable tale, is pleasing and upon the whole
not immoral, though in some passages very indelicate. And
Sir Launcelot Greaves, though still more improbable, has
great merit; and is truly original in the execution, notwithstanding that the hint is borrowed from Don Quixote. [64]

The notable points in this passage are the praise of Smollett's
narrative style, hitherto almost entirely neglected, and the
eccentric ranking of the novels - with *Humphry Clinker* not even
mentioned. Some additional light is shed on Beattie's attitude
toward fiction and his competence to criticize it, by a paragraph
from a 'Character of Mr. James Beattie' by his father, printed in
a magazine in 1795.

> There is another fashionable recreation, to which he
> could not reconcile his mind, the reading of romances.
> The time employed in that way he held to be lost. Don
> Quixote, however, Robinson Cruesoe, and Cecilia, he read
> with pleasure, and began, but he could not get through,
> Gil Blas. Hearing that an acquaintance of his had almost
> had his brain turned with the Adventures of Roderick Ran-
> dom, he had the curiosity to ask for the book, but quickly
> laid it aside, and would never afterward resume it. [65]

We also learn that the son went on to read Fielding, and enjoyed
him, but still he felt that the time so spent was lost.

At about this time, Clara Reeve was writing what might, with
some mental reservation, be called the first history of the novel
to be written in English. Smollett is introduced into the discussion as though by an afterthought.

> *Euphrasia* - Whenever you recollect any books of this
> kind that are worthy of our notice (i.e., novels), and
> that are not mentioned in my notes, you will oblige me by
> reminding me of them.
> *Hortensius* - I will then put you in mind that Dr.
> *Smollett* was a novel writer.
> *Euphrasia* --Dr. Smollett's Novels abound with wit,
> and humour, which some Critics think is carried beyond the
> limits of probability; all his characters are over charged,
> and he has exhibited some scenes that are not proper for
> all readers; but upon the whole, his works are of a moral
> tendency, - their titles are, *Roderick Random - Peregrine
> Pickle - Sir Launcelot Greaves- Ferdinand Count Fathom -
> Adventures of an Atom.* Many years after these he gave
> the public another, in no respect inferior, and in some
> superior to them all, called *Humphry Clinker.*
> *Hortensius* - Honest *Humphry* is an acquaintance of
> mine, and he is really a pleasant fellow. - But as you
> say many of the characters are *outree.* [66]

These opinions were all conventional by this time; in fact, her
discussion of Smollett was so perfunctory that in its review of
Clara Reeve's work the *Critical Review*, after complaining that

64 James Beattie, *Dissertations Moral and Critical*, II, 316-317.
65 *Universal Magazine of Knowledge and Pleasure*, XCIIII (1793), 405.
66 Clara Reeve, II, 10.

she praised Richardson too highly, and Fielding too little, said:
'To Dr. Smollett, the fair critic is somewhat more complaisant;
but her account of his novels is so very trifling, that we are
almost ready to suspect that she has not yet read them.'[67]   The
Monthly, however, did not seem to think that Smollett had been
slighted; it observed that in her discussions of the later novels
'the productions of *Richardson* and *Fielding* very properly take
precedence.'[68]

We also find, among these lesser writers, some remarkably
ardent admirers of Smollett. One was Jeremiah Newman, who, in
his *Lounger's Common Place Book* (1792), was quite unequivocal in
his preference for Smollett, of whom he said:

> I notice him as a novel writer, a literary depart-
> ment in which he pleases *me* more than the moral, the
> pathetic, but tiresome Richardson, or the ingenious, but
> diffuse Henry Fielding, with all his knowledge of the
> human heart.
>
> I am aware, that in this decision, many readers will
> differ from me; but can they with truth declare, that
> they have not sometimes yawned, and sometimes slept, over
> the wire-drawn pages of Grandison and Clarissa, or the
> common-place introductory discussions, and tedious nar-
> ratives of Jones, Joseph Andrews, and Amelia.
>
> That Fielding repeatedly displays considerable humor,
> and that passages may be pointed out in Richardson, which
> do credit to his imagination and understanding, equal to
> the best efforts of Smollett, I cannot deny; yet, after
> perusing their works, I never quit them with such reluc-
> tance as I feel on closing the pages of the latter.[69]

Another and even more emphatic enthusiast was Lord Gardenstone,
whose *Miscellanies*, published in 1792, contain two verse tributes to Smollett[70] and an essay with some extravagant and in-
discriminate praise, of which this is a sufficient example: 'For
the talent of drawing a natural and original character, Dr. Smollett, of all English writers, approaches nearest to a resemblance
of our inimitable Shakespeare. What can be more chaste, amusing,
or interesting, than Random, Trunnion, Hatchway, Lismahago, . . .'
But the accuracy of the following observation is supported by the
evidence cited in this chapter:

> In this age, many gentlemen publish volumes of criti-
> cism, and attempt to illustrate the human mind upon metaphy-
> sical principles. In their works, it is usual to cite pas-
> sages from poets, and other writers in the walk of invention;
> yet it is singular that they have seldom or never quoted
> Smollett, whose talents reflect honour on his century, and
> who, next to Buchanan, is by far the greatest literary genius
> of whom North Britain has to boast. The admiration of the
> public bestows an ample atonement for the silence of our pro-

---

67 *Critical Review*, LX (1785), 58-
68 *Monthly Review*, LXXIII (1785), 418.
69 Jeremiah Newman, III, 191.
70 Francis Garden, Lord Gardenstone, pp. 103, 222-223.

fessed critics. His volumes are in every hand, and his praises on every tongue.[71]

It has already been mentioned that Smollett's name found its way into several travel books, such as the *Sentimental Journey* and the works of Thicknesse. In 1792 he was mentioned in another work of this kind, the famous *Travels in France* by Arthur Young. Young quoted Mr. Green, the British consul at Nice, as follows:

> He remarked, that Dr. Smollett, in his description, has done great injustice to the climate, and even against the feelings of his own crazy constitution; for he never was so well after he left Nice as he had been at it, and made much interest with Lord Shelburne to be appointed consul, who told him, and not without some foundation, that he would on no account be such an enemy to a man of genius; – that he had libelled the climate of Nice so severely, that if he were to go again thither the Nissards would certainly knock him on the head. [72]

One could hardly blame the people of Nice for their attitude, if this were it; but it later changed sufficiently so that they named a street in their city after Smollett.

We have found several people who declared that Smollett must have lived a very low life, judging from the kind of novels he wrote, and there were to be many such judgments on him, as there were on Fielding, in the succeeding century. But even by the latter part of the eighteenth century these ill-advised attempts at determining the facts of an author's biography from what he had written had become so numerous that Isaac D'Israeli, in his *Essay on the Manners and Genius of the Literary Character* (1795), was moved to include a chapter entitled 'The Characters of Writers not discoverable in their Writings.' One of the examples he cited therein is as follows: 'Smollett's character is immaculate, yet what a description has he given of one of his heroes with Lord Straddle.' [73]

In the same year Richard Cumberland, the playwright and novelist, drew a picture of Fielding, Richardson, and Smollett in his novel *Henry* which, it seems to me, is as pleasantly written and, for its length, as illuminating as any of the much more famous dicta of the great nineteenth-century writers upon these classical novelists. The three descriptions are as follows:

> An eminent author, whose talent for novel-writing was unequalled, and whose authority ought greatly to weigh with all, who succeed him in the same line, furnished his baiting-places with such ingenious hospitality, as not only to supply his guests with the necessary remissions from fatigue, but also to recruit them with viands of a very nutritive as well as palatable quality. According to this figure of speech, (which cannot be mistaken, as

71 *Ibid.*, pp. 194–195.
72 Arthur Young, I, 398.
73 Isaac D'Israeli, *Essay on the Manners and Genius of the Literary Character*, p. 140.

alluding to his prefatory chapters) he was not only a pleasant facetious companion by the way, but acted the part of an admirable host at every one of the inns. Alas! it was famous travelling in his days: I remember him full well, and despair of ever meeting his like again, upon that road at least.

Others there have been, and one there was of the same day, who was a well-meaning civil soul, and had a most simpering kind of address, that took mightily with the ladies, whom he contrived to usher through a long, long journey, with their handkerchiefs at their eyes, weeping and wailing by the way, till he conducted them, at the close of it, either to a ravishment or a funeral, or perhaps to a madhouse, where he left them to get off as they could. He was a charming man, and had a deal of custom, but the other's was the house that I frequented.

There was a third, somewhat posterior in time, not in talents, who was indeed a rough driver, and rather too severe to his cattle; but in faith, he carried us on at a merry pace over land or sea; nothing came amiss to him, for he was up to both elements, and a match for nature in every shape, character, and degree; he was not very courteous, it must be owned, for he had a capacity for higher things, and was above his business: he only wanted a little more suavity and discretion to have figured with the best. [74]

We have opinions from many more people, saying many different things: Arthur Henderson, for example, pouring out stupid abuse against Smollett, such as that he 'was a man of very little learning' or that Patrick Gordon was 'the real compiler of Roderick Random';[75] John Hall Stevenson, versifying his attacks, which were stupider still;[76] Pye,[77] Samuel J. Pratt,[78] Mathias,[79] and Bisset,[80] all expressing a distinct preference for Fielding, but all speaking favorably of Smollett too; Nathan Drake,[81] praising Smollett's Gothic effects; Murphy, in his life of Garrick, praising the humor;[82] Davies, in *his* life of Garrick, praising Smollett not at all;[83] Alexander Carlyle, Smollett's cordial friend, yet a discriminating man in judging his friends, praising Smollett's character and ability;[84] Dermody, the precocious Irish poet, singing the charms of *Launcelot Greaves* in inflated, unlovely verses;[85] Woodhouselee, holding no great admiration for Smollett's ability as a translator, but applauding the man warmly for his achievements in other lines;[86] Edward Topham

74 Richard Cumberland, I, 97–98.
75 Arthur Henderson, p. 12.
76 J. H. Stevenson, pp. 75–76.
77 Henry Pye, p. 437.
78 Samuel J. Pratt, III, 124–125.
79 T. J. Mathias, p. 59, n.
80 Robert Bisset, *The Historical, Biographical, Literary, and Scientific Magazine*, I (1798), 55–56.
81 Nathan Drake, I, 274.
82 Arthur Murphy, pp. 203–204.
83 Thomas Davies, I, 282–283.
84 A. Carlyle, p. 216.
85 T. Dermody, II, 97–98.
86 Lord Woodhouselee, *Essay on . . . Translation*, pp. 282–283; *Memoirs of . . . Henry Home*, I, 164, 316, n.

and the anonymous author of the *Letters concerning the present state of England,* deprecating Smollett's poverty and his failure to receive due recognition;[87] Mrs. Anne Grant, mentioning Smollett six times, and with admiration, in her *Letters from the Mountains;*[88] young William Stevenson, father of Mrs. Gaskell, described incongruously by his classmates as being 'a good classical scholar, as fond of Fielding and Smollett, but as having no taste for sports';[89] and the staunch Richardsonian, Anna Seward, writing that *Peregrine Pickle* had made so little impression that she had no remembrance of Commodore Trunnion, but complaining thus, in another letter, of the tide of affairs: 'If I could write like Richardson, I would turn novelist; but then my work would be too good to be popular; - for how is Richardson neglected?'[90]

There is no doubt that this complaint was justified, or that, on the other hand, Smollett was forging toward the front. All the evidence is consistent in support of both points. In the absence of a Gallup poll, we have testimony from two men who should be almost equally informing: booksellers. One is William Creech of Edinburgh, a stout Calvinist, whose *Fugitive Pieces* were published in 1791. In a series of letters signed 'Beelzebub,' there is outlined the system of education which he (the devil) would recommend. Modern novels have an important place in the scheme, and 'To the honour of this country, a Scotchman was one of the first and the ablest writer in this delightful species of composition, and most rapidly did his labours increase the number of my votaries, many of whom are now reaping the fruits of the instruction.'[91] Another letter to the newspaper signed 'Gamaliel Pickle' complained that the writer's wife was neglecting her household duties for constant reading. There seems, said Pickle or Creech, to be no method or purpose to her selection. She 'breakfasts on Tillotson, dines on the Thirty-nine Articles, drinks tea with Roderick Random, and goes to bed with Humphry Clinker.'[92] Perhaps the last two titles were selected as being most antithetical to the two first. But Creech himself read this accomplice of the devil, for elsewhere he wrote:

> I must state a superiority which a reader has over him who keeps company. It consists in the patience and meekness with which books bear whatever you may advance against their arguments. I have condemned parts of Swift with great indignation, but he never reviled me; and I have thrown Smollett on the table in disgust, and he never said, Why do you so?[93]

87 Edward Topham, I, 205; *Letters concerning the present state of England,* p. 397.
88 Mrs. Anne Grant, I, 24, 28-29, 56, 205; II, 35, 217.
89 G. D. Sanders, p. 1.
90 Anna Seward, II, 185; III, 172.
91 William Creech, p. 277.
92 *Ibid.,* p. 342.
93 *Ibid.,* p. 155.

Thus Creech paid grudging tribute to Smollett's fascination and his wide following, and but for an over-zealous conscience he would have enjoyed the novels as much as anyone. Or perhaps he did.

In the same year, 1791, we have the *Memoirs* of James Lackington, who made a fortune from his London bookshop and probably knew the reading habits of the people as well.as anyone.

> Before I conclude this letter, I cannot help observing, that the sale of books in general has increased prodigiously within the last twenty years. . . . The poorer sort of farmers, and even the poor country people in general, who before that period spent their winter evenings in relating stories of witches, ghosts, hobgoblins, &c. now shorten the winter nights by hearing their sons and daughters read tales, romances, &c. and on entering their houses, you may see Tom Jones, Roderick Random and other entertaining books, stuck up on their bacon racks, &c. If *John* goes to town with a load of hay, he is charged to be sure not to forget to bring home 'Peregrine Pickle's Adventures;' and when *Polly* is sent to market to sell her eggs, she is commissioned to purchase 'The History of Pamela Andrews.' [94]

But Smollett was equally at home in other surroundings than bacon racks and loads of hay. A writer in the *Westminster Magazine* in 1785 stated that literary ladies do not read Addison, for to do so before going to an assembly would uncover too many defects in the company. 'Such readers, therefore, must confine themselves to the light, and least moving of writings; and Humphry Clinker would unquestionably be preferred to all the histories, and moral writings that ever were published.' [95]   In Lady Anne Hamilton's *Epics of the Ton* a bit of gossip again has Smollett in milady's chamber, somewhat more snugly.

> Peregrine Pickle adorns many a toilet, where Aristotle's Master-piece would be thought to carry indelible pollution. It is said that my Lord ---, on entering her ladyship's apartment one morning, perceived the third volume of Peregrine Pickle under her pillow. As she was asleep, he gently withdrew it, and substituted in its room a Common Prayer Book. One may imagine her ladyship's surprise, when on awaking, and resorting to her dear morning treat, she found the amours of Mrs. B converted by magic art, into the Litany. [96]

But the contemptuous tone of these last two references, we must remember, is only a tiny part of the whole story. Smollett was being read by the weighty Johnson and Burke, by the learned Kames and Woodhouselee, by the gifted Burns and Cowper, by the ungifted Dermody and Gardenstone, by Farmer Brown and Lady Jane, and by their servants, their parsons, their magazine editors, and their tradesmen. Small wonder that reprints of one novel or another were being ticked off at a rate of better than two every twelvemonth.

94 J. Lackington, p. 257.
95 *Westminster Magazine*, XIII (1785), 137.
96 Lady Anne Hamilton, p. 6. The footnote is not by the author of the poem.

It is hard to understand why so many years elapsed before
anyone published an adequate biography of Smollett or a collected
edition of his works. Eight years ater Fielding's death there
appeared the Murphy edition, a fine-looking set, though the biography was wretched. Sterne's admirers had to wait only twelve
years after his death for a praiseworthy edition in ten volumes.
But the first collected edition of Smollett's works did not appear until 1790, and the first adequate biographies came only in
1796 and 1797. Unquestionably the demand amply justified these
ventures. Not only were Smollett's single works selling rapidly
during these years, as we have seen, but the collection edited
by Anderson, which seems to have struck the popular fancy more
than its rivals, reached a sixth edition by 1820.

Before writing his biography for the collected works,
Anderson had included a sketch of Smollett, some ten pages long,
in his *Works of the British Poets*, 1795. Here Anderson paid
little attention to the novels, his chief interest being elsewhere. More than that, we find, in the bare page devoted to the
novels, that Anderson cribbed unblushingly from two earlier criticisms of Smollett's work, that which first appeared in the *Westminster Magazine* and was reprinted in several other places, and
that in the *Lounger's Common Place Book* of Newman. Three of the
passages I refer to are as follows:

> His Trunnion, Hatchway, and Pipes, are highly finished
> originals; but Lieutenant Bowling exceeds them, and perhaps
> equals any character that has yet been painted by the happi-
> est genius of ancient or modern times. This is, indeed,
> nature itself; original, *unique,* and *sui generis.*

> *Count Fathom* and *Sir Launcelot Greaves* are still in the
> list of what may be called reading novels; but there is no
> injustice in placing them in a rank below *Roderick Random*
> and *Peregrine Pickle.*

> *Roderick Random, Peregrine Pickle,* and *Humphry Clinker*
> are efforts of genius and fancy which rival the moral, the
> pathetic, but tiresome Richardson, and the ingenious but
> diffuse Fielding, with all his knowledge of the human heart
> . . . after perusing the wire-drawn pages of 'Grandison' and
> 'Clarissa,' or the common place introductory discussions and
> diffuse narrative of 'Tom Jones,' 'Joseph Andrews,' and
> 'Amelia,' we never quit them with such reluctance as we feel
> on closing the pages of Smollett.[97]

By 1820, Anderson's life of Smollett had swelled to 161 pages,
besides 40 pages of letters. Where had he found all this additional material? A quick glance over his work tells much of the
answer. Page after page is quoted from Moore, Cumberland, and
other writers, and elsewhere we find passages that are not quoted
but seem none the less to be unoriginal, such as a warning on page
27; strongly reminiscent of similar remarks in Moore, that we must

---

[97] See pages 52 and 59 , *supra,* and *Miscellaneous Works of Tobias Smollett, M.D.,* ed.
R. Anderson, I, 125, 126, 133.

not press too far the similarities between Roderick Random's career and the life of the author.

It must be admitted, however, that Anderson was an enthusiastic admirer of Smollett, and that his widely read biography must have had marked influence for at least a generation. Devoid of the literary distinction which could have kept it alive even longer, the biography made itself felt far beyond its proper span of life when Scott, as he tells us, borrowed so heavily from it in writing his own account of Smollett. Anderson does take notice of Smollett's alleged shortcomings, but only in such a way as to accentuate his praise. Thus, after placing Smollett above Richardson and Fielding, he said, 'With so much merit, he is not without his faults,' and he instanced coarseness, indelicacy, overcharged characters, and the absence of any fine pictures of grace, elegance, and dignity. 'His novels, however, are of a moral tendency,' despite all the rogues and scenes of low life. Similarly, though *Ferdinand Count Fathom* and *Launcelot Greaves* are placed somewhat below the other novels, it is not by censure so much as by less fervent praise that the distinction is made. On the whole, the following statement summarizes Anderson's position accurately:

> As a writer of that species of modern romance which has been denominated a *novel*, he is entitled to the praise of being one of the greatest that our nation has produced. He ranks with Cervantes, LeSage, Marivaux, Rousseau, Richardson, and Fielding, the great masters of prosaic fiction; and though we cannot say he has surpassed them, he has entered into a noble competition. [98]

The other early biography was written by Dr. John Moore, Smollett's close friend and a successful novelist in his own right. With these qualifications, he might have produced a definitive work. Moore's life is certainly not that. Although it remains one of the chief primary sources for our knowledge of Smollett, it is for the most part undocumented, and the materials in general are vague and scanty. With a little effort, Moore could probably have laid his hands on a good part of Smollett's correspondence; and we should judge, from the more than common interest of the extant letters, that the task would have been much more worth his while than his preliminary essay on romance.

As for the critical parts of his work, the first point to notice is that Moore made some use of Anderson's material, though only in moderation and with proper acknowledgment. But Anderson in turn borrowed so much from Moore that it is not inaccurate to describe the later editions of his work as the composite product of the first two biographers.

98 *Ibid.*, I, **124.**

The tone of Moore's comments is generally more restrained than Anderson's. There is no general estimate of Smollett as a novelist, no summing-up of the man's work, but in his specific remarks Moore said fewer things than Anderson to which the average modern critic would take exception. He resembles Anderson, however, in that his work lacks distinction. The writing of both men is little more than commonplace. They could praise Smollett, they could point to the things they liked or did not like and give superficial reasons for their opinion, but they lacked the critical faculty and discernment to shed new light on the value of Smollett's work, or the vigor to impress their views on other people. At least, this would certainly be the judgment of any modern reader - a judgment which would, however, be tempered by the reflection that little more can be said for most of the criticism of fiction written at this time. Neither man was a maker of phrases.

Moore did, nevertheless, perform one valuable service in emphasizing that Roderick Random is not Smollett.

> Roderick Random unquestionably is sometimes placed in situations similar to those in which Smollett had been; but it is equally certain that other circumstances in Random's story are so different from those which belonged to the Doctor himself, that he believed the application would never have been made. [99]

To prove his point, Moore cited several important differences between the early careers of Roderick and Tobias. Moore also made the just observation, applicable to so many authors but especially to this one, that Smollett revealed far less knowledge of human nature in his own life than in his comments on his characters. Beyond that, he lauded *Roderick Random* and *Humphry Clinker* highly, singling out Bowling, as Anderson did (perhaps influenced by the same sources) for special praise; *Peregrine Pickle* is also highly commended, but censured as well, especially on matters of taste; *Ferdinand Count Fathom* is defended from the charge that the central figure is an improper choice; and *Launcelot Greaves* held to have been hardly likely to benefit from more time than Smollett was enabled to bestow upon it, because of its ill-conceived plan. Except for their length, we find nothing in the critical comments of Moore and Anderson which distinguishes them from many that had already been penned.

Anderson's edition seems to have attraced little attention from the periodicals, but somewhat more notice was paid to Moore's work. The *European Magazine* began its comments as follows:

> The Works of Dr. Smollett are at length partially collected, and published in a more respectable form than they have hitherto been. At the present period, when prejudice

---

[99] *The Works of Tobias Smollett, M.D.*, ed. John Moore, I, cxiii.

and partiality have in a great measure subsided, his merit
may be fairly estimated. His excellencies were certainly
many and great, and his defects trifling and insignificant.
He has, however, had the lot to be more read than applauded,
and less applauded than many other writers who have not possessed a tythe of his genius. [100]

The *British Critic*, in its notice, also testified to Smollett's
popularity at this time.

> To collect the works of a deceased author in an uni-
> form and handsome edition, with some account of his life,
> and other appropriate illustrations, is a tribute due to
> a certain rank of merit, which the public usually re-
> ceives with pleasure and supports with liberality. That
> Dr. Smollett well deserved this distinction, few inhabi-
> tants of Great Britain can without ingratitude deny: since
> there are few, if any, who have not been amused and de-
> lighted by some or all of his productions. As an able
> predecessor, in the honourable walk of Criticism, we owe
> him an additional respect. [101]

Professor Blanchard, in his exhaustive study of Fielding's
reputation, tells us that 'in the closing years of the century,
the old battles raged over the respective merits of Fielding
and Richardson, with occasional debates on the subject of Fielding and Smollett. Compared with the popularity of Richardson,
however, that of Smollett, in spite of his Scotch supporters,
was not at all formidable,' and again he tells us that the 'real
struggle for supremacy' was between Fielding and Richardson. [102]
He mentions some of Smollett's champions, Moore, Anderson, Alexander Carlyle, Gardenstone, Campbell, and Godwin, but quotes remarks from Andrew Lang to support his contention. Andrew Lang's
conclusion is based on a single kind of evidence, the fact that
novels by Fielding and Richardson were abridged for children
about 1780, whereas Smollett's novels were not. As for Chateaubriand, who wrote about the relative popularity of Richardson,
Fielding, and Sterne in the latter part of the century but did
not even mention Smollett, it is enough to say that he was a
Frenchman.

The danger of making statements about the relative popularity of these authors is obvious. Unless one has investigated the
fate, not of one, but all of them, how are reliable conclusions
to be reached? The evidence cited in the present study would seem
to make for a modification, and perhaps more than that, of Blanchard's remark that Smollett's popularity 'was not at all formidable.' The frequency and the tone of the references to Smollett in the periodicals, the statement of such an unusual authority as James Lackington, the opinions of major literary figures

---

100 *European Magazine*, XXXIII (1798), 100–104.
101 *British Critic*, XII (1798), 59–60.
102 F. T. Blanchard, pp. 238 and 264.

like Burke, Boswell, Cowper, and Burns, all point in a different direction. A count of editions of single titles reveals that Smollett was at least so formidable that, with the help of his five major pieces of fiction as against Fielding's three, there were about an equal number of British editions of the two men for the last quarter of the century. *Tom Jones* was far out in front; *Joseph Andrews* sold about as well as Smollett's most popular works; and *Amelia* lagged badly. As between Richardson and Smollett, Smollett seemed to be assuming a leading position among three important groups: the major authors, the literary periodicals, and the general reading public. Richardson was still the favorite with conservative and orthodox circles, with the increasing number of literary ladies, and with many minor authors; and like their leader, his disciples were usually anything but reticent. Moreover, the fortunes of Smollett, like those of Fielding, were on the upgrade, while the number of Richardson's admirers seemed to be growing fewer and fewer.

Another point which must be repeated here is the disparity between Smollett's popularity and his reputation. While writers were testifying that his works were in the hands of everyone, and editions of his novels were keeping pace with those of Fielding, why were references to him so much less common? For one thing, he must have been a favorite with great numbers of the common people, whose opinions would not have gone into print. Additional evidence in support of this conjecture will be introduced in succeeding chapters. But the possibility that he was a Zane Grey of his day is ruled out by his treatment at the hands of many of the best authors of the times. It seems, then, that it was the large number of lesser writers, ranging from fairly well known figures down to the least of those who managed to get their names on a title-page, who did not care for him. We have two specific statements, the one by Gardenstone and the other by the reviewer in the *European Magazine,* that the praise bestowed upon him was very unequal to the popularity he enjoyed. Certainly the evidence supports this idea. The neglect which he met with from the critics during his lifetime was only partially redressed by their descendants of the next generation. Smollett was still, there is no doubt, 'more read than applauded.'

CHAPTER IV

At the Height of Fame
1801 - 1832

It may be doubted whether any competent critic, not,
like Scott, bribed by compatriotism, ever put Smol-
lett above Fielding, or even on a level with him.
                                          George Saintsbury

The first third of the nineteenth century brings the crisis in
our story. During most of this time Smollett seems to have been
as popular as before; and this means that, if he was not the most
popular novelist in England, at least there was none other we
could assuredly place ahead of him. During this same time, most
of our major authors testified to their profound admiration for
him. A critic writing in 1820 could have complimented the English
on their taste, since their greatest novelist was also the most
widely read; and ample if not convincing evidence was at hand to
support both parts of his statement. This chapter will present
some of that evidence, but it must also point out the forces then
at work which were to effect such a sudden and dramatic change in
Smollett's literary standing. These forces were not all inimical
to Smollett. Of course, enemies of his were abroad, perhaps best
represented by those female moralists who have caused Agnes
Repplier to cast a nostalgic glance at an age when one could, by
writing such vapid stuff as theirs, achieve wealth, popularity,
and prestige. But at this time they were more prophetic than
powerful.

Now, however, a new novelist appeared, the first great novelist
whom even the female moralists could countenance without a quibble.
Scott is important in our story in more ways than one. Not only
did he write the best known account of Smollett's life and works
which has yet appeared, but he inadvertently helped to remove
Smollett from the list of widely read authors by being so much
more popular himself. He praised Smollett handsomely - many have
thought inordinately - and supplanted Smollett effectually with
those future generations of readers who have turned to the novel
for stories of adventure. While Smollett's fortunes were stagger-
ing from the blow dealt by the Waverley novels, a doughty new
champion appeared on his side. Dickens, like Scott, praised
Smollett so highly that later critics have had to apologize for
him; and Dickens gave a mighty impetus to the process begun by

Scott when he created caricatures and scenes of ludicrous humor that have put Smollett's efforts of the kind completely out of the ken of the ordinary reading public. The early decades of the nineteenth century saw Smollett moved from his proud position as perhaps the most popular English novelist to a not very accessible shelf in the gentleman's library, where he has naturally taken on a somewhat dusty aspect.

Momentum operates in the literary as well as in the physical world, and it is not surprising that Smollett continued to figure prominently and favorably in the periodicals during this period The editor of the *European Magazine*, commenting on a 'Letter to a Young Lady on Novels and Novel Reading,' suggested that his correspondent had omitted humorous novels, and 'without presuming to advocate *the whole*,' asked for an opinion on the works of Cervantes, Le Sage, Fielding, Smollett, 'and many others, who have pursued *nature* through all her varied forms, animated her with the flame of genius, and decorated her with the brilliancy of wit.'[1] In 1815, the *Edinburgh* repeated the commonly heard remark that Smollett and Arbuthnot alone 'are sufficient to rescue Scotland from the imputation of wanting talent for pleasantry.'[2] Such a pious organ as the *Anti-Jacobin Review* said of E. F. Lantier's *Travellers in Switzerland* that 'We mean no disrespect to M. Lantier, when we say that the reader will not find in these volumes, that delicate discrimination of character, and that intimate knowledge of human nature in all its different modifications, which charm us in Fielding, Richardson, and Smollett: for these mighty masters have hitherto stood unrivalled and alone.'[3] The *Literary Gazette*, one of the early weeklies in the field, seems to have been a consistent admirer of Smollett,[4] while the *Westminster Review* said in 1827 that doctrinal novels are 'infinitely inferior to the productions of Smollett, . . . so prodigiously inferior, that, in humble but significant phrase, it may be said that they ought not to be mentioned on the same day.'[5]

So far we are on familiar ground. Is there anything in the periodicals, then, to foreshadow coming events, to warn us that Smollett is about to tumble like Icarus? Not in an occasional complaint over the vicious influence of Fielding and Smollett, such as appeared in the *Northumberland and Newcastle Magazine* in 1818,[6] for this sort of thing had turned up from time to time since the beginning. But the establishment of a periodical whose subscription list would be almost unanimously hostile to Smollett would be something both new and ominous. Such an organ was the *Christian*

1 *European Magazine*, LVIII (1810), 21.
2 *Edinburgh Review*, XXV (1815), 483.
3 *Anti-Jacobin Review*, XXI (1805), 449.
4 *Literary Gazette*, V (1817), 69; LXXXVI (1818), 591; No. 160 (1820), 97; No. 283 (1822), 386.
5 *Westminster Review*, VII (1827), 343.
6 *Northumberland and Newcastle Magazine*, I (1818), 247.

Observer, The name will recall the well known prank of young Macaulay at the expense of his father, who was editor of the magazine. Answering a letter by 'A.A.' in which all novels had been condemned, Macaulay, under the name of 'Candidus,' smuggled some praise of Fielding and tacit approval of Smollett into the pious pages of the *Observer.* Replies to 'Candidus' in turn were not long in forthcoming. 'Candidior' agreed so far as to say that not all novels should be condemned, but 'I was particularly disgusted at the tenderness with which he treats the works of Fielding and Smollett, works whose licentiousness seems to demand an universal proscription. It is not possible to wade through the filth of such a slough, without contracting some pollution.' Another subscriber, 'Excubitor,' had to write twice to relieve his wounded feelings. Discussing the morality of several novelists, he referred to Fielding, Smollett, and Sterne, as 'registered in the *index expurgatorious* even of accommodating moralists, and to be found, I presume, in no decent family.'[7]

But the *Christian Observer,* after all, was only a minor phenomenon of an age which witnessed far-reaching changes in its periodicals. By 1825 most of the great eighteenth-century magazine and reviews, if they had not vanished, were moribund or insignificant. Their literary functions had been assumed by the quarterlies. The kind of reviewing done by Johnson, Smollett, and Goldsmith gave way, before the irresistible march of progress, to the work of Croker, Jeffrey, and Lockhart.

Let us look at two great periodicals, one old and one new, to see what effect these changes were having on the fame of Smollett. For the older one, we shall select that most closely linked with his name, the *Critical Review.* Long after he had severed his connection with it, long after his death, his name was constantly referred to, not more favorably, perhaps, than in some other publications, but more frequently and more affectionately. It may be that for many years his associates in its founding, yoked in respect and good will for their chief, remained to do homage to him. Even after the last of them was gone, Smollett must have lingered on as a legendary figure about the offices, the subject, no doubt, of many an anecdote rising out of his talent and his temper - a fruitful combination for the making of anecdotes. For nearly half a century the spirit of Smollett stalks through the pages of the *Critical.* Nearly half a century - for in this too we find a change. In the first few years of the century, the series of favorable allusions continues,[8] but after 1804, strangely enough, they seem to cease and when his name reappears in 1814, a different tone is evident. In that year, it is true, a writer in the *Critical* lamented the decline of the novel, in-

7 *Christian Observer,* XVI (1817), 230, 372.

8 *Critical Review,* Second Series, XXXII (1801), 106, 232; XXXIV (1802), 449; XXXVII (1803), 55; XXXIX (1803), 236; Third Series, II (1804), 348.

quiring: 'Where are now the Bowlings, the Trunnions, and the
Lismahagoes of Smollett?'[9] But in the following year the reviewer had so far forgotten his Smollett as to say that 'though
Smollett was one of the best historians of our own country, we
do not find a single historical fact interwoven with his novels.'[10]
And then, in 1816, the reviewer of *The Antiquary* decided that the
era of the novel was not passing away after all. The author of
this work was placed in the first rank. 'Smollett was always a
caricaturist, and Fielding sometimes a libeller of human nature;
but this author paints her as she is, with her frailties, her
follies, her affections, and her passions, without exaggeration:
if he have not the humour of Smollett he is also without his
grossness.'[11] Thus we see that the old attitude of intimate familiarity and almost unquestioning reverence had given way to something new.

The *Quarterly Review*, established in 1809, had no tradition
from a departed century behind it; it was a product of the new
age with a set of criteria fresh and bright to reflect the taste
of its times. These times saw fit to honor Smollett, and so in
the first volume we find him being praised for his pictures of
naval life,[12] and as late as 1833, a review of a work titled *The
Port-Admiral* begins with this high praise:

> Some few attempts have of late years been made to in-
> troduce a species of nautical novels into the light and
> popular literature both of this country and of the United
> States; but we cannot very highly compliment *our* authors,
> at least, on their success in this department. The truth
> is, they come forward under the great disadvantage of their
> readers being constantly reminded of something better, and
> compelled to contrast those original and incomparable pro-
> ductions of Roderick Random and Peregrine Pickle with the
> comparatively feeble and spiritless compositions of the
> present day.[13]

On the other hand, these same times were making some new demands
upon novelists, and Smollett fared ill when his works were thrown
into comparison with the moral tales of Miss Edgeworth.

> In Tom Jones, Peregrine Pickle, and Amelia, we have a
> most accurate and vivid picture of real life; but it is,
> if we may venture to say so, *too* real. A novel, which is
> not in some degree a lesson either of morals or conduct,
> is, we think, a production which the world might be quite
> as well without, and, it must be admitted, that the per-
> sonages of the (otherwise) excellent works which we have
> mentioned, are brought together, without any such leading
> object in the association - without reference to any par-
> ticular principle, and without inculcating any specific
> system of moral duty . . . we are convinced that the gay
> immoralities, the criminal levities, and the rewarded

9 *Ibid.*, Fourth Series, V (1814), 405–406.

10 *Ibid.*, Fifth Series, II (1815), 104.

11 *Ibid.*, III (1816), 487.

12 *Quarterly Review*, I (1809), 338.

13 *Ibid.*, XLIX (1833), 485.

dissipation of Tom Jones and Peregrine Pickle have contributed to inflame, and we will venture to add, to debauch
many a youthful imagination.[14]

The reviewer returned to this theme upon the appearance of
Waverley. 'We do not believe that any man or woman was ever im-
proved in morals or manners by the reading of Tom Jones or
Peregrine Pickle, though we are confident that many have profi-
*.ed by the Tales of Fashionable Life, and the Cottagers of
Glenburnie.'[15] Again, in 1826, the *Quarterly* ranked Scott above
Fielding and Smollett.[16] Two years previously *Blackwood's* had
done the same.[17]

The evidence of the periodicals, then, is confusing, but the
meaning of this confusion, from our vantage point, is clear.
Smollett was losing ground; the tide was running against him,
though for a time its flow was languid and barely perceptible.
For example, the decade after Waterloo, like the decade after
the World War, witnessed a strong interest in his works. Play-
wrights found it profitable to dramatize his novels. In 1818
alone we find Dibdin's *Roderick Random*, *Humphry Clinker*, and
Ferdinand Count Fathom all being produced at the Royal Circus,
and *Peregrine Pickle; or, Hawser Trunnion on Horseback*, by an
unknown author, at the Royal Amphitheatre.[18] Anderson tells us in
his 1820 edition that 'A farce called "Roderick Random" was lately
acted at Manchester, written by Mr. Riley.'[19] In 1828, another
version of *Humphry Clinker* by Dibdin was performed at Sadler's
Wells Theatre, which sent 'many laughing audiences' away and
'added greatly' to the fame of the leading actor.[20]

In this same decade we learn that Smollett's tomb at Leghorn
had now become a national shrine. In 1818 the following remark
from an anonymous letter written from Rome appeared in the *Gentleman's Magazine:*

> The tomb of Dr. Smollett, which is situated on the
> banks of the Arno, between Leghorn and Pisa, is now so
> covered with laurel, that it can scarcely be seen; and the
> branches are even bound up to clear the entrance to the
> doors; so many of his countrymen having planted slips in
> honour of departed genius.[21]

In the same year, the *Literary Gazette* printed a lengthier contribution about the tomb, informing us that

> The English who visit it from the port of Leghorn,
> have erected a plain marble table, surrounded by stone

14 *Ibid.*, VII (1812), 331–332.
15 *Ibid.*, XI (1814), 355.
16 *Ibid.*, XXXIV (1826), 376.
17 *Blackwood's Edinburgh Magazine*, XV (1824)), 407–408, 414.
18 A. Nicoll, I, 96, N. 1; II, 508.
19 *Miscellaneous Works of Tobias Smollett, M.D.*, ed. R. Anderson, I, 108, N.
20 A. Nicoll, I, 96, N. 1.
21 *Gentleman's Magazine*, LXXXVIII (1818), 267.

seats within; and scarce a vessel arrives, but the officers
and crews pay a visit to Smollett's tomb, and do homage to
his memory in *sacrifices* of the finest fruit, and copious
libations of the most generous 'lachrymae christi' wine.

Inside the tomb, the account went on, are inscriptions in honor
of the author in Italian, Latin, Greek, and English, translations
of which are given.[22] Most of this was reprinted in the *European
Magazine* in 1819.[23] In 1822, the *London Magazine* was printing a
series of essays called 'Sketches on the Road.' In the sixth,
among the remarks on Leghorn, we find this:

> There is a plain and modest monument here to which
> every Englishman repairs: a thousand names are scratched
> upon it, sure, though unsightly testimonials, that no
> common dust lies there. Poor Smollett! the ocean rolls
> between his country and his grave; but, perhaps, he is
> fortunate, for here he will be remembered, and there he
> will not be forgotten.[24]

Laurel for Smollett! There is a wistful air about these remarks of over a hundred years ago. In showing us a different
literary taste, they show us a different world. Smollett would
have felt at home in an age which planted laurel and poured sacrifices 'in the manner of the ancients.' But if we may feel safe
in surmising that no laurel has been planted at his tomb for many
years, there is yet one tribute to his memory in this region which
still endures. As early as 1826 it was noted that 'It was Smollett who first made Nice so popular among the English, who before
that time had generally frequented Montpellier.'[25] The fact that
for many years there has been a Rue Smollett in Nice seems to
attest the truth of this writer's observation.[26]

It is astonishing to see how many different kinds of writers
during these years commented on Smollett. Aside from such obvious people as poets and critics, we find bibliographers, ex-
plorers, novelists moral and immoral, historians, clergymen,
humorists, reformers, topographers, and diarists among those who
mentioned him in their works - often for no other reason than that
everybody knew him, that it was customary to talk about him. It
would be tedious and unprofitable to examine all this material in
detail, but certain portions of it are worth brief notice.

The inclusion of Smollett's name in several standard reference
works indicates that his position was steadily becoming more firm-

22 *Literary Gazette*, LXXXVI (1818), 591.
23 *European Magazine*, LXXVI (1819), 512.
24 *London Magazine*, V (1822), 64.
25 *Gentleman's Magazine*, XCVI (1826), 531.
26 Mr. Horace Remillard, American consul at Nice, informs me in a letter dated Nov. 4, 1939,
    that the street has been there since 1885 at least. Earlier archives have been
    removed because of the war. 'It is understood that the name of Smollett was
    given to that street because he had written certain literature on Nice.'

ly established. The *Encyclopedia Britannica* noticed him for the
first time in its third edition, 1797, as 'an author whose writings
will transmit his name with honour to posterity.' Most of its
article consisted of the ubiquitous remarks which we found above to
have appeared first in the *Westminster Magazine* for 1775. In 1814
the *General Biography* of Aikin and Johnston gave him some very
qualified praise. 'He is perhaps best known as a novelist, and
they who read these compositions for amusement solely, without
much nicety of taste, seldom fail of being entertained by him.'[27]
In the same year we find Smollett in another scholarly work, the
still celebrated *History of Fiction* of Dunlop. This pioneering
work was very favorable to Smollett, though it gave him and Fielding what seems to us to be a disproportionately small amount of
space. Dunlop's most interesting remarks concern *Humphry Clinker,*
the true purpose of which he was among the first to perceive. He
said that in this work 'the author most successfully executes,
what had scarcely ever been before attempted – a representation of
the different effects which the same scenes, and persons, and
transactions, have on different dispositions and tempers. He ex-
hibits through the whole work a most lively and humorous delineation, confirming strongly the great moral truth, that happiness
and all our feelings are the result, less of external circumstances,
than the constitution of the mind.'[28]

Meanwhile, the year 1810 had been an important one in our record,
for it saw the publication of three anthologies which included the
work of Smollett. The best known is the collection of novels edited by Mrs. Barbauld, who, thorough Richardsonian as she was, might
be expected to have little sympathy for Smollett. As a matter of
fact, though her moral objections were strong, they were not violent,
nor did they keep her from pointing out certain praiseworthy elements which she found to exist in Smollett's work. Her most interesting comment, perhaps, is that it is 'to the praise of the present
generation that this author's novels are much less read now than
they were formerly.'[29] This remark seems premature. For one thing,
it stands alone at this time; furthermore, all the evidence seems to
point the other way. In fact, her statement led Sir James Mackintosh to query in his memoirs for 1811: 'Is it true, as Mrs. Barbauld
says, that the coarseness of Smollett makes him less read now than
he was formerly?'[30]

Another collection of novels was published in 1810, this under
the editorship of William Mudford. The title is *The British novelists; comprising every work of acknowledged merit which is usually
classed under the denomination of novels,* and it is interesting to
note that the first two of the five volumes compiled to fulfill the

27 John Aikin and William Johnston, IX, 177 f.
28 John Dunlop, II, 407 f.
29 *The British Novelists,* ed. Mrs. Barbauld, XXX, v.
30 Sir James Mackintosh, II, 104–105.

claims of this title were given over entirely to the works of Smollett, even *Fathom* and *Launcelot Greaves* being included. Nothing stands out in Mudford's critical remarks, which in general are orthodox, except a few most unusual opinions: that Peregrine 'preserves the goodwill of the reader even in the midst of all his excesses'; that the letters of Tabitha and Mrs. Jenkins are 'tedious,' their malapropisms 'puerile'; and, most astonishing of all, in the discussion of the style of the novels, that Smollett was incapable of writing with 'energy.'[31]

The third anthology from 1810 was a collection of British poets edited by Alexander Chalmers. His remarks so well typify the changing attitude toward Smollett, the legacy of deep respect combined with the swelling note of opposition to the moral defects, that it will be useful to consider Chalmers a little more in detail. *Roderick Random,* he said, 'was the most successful of all his writings, and perhaps the most popular novel of the age. . . . If, indeed, we consider its moral tendency, there are few productions more unfit for perusal; yet such were his opinions of public decency that he seriously fancied he was writing to humour the taste, and correct the morals of the age.' But the critic was impartial enough to point out that 'real life' was Smollett's object in his novels, which have 'none of those perfect beings who are the heroes of the more modern novels.'[32] Chalmers' position, and the position of a number of his contemporaries, is summarized in a few passages toward the end of his remarks. First we have a eulogy, expressed in no uncertain terms; then, after a discussion of the morality of the novels, the effect of anything favorable he might have said about Smollett is quite destroyed by what follows.

> But if the morals of the reader were in no danger, his taste can hardly escape being insulted or perverted. Smollett's humour is of so low a cast, and his practical jokes so frequently end in what is vulgar, mean, and filthy, that it would be impossible to acquire a relish for them, without injury done to the chaster feelings, and to the just respect due to genuine wit. No novel writer seems to take more delight in assembling images and incidents that are gross and disgusting: nor has he scrupled to introduce, with more than slight notice, those vices which are not fit even to be named. If this be a just representation of his most favourite novels, it is in vain to oppose it by pointing out passages which do credit to his genius, and more vain to attempt to prove that virtue and taste are not directly injured by such productions.

An illuminating comment follows these criticisms. Confessing his debt to Moore and Anderson for biographical material, Chalmers said: 'If I have not been able to join in their opinion of Dr.

31 Wm. Mudford, ed., *The British Novelists*, I (*Peregrine Pickle*), 6; I (*Humphry Clinker*), ii; II (*Ferdinand Count Fathom*), iii.
32 A. Chalmers, XV, 543.

Smollett, it is some excuse that I have been indebted to them for the principal reasons which have induced me to differ.[33]

Among the many references to Smollett during these years, a number possess special interest as showing the attitude of his literary descendants, either direct or collateral. Smollett never stood higher with novelists than in the first half of the nineteenth century. Besides the enthusiasm of Dickens and Scott and the more tempered admiration of Thackeray, we have the favorable opinions of many lesser novelists - and a few strictures. The attitudes are not always what we might expect. The moral and carefully nurtured Maria Edgeworth, for example, referred to Smollett several times, twice in a tone of intimate acquaintanceship with his works,[34] and again, on finding in Cooper's *Spy* 'a surgeon worthy of Smollett,'[35] apparently expressing her approval. The equally moral Mrs. Brunton considered *Waverley* 'the most splendid exhibition of talent in the novel way, which has appeared since the days of Fielding and Smollett.'[36] Mary Russell Mitford wrote to a friend that her father, in the latest years of his life (he died in 1842) 'had only pleasure in Smollett and Fielding,' and she added that she considered his taste 'about the surest I have ever known.'[37]

Some of the silences are also surprising. We have no closer imitation of *Humphry Clinker* than *The Ayrshire Legatees*,[38] yet Galt seems to have left nothing on record concerning Smollett. Nor has Marryat, except for an insignificant allusion in *Snarleyyow*,[39] though here too the debt was enormous. We have Smollettean influence again in *Tom Cringle's Log* (1833) of Michael Scott, but the only definite evidence is an allusion to Trunnion and the name of one of the characters, Peregrine Whiffle.[40] But in a forgotten nautical novel from two years before, *The Staff Officer,* by Oliver Moore, there are several references to Smollett, including this remark: 'It is somewhere said that no man ought to undertake a long voyage without having Roderick Random to while away the heavy hours.'[41] And in the early pages of Pierce Egan's *Life in London* (1821), we have this appeal:

> Smollett, thy touching heartfelt qualities break in
> upon me so penetratingly, that I must also invoke thy
> friendly shrine! And if a Rory Random, or a Lieutenant
> Bowling should ever cross my path, instruct me to portray
> their noble traits with all that richness of colouring,

33 *Ibid.*, 551-553.
34 M. Edgeworth, *Chosen Letters*, p. 98; A.J.C.Hare, II, 373.
35 A.J.C.Hare, II, 371.
36 Mrs. Brunton, I, lxxxi.
37 A.G.L'Estrange, *Friendships of Mary Russell Mitford*, pp. 409-410.
38 Except for an anonymous continuation, *Brambleton Hall*, published in 1810. To my knowledge
   it is the only sequel to any of Smollett's novels.
39 F. Marryat, p. 11.
40 M. Scott, pp. 238, 255.
41 O. Moore, II, 72.

and peculiar happiness of style, that once embellished
thy truly characteristic pen.[42]

Again, in the *Life of an Actor*, Egan not only named his hero
Peregrine Proteus, but himself made a comparison with the more
famous Peregrine.[43]

Among the detractors of Smollett in this group of lesser
novelists are Maturin[44] and Eaton Stannard Barrett.[45] The latter's animadversions brought a quick response from the *Literary
Gazette*, which hoped that 'the taste of Englishmen is not so
corrupted as to reject the sterling wit and humour' of Fielding
and Smollett.[46] What seems to be an accurate commentary on Smollett's position at this time is found in Susan Ferrier's novel
The Inheritance, 1824. Several members of a party are discussing whether most fame does not attach to those writers who have
been pious as well as gifted, one of them naming Milton, Klop-
stock, Dante, Young, and others as examples. A second speaker
replies to this by citing 'these two great writers' Fielding
and Smollett. 'I suspect there's none of these you have mentioned will ever be half so popular as Tom Jones and Humphry
Clinker.' Here a third speaker, a clergyman, remarks: 'The
works of Fielding and Smollett, even the more highly gifted ones
of Voltaire and Rousseau, are passing away like noxious exhala-
tions.'[47]

Similarly revealing of the age are the works of two essayists
who otherwise would scarcely deserve mention. Murray's *Morality
of Fiction*, 1805, is less severe on Smollett than the title suggests; Murray based his criticism on aesthetic as well as moral
principles, but the burden of his argument is, of course, distinctly unfavorable.[48] A much more extreme work is Mangin's *Essay on
Light Reading*, 1808, where one can find some of the most violent
attacks on Smollett ever penned. Mangin hopes for the day when
novels like those of Smollett 'will either not be found at all,
or only in the cabinets of the curious and the reprobate.' They
are 'fit manuals for the rake and the courtesan'; 'the female who
has read these novels has nothing bad to learn.' Yet even Mangin
reveals that he is writing in the heyday of Smollett's fame by
dropping in an occasional phrase in tribute to his talent and
popularity, as when he called Swift and Pope 'two capital crimi-
nals . . . who, for abilities and popularity might be compared
with the authors of Tom Jones and Roderick Random.'[49]

42 P. Egan, *Life in London*, pp. 3–4, 6.
43 P. Egan, *Life of an Actor*, p. 131.
44 *British Review*, XI (1818), 40–42.
45 E. S. Barrett, p. x.
46 *Literary Gazette*, V (1817), 69.
47 S. Ferrier, p. 392.
48 Hugh Murray, 106 f.
49 E. Mangin, pp. 30–31, 46, 21–33.

Among the evidences of this popularity we might cite the many
boyish admirers of Smollett. Coleridge, Hazlitt, Hunt, Lamb,
Carlyle, Dickens, Macaulay, all were Smollett fans in their
younger years; and to their names can be added Jerrold,[50] Blackie,[51] Aytoun, all born in the first fifteen years of the century.
Aytoun, we are told, had to filch *Humphry Clinker* from his
father's library and conceal it as best he could from his mother,
who did not approve,[52] and no doubt many another boy read his
Smollett under similar circumstances. Thomas Campbell in his
college days was thrown 'into paroxysms of laughter' by Smollett,[53] and as late as 1817 was still fond enough of his early
favorite to champion him in a friendly argument with Crabbe, who
preferred Fielding.[54] Two years later, by the way, Campbell said
Roderick Random was 'the most popular of all the novels on which
his (Smollett's) high reputation rests.'[55] It seems that *Roderick
Random* had never lost its favored position.

It is impossible to mention all the other readers of Smollett
during these years who have left any record of their reading.
Many of the allusions are interesting, like that of Granville,
who, born in Italy and coming to London about 1808, read Smollett
(on the advice of friends) to become acquainted with the English
language, thus reminding us of Smollett's own Scotch doctor who
set up in London to teach the pronunciation of English. With
Granville, however, the experiment was highly successful; he felt
that his reading had 'converted me almost into an Englishman at
once.'[56] And, though most of the readers were also admirers, we
find a great variety of opinions, ranging from the enthusiasm of
Boaden, Garrick's biographer, who unqualifiedly preferred Smollett to Fielding,[57] through the very moderate admiration of Mrs.
Jane West[58] and Wraxall,[59] to an occasional expression of strong
dislike. Thus the bibliographer Brydges not only despised Smollett,[60] but was moved to ask, 'Who now reads Fielding, Smollett?'
Yet in this same year, 1825, Brydges visited Leghorn, but made
no mention of the novelist on that occasion.[61] Had he taken the
trouble to look at Smollett's tomb, which, we have seen, was at
this very time a Mecca for visiting Englishmen, he would have
found the answer to half his question at least.

50 W. Jerrold, I, 22.
51 J. S. Blackie, p. 4.
52 T. Martin, p. 11.
53 Wm. Beattie, I, 57, 163, N.
54 Geo. Crabbe, I, 239, 243.
55 T. Campbell, *Specimens of the British Poets*, VI, 221.
56 A. B. Granville, I, 273.
57 *The Private Correspondence of David Garrick*, I, xxxiii.
58 Mrs. Jane West, pp. 320, 311.
59 N. Wraxall, I, 37.
60 E. Brydges, *Censura Literaria*, IV, 81.
61 E. Brydges, *Recollections of Foreign Travel*, I, 40, 63.

But it is time to take leave of these lesser figures, and we do so by noticing one who serves as a link with many of the greater names of the period: Henry Crabb Robinson. With respect to his opinion on Smollett, at least, he was an eccentric planet, guided by other forces than those residing in the suns round whom his orbits ran. His attitude is shown most clearly in this comment on the opinions of Tieck: 'He was warm in his praise of our English novelists; Sterne, Fielding, Richardson all praised, even Smollett's *Peregrine Pickle*. This is descending low.'[62]

When we look at the great figures of this great age, we are brought up against the fact that the novel was by no means following a course parallel with that of poetry. Not only was the poetry different in many ways from what had gone before, but in theory and practice it often represented a conscious rebellion against the work of the principal eighteenth-century poets. In fiction (and we are still speaking of the major authors those who wrote or criticized novels) signs of this rebellion are much less in evidence. Histories of literature often violate chronology to include Maria Edgeworth and Jane Austen among the 'classical' writers. Scott is romantic enough, but he borrowed from the older novelists when he liked, acknowledged his debt freely, and praised them whole-heartedly. In this latter respect he well represented his age. Not only was there no reaction against the earlier fiction (except, occasionally, on the single count of morality), but the great eighteenth-century novelists, we find, have never been in such high repute with the principal writers of any other age from their own to the present one. Moreover, it was not Richardson and Sterne who were praised most, but the two who seem to be most anti-romantic in their work, Fielding and Smollett. It is hardly an exaggeration to say that no authors of the preceding century were more highly regarded than these two men; and (especially in view of the place he holds today) it was Smollett who fared best of all.

Turning to Wordsworth, we find evidence both for his high opinion of Smollett and for his knowledge of that writer's lesser known works. Thus, among his opinions recorded on prose style, there is this: 'He considers Lord Chesterfield the last good English writer before Johnson. Then came the Scotch historians, who did infinite mischief to style, with the exception of Smollett, who wrote good pure English.'[63] In a letter of 1822 to Richard Sharp, Wordsworth wrote: 'You, like myself, are,

62 *Henry Crabb Robinson on Books and Their Writers*, I, 375.
63 Christopher Wordsworth, II, 459.

as Smollett says in his translation of the French phrase, "d'un
certain age," no longer a chicken.[64] If we may credit a modern
student of Wordsworth's theory of poetic diction, Smollett was
among the eighteenth-century poets laid under contribution by
him.[65] Lockhart supplies additional evidence in his account of
Wordsworth's visit to Scott in 1831.

> Sitting that evening in the library, Sir Walter said
> a good deal about the singularity that Fielding and Smol-
> lett had both been driven abroad by declining health, and
> never returned - which circumstance, though his language
> was rather cheerful at this time, he had often before
> alluded to in a darker fashion; and Mr. Wordsworth ex-
> pressed his regret that neither of those great masters of
> romance appeared to have been surrounded with any due marks
> of respect in the close of life.[66]

But the clearest information is that supplied by one who was himself no friend of Smollett - De Quincey. Commenting on Wordsworth's
taste for novels, De Quincey remarked that he almost certainly never
read a page of Scott; he read *The Italian*, but only to laugh at it;
'whilst, on the other hand, the novels of Smollett, Fielding, and
Le Sage - so disgusting by their moral scenery and the whole state
of vicious society in which they keep the reader moving: these, and
merely for the ability of the execution, he read and remembered
with extreme delight.'[67] So we see that the first of the Romantics
was not only unromantic, but seemingly anti-romantic, in his taste
for fiction.

De Quincey stands quite alone in his strong aversion to the old
masters. His attitude is seen more plainly in his review of Forster's *Goldsmith*, where, arguing that novels are an ephemeral kind
of writing which soon lose much of their appeal, he wrote: 'How
bestial and degrading at this day seem many of the scenes in Smollett! How coarse are the ideals of Fielding! - his odious Squire
Western, his odious Tom Jones!'[68] Richardson is also castigated.

Coleridge's opinions on the early novelists were about the
same as those of Wordsworth, but through the course of all his
critical works he naturally expressed himself at greater length.
Two at least of his remarks on Fielding have become commonplaces
of criticism; that he also had a very high opinion of Smollett is
much less generally recognized. If he ever made a comparison of
the two novelists, it does not seem to have been recorded, but in
its absence, we can safely say that he would have put Fielding
first. His references to Smollett, however, extending over the
last thirty years of his life, are anything but lukewarm. The
first reference, recorded by Dorothy Wordsworth in her journals,

64 *Letters of William and Dorothy Wordsworth. The Later Years.* I, 65.
65 M. L. Baratow, p. 93.
66 J. G. Lockhart, *Memoirs of . . . Sir Walter Scott,* V, 358.
67 T. De Quincey, III, 617-618.
68 *Ibid.,* V, 348.

concerns their visit to Smollett's monument during a walking tour in 1803.

> In a small enclosure by the wayside is a pillar erected to the memory of Dr. Smollett, who was born in a village at a little distance, which we could see...There is a long Latin inscription, which Coleridge translated for my benefit. The Latin is miserably bad - as Coleridge said, such as poor Smollett, who was an excellent scholar, would have been ashamed of.[69]

Some years later, Coleridge's admiration for Smollett got him into a dilemma. He was inveighing against the Scotch, denying humor to the nation, when one of his listeners managed to get a word in and appealed on behalf of Smollett. 'Coleridge endeavoured to make a distinction: that is, maintain his point and yet allow the acknowledged merits of Smollett.'[70] And no doubt he succeeded. But as if to make amends for any unfairness to Smollett that he might have been led into as a result of his generalizations on the Scotch, we find him, in one of his 1818 lectures, while trying to give a distinctive meaning to the word 'humor,' saying this:

> Thus again (to take an instance from the different works of the same writer), in Smollett's Strap, his Lieutenant Bowling, his Morgan the honest Welshman, and his Matthew Bramble, we have exquisite humor, - while in his Peregrine Pickle, we find an abundance of drollery, which too often degenerates into mere oddity; in short, we find that a number of things are put together to counterfeit humor, but that there is no growth from within.[71]

In his notes to another lecture in this series Coleridge commented that *Ferdinand Count Fathom* fails because there is no goodness of heart in any of the prominent characters, in this resembling *Volpone* and *Zeluco*.[72] But Coleridge's most interesting references are those occasioned by his reading of the Waverley novels. In a letter to Allsop in 1820 he wrote that in Scott's novels he 'cannot pretend to have found . . . a character that even approaches in genius, in truth of conception, or boldness and freshness of execution, to Parson Adams, Blifil, Strap, Lieutenant Bowling, Mr. Shandy, Uncle Toby and Trim'; nor can any of Scott's comic female characters compare with Tabitha Bramble.[73] The following year, he returned to the comparison between Scott and his predecessors. He said that Scott's works supply what is required in the present age for popularity, 'to amuse without requiring any effort of thought, and without exciting any deep emotion.' Continued Coleridge:

> The age seems *sore* from excess of stimulation, just as, a day or two after a thorough debauch and long sustained

69 Dorothy Wordsworth, I, 218.
70 *Henry Crabb Robinson on Books and Their Writers,* I, 28.
71 S. T. Coleridge, *Works,* IV, 277.
72 T. M. Raysor, p. 55.
73 T. Allsop, p. 27.

drinking match, a man feels all over like a bruise . . . .
Compare Waverley, Guy Mannering, and Co., with works that
had an *immediate run* in the last generation, Tristram Shandy,
Roderick Random, Sir Charles Grandison, Clarissa Harlowe,
and Tom Jones (all which became popular as soon as published,
and therefore instances fairly in point), and you will be
convinced that the difference of taste is real, and not any
fancy or croaking of my own.[74]

Finally, a passage from his *Table-Talk* dated March 5, 1834, shows
that Coleridge remained fond of Smollett until the very end. 'I
have received a great deal of pleasure from some of the modern
novels, especially Captain Marryat's "Peter Simple." That book
is nearer Smollett than any I remember.'[75]

Hazlitt's attitude was, in the main, the same as Coleridge's.
Both men preferred Fielding, Hazlitt stating his opinions with un-
mistakable clearness, but both seem very different from those
modern critics who tell us, as by rote, of the superiority of
Fielding over Smollett. Wherein lies this difference? Today,
with a very few exceptions, it is a matter of intellectual judgment; the mind (or the force of tradition) gives the answer, and
there is an end of the matter. But Coleridge and Hazlitt, and
many others of their age, not only thought about the old novelists;
they felt. These two critics loved Fielding, and Smollett too;
yet, having the discriminating mind of the true critic, they were
not content with a state of feeling; they went on to examine, to
differentiate, and to judge. This done, however, they seemed to
think it less important than to enjoy and admire both men. Sin-
cere, warm-hearted, enthusiastic, their references to Smollett
reveal an abiding affection.

Thus, although Hazlitt set up as one of the marks of the commonplace critic that he prefers Smollett to Fielding,[76] and counted
it a great triumph when he induced Lamb to switch allegiance from
the first to the second,[77] and asked and answered the question
'What, then, is it that gives the superiority to Fielding?', we
have but a very imperfect picture of his mind if we stop there.
In the discussion of the two writers in the *English Comic Writers,*
for example, we find much to the credit of Smollett. *Roderick
Random* has 'a more modern air to it' than *Tom Jones.* Its style
is 'more easy and flowing'; 'the incidents follow one another more
rapidly (though, it must be confessed, they never come in such a
throng, or are brought out with the same dramatic effect); the
humour is broader, and as effectual; and there is very nearly, if
not quite, an equal interest excited by the story.' *Humphry
Clinker* is perhaps 'the most pleasant gossiping novel that ever
was written; that which gives the most pleasure with the least

74 *Ibid.*, p. 79.
75 S. T. Coleridge, *Table Talk*, II, 151.
76 W. Hazlitt, IV, 138.
77 *Ibid.*, XII, 36.

effort to the reader.' And, after a discussion of some of its
characters, 'But Lismahago is the flower of the flock. His tena
ciousness in argument is not so delightful as the relaxation of
his logical severity, when he finds his fortune mellowing in the
wintry smiles of Mrs. Tabitha Bramble. This is the best-preserved,
and most severe of all Smollett's characters.' *Ferdinand Count
Fathom*, along with certain animadversions, also gets high praise:
'there is more power of writing occasionally shewn in it than in any
of his works.' Citing several scenes, he concluded. 'It would be
difficult to point out, in any author, passages written with more
force and mastery than these.'[78]

   There are also many occasional reference which show how well
versed Hazlitt was in the novels of Smollett;[79] also a group of
more personal and intimate, and hence more interesting allusions.
Reminiscing of twenty years past, he wrote: 'I knew Tom Jones by
heart, and was deep in Peregrine Pickle.[80] 'We passed Smollett's
monument on the road (somehow these poets touch one in reflection
more than most military heroes).'[81] 'I do not think any one can
feel much happier - a greater degree of heart's ease - than I used
to feel in reading Tristram Shandy, and Peregrine Pickle, and Tom
Jones.'[82] In an essay on Merry England we have this:

        Our cloud has at least its rainbow tints; ours is not
     one long polar night of cold and dulness, but we have the
     gleaming lights of fancy to amuse us, the household fires
     of truth and genius to warm us. We can go to a play and
     see Liston; or stay at home and read Roderick Random.[83]

An interesting statement of what his favorite novelists meant to
him is found in 'On Reading old books':

        My father Shandy solaced himself with Bruscambille.
     Give me for this purpose a volume of Peregrine Pickle or
     Tom Jones. Open either of them anywhere . . . and there
     I find the same delightful, busy, bustling scenes as ever,
     and feel myself the same as when I was first introduced in-
     to the midst of it. Nay, sometimes the sight of an odd
     volume of these good old English authors on a stall, or the
     name lettered on the back among others on the shelves of a
     library, answers the purpose, revives the whole train of
     ideas, and sets 'the puppets dallying.' Twenty years are
     struck off the list, and I am a child again. . . . Ah!
     never again shall I feel the enthusiastic delight with
     which I gazed at the figures, and anticipated the story
     and adventures of Major Bath and Commodore Trunnion.[84]

He quoted Leigh Hunt, of whom he said 'no one is better qualified than he to judge,' as thinking 'that the most pathetic story

78 *Ibid.*, VI, 115–117.
79 *Ibid.*, XVIII, 245–246, 298; IX, 58; VII, 37; VII, 194; IV, 80.
80 *Ibid.*, X, 64.
81 *Ibid.*, IX, 140.
82 *Ibid.*, XII, 303.
83 *Ibid.*, XVII, 161.
84 *Ibid.*, XII, 221–223.

in the world is that of Smollett's fine gentleman and lady in
gaol, who have been roughly handled by the mob for some paltry
attempt at raising the wind.'[85] In still another vein he declared
that the robber scene in the *Monk* 'is only inferior to that in
Count Fathom'[86]; and that not only Sir Anthony Absolute and Mrs.
Malaprop, but 'the whole tone, as well as the local scenery of
"The Rivals," reminds the reader of "Humphry Clinker."'[87] Concerning the assertion of some people that the Scotch have no
humor, he wrote: 'It is in vain to set up this plea, since Smollett was a Scotchman.'[88] In short, though Hazlitt's differentiae
are by no means unimportant, the essential element in his attitude toward Smollett is, simply, that *multum amavit*.

And so did Lamb; though with him Smollett was long the favorite. Lamb's position may have been due to his preference
(other things being fairly equal) for the outre, or to his desire
not to end a good subject for conversation. It was not until
'after some years' difficulty,' Hazlitt tells us, that he effected
his conversion, that is, made him a Fieldingite.[89] The intervening
talks were surely more important for Lamb than the outcome; and
the conversion, like many another, may have lasted until the dry-
ing up of the baptismal water. As a matter of fact, Lamb himself
never took the trouble to expatiate on the relative merits of
these two favorites of his, Fielding and Smollett. The nearest
thing to an explanation of his love for Smollett is found in a
letter to Wordsworth written in 1801, where he objected to the
direct preaching in some of Wordsworth's poems.

> An intelligent reader finds a sort of insult in being
> told, I will teach you how to think upon this subject. This
> fault, if I am right, is in a ten-thousandth worse degree to
> be found in Sterne and many other novelists & modern poets,
> who continually put a sign post up to shew where you are to
> feel. They set out with assuming their readers to be stupid.
> Very different from Robinson Crusoe, the Vicar of Wakefield,
> Roderick Random, and other beautiful bare narratives.[90]

Lamb's other references merely attest to his appreciation of Smollett. Saying that a little good nature overpowers a lot of bad,
and having cited Tom Jones and Blifil as an example, Lamb continued: 'One homely expostulating shrug from Strap, warms the
whole air which the suggestions of a gentlemanly ingratitude from
his friend Random had begun to freeze.'[91] In 'Imperfect sympa-
thies,' discussing the idiosyncrasies of the Scotch, he wrote:

85 *Ibid.*, XVII, 184.
86 *Ibid.*, VI, 127.
87 *Ibid.*, IX, 68.
88 *Ibid.*, XVII, 101, n. 1.
89 *Ibid.*, XII, 36.
90 C. Lamb, VI, 209.
91 *Ibid.*, I, 83.

Thomson they seem to have forgotten. Smollett they
have neither forgotten nor forgiven for his delineation of
Rory and his companion, upon their first introduction to
our metropolis. — Speak of Smollett as a great genius, and
they will retort upon you Hume's History compared with *his*
Continuation of it. What if the historian had continued
Humphrey Clinker?[92]

More praise of Smollett appeared in his "Detached Thoughts on
Books,' where he wrote: 'In some respects the better a book is,
the less it demands from binding. Fielding, Smollett, Sterne,
and all that class of perpetually self-reproductive volumes —
Great Nature's Stereotypes — we see them individually perish with
less regret, because we know the copies of them to be "eterne."'[93]
And that his fondness for the old novelists was of life-long dura-
tion may be inferred from these lines from his verses 'To T.
Stothard, Esq.,' written in 1833:

> In my young days
> How often have I with a child's fond gaze
> Pored on the pictured wonders thou hadst done:
> Clarissa mournful, and prim Grandison!
> All Fielding's, Smollett's heroes, rose to view;
> I saw, and I believed the phantoms true.[94]

Southey seems to have had very little to say about Smollett,
but that little implies a favorable opinion. In *The Doctor* he
humorously appealed to an imaginary reader to banish Smollett and
his three great contemporaries, but not 'the Doctor, true Doctor
Dove.'[95] In his *Journal in Scotland*, he referred to Smollett's
monument thus: 'The family did well in erecting it: it would become them to keep it in a proper state of repair.'[96]

In Byron s works, on the other hand, references to Smollett
abound, but owing to his practice of alluding to authors very
often, and criticizing them (except in most general terms) very
seldom we do not learn much more than that his opinion of Smollett was favorable. Several times in his letters Byron defended
Don Juan against the charge of indecency by saying that the ob-
jectors found no fault with Smollett, who, we are told on one
occasion, was 'ten times worse,' and Fielding 'no better.' In
another letter he was careful to say that he made no pretence of
competing with these and other honored names 'in any thing but
decency.'[97] He even answered his critics in the poem itself:

> 'Tis all the same to me; I'm fond of yielding,
> And therefore leave them to the purer page
> of Smollett, Prior, Ariosto, Fielding,
> Who say strange things for so correct an age.'[98]

92 *Ibid.*, II, 61.
93 *Ibid.*, II, 173.
94 *Ibid.*, V, 75.
95 R. Southey, *The Doctor*, p. 45.
96 R. Southey, *Journal of a Tour in Scotland in 1819*, p. 250.
97 Lord Byron, XI, 366–367, 381; XIII, 155–156.
98 *Ibid.*, VI, 210.

Byron, of course, never attacked the immorality of Fielding and Smollett. Still, in defending himself by citing them as precedents he did not aid their cause. By nosing again and again to the same sources of indecency he was establishing in the minds of his readers various unpleasant associations with the names of Fielding and Smollett. Inadvertently, perhaps, he spoke only too well for his age in denigrating them, if not in exculpating himself.

Some of his other references serve to show his detailed knowledge of Smollett's writings. Twice, in his letters, he used Mrs. Jenkins' phrase 'the handsome thing';[99] in the notes to *Childe Harold* he mentioned 'Smollett's Lismahago, who maintains that the purest English is spoken in Edinburgh';[100] in another letter, in the tone of an *ipse dixit*, he wrote: 'You know, laughing is the sign of a rational animal; so says Dr. Smollett';[101] he brought in a phrase from *Roderick Random*;[102] he defended one of his rhymes by citing as authority 'Smollett's famous *Tears of Scotland*.'[103] He pointed out in a letter to Murray that Campbell was in error in seeing the influence of *Humphry Clinker* in the *New Bath Guide*,[104] and he made an error of his own in attributing to Smollett, in the *Adventures of an Atom*, credit for originating the phrase 'blatant beast.'[105] All this tells us as clearly as any direct statement could that Smollett occupied a high and honorable place in Byron's estimation.

When we consider Shelley, the results are purely negative. His own attempts at fiction apparently aroused in him no interest in the works of the English masters. Medwin tells us that at the circulating library near Shelley's first school, 'Richardson, Fielding, and Smollett, formed the staple of the collection. But these authors were little to Shelley's taste, for they exhibited life pretty much as it is, and poets of all ages have despised the real.'[106]

Medwin's generalization, as is common, holds just as long as it is applied to the particular instance which caused its formulation. We have seen the attitude of the poets Wordsworth, Coleridge, and Byron, and with them must be classed Keats. Moreover, in one of his letters Keats used Smollett and Scott as exemplars of the real and unreal in fiction and cast his vote for the former. The passage, found in a letter to his brothers written in 1818, is as follows:

99 *Ibid.*, II, 248; II, 153.
100 *Ibid.*, II, 203.
101 *Ibid.*, VIII, 197, 198.
102 *Ibid.*, X, 172.
103 *Ibid.*, IX, 155.
104 *Ibid.*, XII, 23.
105 *Ibid.*, II, 40.
106 T. Medwin, p. 25.

You ask me what degrees there are between Scott's Novels and those of Smollett. They appear to me to be quite distinct in every particular - more especially in their aim — Scott endeavours to throw so interesting and romantic a colouring into common and low Characters as to give them a touch of the Sublime - Smollett on the contrary pulls down and levels what with other Men would continue Romance. The Grand parts of Scott are within the reach of more Minds that (for than) the finest humours in Humphrey Clincker.[107]

A very interesting passage from a letter to Woodhouse in the following year shows how Smollett's novels had caught Keats's fancy. He has been imagining here a continuation of *Humphry Clinker*.

Have you seen old Bramble yet - they say he's on his last legs. The gout did not treat the old Man well so the Physician superseded it, and put the dropsy in office, who gets very fat upon his new employment, and behaves worse than the other to the old Man. But he'll have his house about his ears soon. We shall have another fall of Siege-Arms. I suppose Mrs. Humphrey persists in a big-belley - poor thing she little thinks how she is spoiling the corners of her mouth - and making her nose quite a piminy. Mr. Humphrey I hear was giving a Lecture in the gaming-room - when some one call'd out Spousey! I hear too he has received a challenge from a gentleman who lost that evening. The fact is Mr. H. is a mere nothing out of his Bathroom. Old Tabitha died in being bolstered up for a whist-party. They had to cut again. Chowder died long ago - Mrs. H. laments that the last last time (sic) they *put him* (i.e. to breed) he didn't take. They say he was a direct descendent of Cupid and Veney in the Spectator. This may be eisily known by the Parish Books.[108]

It is possible that one of the attractions Keats found in Hunt was a common taste in fiction, for Hunt was one of Smollett's most fervent admirers and expressed himself frequently on the matter. Among his many references, it is not surprising - rather, the soundness of his general attitude is only affirmed thereby - to find a few that are unfavorable. He granted Smollett 'generosity in money matters,' but thought him lacking in delicacy; 'otherwise he never would have given "ostentatious" Sunday dinners to poor authors, upon whose heads he took the opportunity of cracking sarcastic jokes!'[109] In discussing rogues in literature, he contrasted Jonathan Wild, 'caviare to the multitude,' with Count Fathom, 'a thief not at all to our taste. We are continually obliged to call his mother to our recollection, in order to bear him.'[110] While in prison, he recorded among the books read Smollett's *Travels*, 'which disgusted me, as they have some others. There is a vein in Smollett - a Scotch vein - which is always disgusting to people of delicacy; but it is enough to say of him in this work, that he is an invalid with whom even invalids cannot

107 J. Keats, I, 81.
108 *Ibid.*, II, 426–427.
109 L. Hunt, *Men, Women, and Books*, p. 218.
110 L. Hunt, *Indicator*, p. 110.

sympathise - one has no patience with his want of patience.'[111]
But on viewing the Venus de Medici, Hunt said he shared the disappointment of the 'Smelfungus' of Sterne, instead of the raptures
of perhaps 'all the travelled connoisseurs of the earth, Smollett
alone and Hazlitt excepted.'[112] Hunt seems to have been one of the
earliest forerunners of those modern critics who have defended and
even praised Smollett's criticisms of the art he examined on his
travels. And Hunt's remaining references to Smollett are all
favorable.

Smollett's attraction for Hunt was, apparently, the matter of a
lifetime. In his autobiography he listed Smollett among some ten
favorite prose authors of his youth,[113] and in his journal for 1822
he again referred to his boyhood reading of the novelist.[114] The
latest reference seems to be one in a letter written in 1846, where
he discussed a book of extracts from eighteenth-century literature
he was planning, to deal with old country houses and to include
passages of terror such as the adventure of Fathom in the robber's
cottage.[115] We have already noted his opinion, as recorded by
Hazlitt, that 'the most pathetic story in the world' is one in
Smollett.[116] In his essay "A Novel Party,' following much the same
plan used in Kidgell's *Card*, he introduced no less than fifteen of
Smollett's characters.[117] Discussing a public official supposed to
be fond of novels, he wrote: "I know not what sort of lawyer he
was; probably none the worse for imbuing himself with the knowledge
of Fielding and Smollett.'[118] Even in treating such an unlikely
subject as the Neapolitan Revolution, he must make allusions to the
famous dinner in *Peregrine Pickle*.[119] In a letter to Shelley in
1819 the mere mention of Italy led him to talk of Smollett and ad-
minister a mild rebuke to Shelley for his lack of interest in the
novelist.

> I should be sorry that you came away from such a country
> without some associations, human as well as inanimate. You
> know, I suppose, that Smollett was buried at Livorno; There
> were some things about his writings very unpleasant, but he
> was an honest man, and an independent one, and is understood
> to have done immense good to the poor wounded sailors in naval
> fights, by those pictures of pitiless surgery and amputation
> in *Roderick Random*.[120]

On his own Italian journey, he failed not to visit Leghorn and set
down some suitable reflections.[121] The most important passage,

111 L. Hunt, *Correspondence*, I, 80–81.
112 L. Hunt, *Autobiography*, II, 158.
113 *Ibid.*, I, 158.
114 L. Hunt, *Lord Byron*, p. 343.
115 L. Hunt, *Correspondence*, II, 83.
116 See pages 84–85, *supra*.
117 L. Hunt, *Men, Women, and Books*, pp. 57–66.
118 L. Hunt, *Autobiography*, I, 237.
119 L. Hunt, *Examiner*, No. 657 (July 30, 1820).
120 L. Hunt, *Correspondence*, I, 148.
121 L. Hunt, *Autobiography*, II, 97.

however, is a section in his Table-talk headed 'Smollett,' which is worth quoting at some length, especially in view of some of the comments that were to be made about Smollett by later writers.

> Though Smollett sometimes vexes us with the malicious boy's-play of his heroes, and sometimes disgusts with his coarseness, he is still the Smollett whom now, as in one's boyhood, it is impossible not to laugh heartily with. He is an accomplished writer, and a masterly observer, and may be called the finest of caricaturists. His caricatures are always substantially true. . . Then as to the objections against his morality, nobody will be hurt by it. The delicate and sentimental will look on the whole matter as a joke (and coarser people will benefit by perceiving that heroes like them are expected to have virtues as well as faults.) Smollett had a strong spice of pride and malice in him (greatly owing, we doubt not, to some scenes of unjust treatment he witnessed in early youth), which he imparts to his heroes; all of whom, probably, are caricatures of himself, as Fielding's brawny, good-natured, idle fellows are of *him*. There is no serious evil intention, however . . . . It is energy, humour, and movement, not particularly amiable, but clever, entertaining, and interesting, and without an atom of ·hypocrisy in it. No man will learn to be shabby by reading Smollett's writings. [122]

This spirited defence of Smollett's moral intention is very fine, but it is regrettable that Hunt felt impelled by the temper of the times to write it and unfortunate that such opinions from his pen and that of other qualified critics had no discernible effect in changing the rapidly spreading opinion that Smollett was unfit to be read by decent people.

The most outstanding contribution which has been made to Smollett literature is still, no doubt, the prefatory essay written by Scott for Ballantyne's *Novelist's Library*. This fact (if it is one) testifies both to the literary power of Scott and to the paucity of good work which has been done on Smollett.. The biographical portion of this essay need not detain us, since, by Scott's own admission, it was not much more than a pasticcio composed from the work of Moore and Anderson. But the critical dicta were, of course, entirely Scott's own.

Scott can hardly be accused of blind partiality. He made no attempt to gloss over the less pleasant things that had been written about Smollett's character and life; he sharply criticized the plan of *Ferdinand Count Fathom;* he took more pains than would seem necessary to point out the weaknesses of *Sir Launcelot Greaves;* he did not care for the *Travels;* and he returned again and again, in other places[123] as well as in this essay, to the point that all of Smollett's novels lack structure.

122 L. Hunt, *Table-talk*, pp. 41–42.
123 *Fortunes of Nigel*, I, xiv–xv; *The Monastery*, I, xxix.

It was in his famous comparison of Fielding and Smollett that Scott fell foul of a host of subsequent writers, including more than one of our own generation. He recognized Fielding's superiority in construction as clearly as anyone could wish. He would not do Jones the 'great injustice' of 'weighing him in the balance with the wild and ferocious Pickle,' nor did he fail to differentiate sharply between the female characters of the two novelists. He granted that *Tom Jones* was superior to anything from the pen of Fielding's rival and even gave it precedence in time for good measure. But he made little or nothing of some others of Fielding's excellences, such as the sound moral tendency of his works (which has, perhaps, been a little too glibly expounded by some modern apologists). He was singularly blind to the author's purpose in *Jonathan Wild*. He refused, moreover, as is the fashion nowadays, to rationalize into positive virtues what he looked upon as defects in a great writer. On the other hand, he gave more weight than most critics to certain of Smollett's virtues: the poetic or romantic elements in his work, his variety, his richness of incident and detail, his animation and broad humor; and it was largely the emphasis he placed upon these which led him to conclude by saying that 'we readily grant to Smollett an equal rank with his great rival Fielding, while we place both far above any of their successors in the same line of fictitious composition.[124]

This much disputed passage should not obscure the excellence of some other parts of the essay. There is an astute comparison of *Roderick Random* and *Peregrine Pickle* which sets forth the relative merits of these two novels so well that later writers have been able to say little more on the subject.[125] Long before Scott's time it had become commonplace to praise the scene in the robber's hut from *Fathom*, but a hitherto neglected element in the book was called to the attention of the public when Scott stated that the character of the Jew was 'the first candid attempt to do justice to a calumniated race.'[126] Scott was also original in pointing out that Aurelia Darnel must be excepted from our generalizations about Smollett's heroines.[127] The remarks on *Humphry Clinker*, on the other hand, although containing nothing strikingly new, were so happily phrased[128] that Scott no doubt did much to confirm the high place which that work has had in the estimation of the critics and the public.

Scott's allusions to Smollett in other places, except for those already referred to, are of so little importance in comparison with this essay that they may be passed over. The essays on the

124 W. Scott, *Lives of the novelists*, pp. 106–112.
125 *Ibid.*, pp. 79–80.
126 *Ibid.*, p. 84.
127 *Ibid.*, p. 93.
128 *Ibid.*, pp. 98–99.

novelists were no doubt widely read (they were quickly extracted from the collection of novels and printed separately) and may have caused a temporary heightening of interest in some of the writers represented. The reviewer in the *Literary Gazette*, for example, said: 'Having read this memoir, we are of opinion that another course of Smollett's novels may be taken with an augmented relish.'[129] But not all the fine things which Scott's generous nature led him to say could effect any permanent change in the taste of the public, which had now, and in his own novels, found something far more to its liking than any of the eighteenth-century classics. Thus, the *Quarterly Review* was saying in 1826 (in an article by Lockhart,[130] however) that 'we are sure every reader will agree with ourselves that Fielding and Smollett have had one successor, who is not merely a rival but a superior.'[131] The same idea had already been voiced in *Blackwood's*, which would have Le Sage far above both Fielding and Smollett, and would place Le Sage 'by the side of two, and two only - the author of Don Quixote and the author of Waverley.' This review is also interesting for its recommendation that Fielding, Smollett, and Sterne, of the older novelists, should be placed in a class by themselves, followed by Richardson, and also for raising the question as to who reads Richardson nowadays.[132]

Lockhart again seemed to be crowning a new monarch of fiction in his life of Scott, when, speaking of *Waverley*, he said: 'In his familiar delineations, he had combined the strength of Smollett with the native elegance and unaffected pathos of Goldsmith.'[133] But, as this indicates, he also retained great respect for Scott's predecessors, including Smollett. In 1813, we find him having in mind to do for the Scotch clergy what Smollett had done for the sailors.[134] In 1823, he asked, in an article in *Blackwood's:* 'Good heavens! what would become of Moliere, Fielding, Smollett, Le Sage, Cervantes - in short, of all the comic writers the world ever saw, if it is to be considered a crime to take a few slaps at "The Three Black Graces," Law, Physic, and Divinity?'[135] In the article in the *Quarterly Review* written in 1826 wherein he declared for the superiority of Scott, he said that the failure of the ancients to write novels cannot be ascribed to lack of suitable material, 'nor can we be persuaded . . . that the author of Peregrine Pickle could have supped with Novidienus, and found no use for his tables. The scattered members of the novelist are found everywhere among the writers of antiquity; and the Journey to Brundisium *in esse* is proof enough

129 *Literary Gazette*, No. 235 (1821), 451.
130 M. C. Hildyard, p. 160.
131 *Quarterly Review*, XXXIV (1826), 376.
132 *Blackwood's Edinburgh Magazine*, XV (1824), 407–408, 414.
133 M. C. Hildyard, p. 110.
134 A. Lang, *Life of Lockhart*, I, 72–73.
135 M. C. Hildyard, p. 91.

that the expedition of a Roman Humphry Clinker might have been.'[136]
Again, in his life of Burns, published two years later, Lockhart
had high praise for Smollett. Speaking of the boldness of Burns's
experiment in making use of the Scottish dialect, he wrote that
even Smollett and Moore dared not use the dialect of their own
country, and referred to Smollett as 'the great master of the art'
and as a 'splendid genius.'[137] And fifteen years later, he wrote
that Hooke, 'in the exuberance of exulting glee with which he
elaborates detached scenes of pretension, affectation,' has 'had
no parallel since Smollett and Foote.'[138]

In the first three decades of the nineteenth century, Smollett
was in high favor everywhere. He was a strong favorite with the
general public and (consequently) with the publishers, and with
the literary journals, with novelists, and with other authors of
various kinds and stature. If it is in this period that we begin
to observe a rising tide of protest against certain qualities in
his work, it is also in this period that we find some of the
warmest praise ever bestowed upon him. Our hero is at the height
of his fortunes, and, as in a well plotted drama, foreshadowings
of his fall must not be lacking.

I think it safe to venture the generalization that when an
author has enjoyed at any time a reputation which seems unwarran-
tably high in the light of present opinion, it is the general
public and the lesser denizens of the literary world who are
found to have been chiefly responsible for elevating him to his
precarious perch. How different the situation was with regard
to Smollett during these years we have seen. If we consider only
the greatest authors of the time, we find him vying for the title
of chief of the English novelists. Not one of these men who
liked Fielding made any such sharp distinction between him and
Smollett as is common with the modern critic. Thus, Coleridge
and Hazlitt, and probably Byron too, awarded the supremacy to
Fielding, but the deep respect and warm admiration which they had
for Smollett has been made apparent. Hunt referred to both men
with such affection that we must count him as being undecided.
Likewise, Wordsworth liked both, but nothing indicates his preference one way or the other. With Keats, Smollett was the
favorite, and with Lamb too, at least for much of his life.
Scott belongs either here or with the neutral group. The total
effect of Lockhart's writings puts him in the camp of the Smollettites; and it is no violation of chronology, but only of con-

136 *Ibid.*, p. 102.
137 J. G. Lockhart, *Life of Burns*, pp. 226–227.
138 *N. C. Hildyard*, p. 76.

ventional literary groupings, to include here the name of Carlyle, who was the most decided of all in his preference for his fellow-countryman. But mention of the Sage of Chelsea leads us on to another chapter in our history, and to a very different state of affairs.

CHAPTER V

The Victorians
1833-1890

*As a novelist, Smollett's reputation, once very high,
is growing less every year with the best portion of
the reading world, and must continue to do so as a
love of moral purity shall continue to increase.*

Charles D. Cleveland

I

(1833-1865)

It would be a grave mistake to assume, despite the material
cited toward the end of the last chapter, that Scott immediately
obscured the older novelists. Indeed, we have seen that such
people as Wordsworth, Coleridge, and Keats continued to prefer
Smollett and his contemporaries to the author of *Waverley,* and
as we turn to figures generally associated with a later period,
we find other great authors standing firm under the banners of
the old masters. Two at least were as staunch Smollettites as
any we shall meet in the course of this study. They belong with
that group already mentioned, whose members had in common a boyish
delight in the works of Smollett; but by their stature in the
literary world and by the eloquence with which they discoursed on
their love for an early (and late) favorite, they stand apart.

It seems a bit strange that one of the greatest admirers Smollett ever had should have been Thomas Carlyle, especially when we
recall that Espinasse, in his *Literary Recollections,* tells us he
waged 'perpetual war' against fiction, 'ever admonishing . . .
novelists to write history or biography.'[1] Several of his earlier
references to Smollett, moreover, reveal no great affection.
Two of them, it is true, were to the history; he spoke of 'Toby
Smollett's eight chaotic volumes,'[2] and several years later said
of the continuation of Hume that 'a worse one can hardly be
imagined than Smollett's.'[3] But even the novels were disparaged
in one of his first mentions of them, when, in a letter of 1823,
he cautioned John S. Carlyle about their morality.[4]

Were this all, Carlyle's attitude toward Smollett could not
be differentiated from that of dozens of his contemporaries.
But other evidence proves that Carlyle placed Smollett apart from

1 F. Espinasse, p. 212.
2 *Early Letters of T. Carlyle,* I, 127.
3 *Ibid.,* II, 28.
4 *Ibid.,* II, 239-240.

all other novelists, and that one of the great events of his
literary life was his first reading of *Roderick Random*. Again
and again, even to his latest years, he liked to speak of that
memorable event, and always in the most glowing terms. Elsewhere Espinasse tells us this: 'I never heard Carlyle speak
of Pope, Swift, and the other Queen Anne men, nor of Fielding,
nor even of Sterne, for whom he had an early love. But he called
the day on which he first read *Roderick Random* one of the sun-
niest of his life (!), and a good biography of Smollett, he
thought, was among the few things of the kind which then remained
to be done.'[5] The final remark, unfortunately, could be made with
equal appropriateness today. In 1859 he referred to his introduction to Smollett again.[6] Six years later, on the evening of the
day he was inaugurated Lord Rector of Edinburgh University, Carlyle retired to a friend's house, where, for a time, he was alone
with Moncure Conway. He began to speak about his past, and again,
in this hour of triumph, he was moved to tell what Smollett meant
to him.

> I remember few happier days than those in which I
> ran off into the fields to read 'Roderick Random," and
> how inconsolable I was that I could not get the second
> volume. To this day I know of few writers equal to
> Smollett. Humphry Clinker is precious to me now as he
> was in those years. Nothing by Dante or anyone else
> surpasses in pathos the scene where Humphry goes into
> the smithy made for him in the old house, and whilst
> he is heating the iron, the poor woman who has lost
> her husband, and is deranged, comes and talks to him as
> to her husband. 'John, they told me you were dead.
> How glad I am you have come!' And Humphry's tears fall
> down and bubble on the hot iron.[7]

It is certainly interesting to find Leigh Hunt (with the approval
of Hazlitt) and Carlyle referring to scenes from Smollett as among
the most pathetic in world literature, when we notice how many
later critics, right up to this day, set down as one of the chief
counts in their indictment of Smollett his brutality and lack of
feeling for his characters. Did those great readers and writers
find more in Smollett than is there, or is it that his 'beautiful
bare narrative' came to seem too bare when read in the light of
the more gelatinous pathos of nineteenth-century fiction? At any
rate, some six or seven years after his talk with Conway, Carlyle
again praised the pathos of that same scene from *Humphry Clinker*.[8]
And in 1873, when he told Charles Eliot Norton about Smollett, we
find his mind running on the same two ideas of Smollett's feeling
and his own first acquaintance with the novels.[9]

5 F. Espinasse, p. 227
6 Anne Gilchrist, p. 63.
7 M. Conway, pp. 31-32.
8 Wm. Allingham, p. 212.
9 C. E. Norton, I, 459.

The unusual distinction which Carlyle made between Smollett and
the other great novelists of that age, pointed out by Espinasse,
is attested to by Carlyle himself. We find him recommending to a
friend *Humphry Clinker* and three other novels, and 'Richardson,
Fielding, &c. if you like such things.'[10] We also have his views
on the relative merits of Smollett and Dickens. He wrote to John
Stuart Mill on July 18, 1837: 'Buller on the Pickwick business
surprised me by speaking of Smollett; I fear that is loose speaking, but I have sent for the Pickwick on the faith of it, and
will see.' His best fears were confirmed. Ten days later he
wrote to John Sterling that he had read Pickwick, 'Buller having
recommended it in the *Review*. Thinner wash, with perceptible
vestige of a flavour in it here and there, was never offered to
the human palate: I will henceforth call Buller not the worst
critic in Britain, but a critic I will not be led by.'[11]

In view of all this, it is not surprising to find Smollett
mentioned here and there in Carlyle's works. Professor Teufels-
drockh knew the 'English Smollett,' and quoted as being possibly
prophetic of the final cessation of war the scene 'where the two
Natural Enemies, in person, take each a Tobacco-pipe, filled with
Brimstone; light the same, and smoke in one another's faces, till
the weaker gives in.'[12] And in *Frederick the Great*, two rhetorical
outbursts were inspired by the author's thoughts of his favorite
novelist.[13]

The story of Dickens' feeling for Smollett is very similar:
youthful love at first sight, eloquent accounts of the affair,
and many tributes in later years as evidence of an admiration
sustained (if not intensified) throughout a lifetime. The chief
difference is that with Dickens Smollett did not stand alone,
but shared his favor with other old novelists, especially Fielding.

The first passage that comes to mind when we think of Dickens
and Smollett, surely, is that where David Copperfield describes
almost the sole 'consolation during his dreary days with the Murd-
stones.

> My father had left a small collection of books in a
> little room upstairs, to which I had access (for it ad-
> joined my own), and which nobody else in our house ever
> troubled. From that blessed little room, 'Roderick Ran-
> dom,' 'Peregrine Pickle,' 'Humphry Clinker' 'Tom Jones,'
> the 'Vicar of Wakefield,' 'Don Quixote,' 'Gil Blas,' and
> 'Robinson Crusoe' came out, a glorious host, to keep me
> company. . . . I have been Tom Jones (a child's Tom Jones,
> a harmless creature) for a week together. I have sus-

10 D. A. Wilson, *Carlyle to Threescore-and ten*, pp. 445-446.
11 *Letters of Thomas Carlyle to John Stuart Mill*, pp. 155, 206.
12 T. Carlyle, *Sartor Resartus*, p. 133.
13 T. Carlyle, *History of Frederick the Great*, IV, 187-188, 386.

tained my own idea of Roderick Random for a month at a
stretch, I verily believe.[14]

He goes on to tell how the whole neighborhood acquired associations with these books.

> I have seen Tom Pipes go climbing up the church-
> steeple; I have watched Strap, with the knapsack on his
> back, stopping to rest himself upon the wicket-gate;
> and I *know* that Commodore Trunnion held that club with
> Mr. Pickle, in the parlor of our little village ale-
> house.[15]

And then, later, David begins to cry when he leaves home, but
stops when he reflects that Roderick Random never cried in try-
ing situations. When he mentions to Steerforth having read
Peregrine Pickle, Steerforth gets him to tell the story.
Again, when going to see Micawber in jail, David is reminded of
Roderick in jail.[16]

Was Dickens recalling his own youth in describing David's
fondness for Smollett? Are we justified in considering these
portions of the novel autobiographical? The warmth of the language and the frequency of his allusions in other places leave
no room for doubt. But positive evidence comes from Forster,
who remarked of the account of David's reading that 'It is one
of the many passages in *Copperfield* which are literally true';
and after quoting the part about Pipes, Strap, and Trunnion,
he added: 'Every word of this personal recollection had been
written down as fact, some years before it found its way into
David Copperfield.[17] Few critics since that time have failed
to notice the influence of Smollett on Dickens' works, a topic
which has been made the subject of more than one special study.
On the other hand, in his study of Fielding's reputation,
Blanchard has given some space to the contention that Dickens
must have preferred Fielding and been more deeply influenced
by him than by Smollett. The arguments of A. W. Ward on this
point are cited; among whose supporting claims is the statement that Dickens and Fielding 'both had that tenderness which
Smollett lacked';[18] but we have seen that for some important
people of Dickens' time and slightly earlier, Smollett did not
lack tenderness. The most positive statement by those who knew
him is a remark by J. T. Fields that Dickens 'preferred Smollett
to Fielding, putting "Peregrine Pickle" above "Tom Jones."'[19]
But one suspects that Dickens would have resented the attempt
to disparage either of his favorties at the expense of the other.
There is enough evidence for arguments either way on the question

14 C. Dickens, *Works*, XXXVI, 80.
15 *Ibid.*, p. 81.
16 *Ibid.*, pp. 92, 134–135, 242.
17 John Forster, *Life of Charles Dickens*, I, 9–10.
18 E. T. Blanchard, pp. 396–397.
19 J. T. Fields, p. 239.

of influence; but when we turn to consider Dickens' preference, it would take jesuitical reasoning to outweigh the testimony of his own words concerning Smollett. There are many mentions of Smollett scattered through his works,[20] but the pleasantest of all the references, though less familiar than the one in *David Copperfield*, is that found in the *Uncommercial Traveller*. Revisiting the town where he had spent his earliest days Dickens told how he looked up an old friend, Joe Specks, now a doctor. 'Through many changes and much work, I had preserved a tenderness for the memory of Joe, forasmuch as we had made the acquaintance of Roderick Random together, and had believed him to be no ruffian, but an ingenious and engaging hero.' Dickens entered his friend's house, and at first Mr. Specks was entirely unable to recognize him, but after a moment he showed a faint sign of recognition. 'Upon that, I saw a boyish light in his eyes that looked well, and I asked him if he could inform me, as a stranger who desired to know and had not the means of reference at hand, what the name of the young lady was who married Mr. Random? Upon that, he said, "Narcissa," and, after staring for a moment, called me by my name, shook me by the hand, and melted into a roar of laughter.' Concluding the episode, Dickens wrote: 'Nor could I discover one single flaw in the good doctor . . . except that he had forgotten his Roderick Random, and that he confounded Strap with Lieutenant Hatchway; who never knew Random, howsoever intimate with Pickle.'[21]

With the appearance of Dickens, critics again were comparing the old masters with the new one. First, however, we have to notice a song of triumph for Scott, which appeared in the *Westminster Review* in 1834.

> Who that can recollect the last thirty years, has not heard a thousand lamentations over the decay of genius for novel-writing? Who has not heard of those unmatchable authors Fielding, and Smollett, and Goldsmith, &c. whose names were to be for ever the wonder and the shame of all succeeding tale-tellers? How would not some profound critic, looking over the unpublished pages of Waverley, have shaken the head, and talked of Tom Jones, or Humphry Clinker, or the inimitable Ratcliffe?

But yet Scott came along to throw 'into comparative darkness the luminaries that were to be for ever bright and unapproachable.'[22]

In 1837, the *Quarterly* reviewer of *Pickwick Papers* and *Boz* asserted that 'Of Fielding's intuitive perception of the springs of action, and skill in the construction of the prose epic - or Smollett's dash, vivacity, wild spirit of adventure and rich poetic imagination, he (Dickens) has none.'[23] But this attitude

20 C. Dickens, *Works*, XVI, iv–v; *Pictures from Italy*, p. 354; *Christmas Stories*, p. 97; *Ibid.*, p. 861; *Letters*, I, 26; *Ibid.*, I, 416–417.
21 C. Dickens, *Works*, XXXIX, 178–180.
22 *Westminster Review*, XX (1834), 153.
23 *Quarterly Review*, LIX (1837), 484.

was not quite typical. The *Westminster Review*, for example, said
that Dickens ought to go on to better things; even *Pickwick Papers*
should not satisfy him. 'The renown of Fielding and Smollett is
that to which he should aspire, and labour to emulate, and, if
possible, to surpass.'[24] And the *Edinburgh Review* considered
Dickens 'the truest and most spirited delineator of English life,
amongst the middle and lower classes, since the days of Smollett
and Fielding.'[25] A year later, in a review in the *Quarterly* of
the *Reports of the Mendicity Society*, it was stated that 'There
is more strength in half a page of Fielding or Smollett than in a
whole ship-load of the diluted, maudlin, sickly sentimentality
with which the so-called *fashionable novelists*, male, female,
and epicene, drench their patients.'[26] If this was written by
the same person who reviewed *Pickwick Papers*, Dickens was probably meant to be included among the 'fashionable novelists.'

So Dickens, like Scott, had to contend against the strongly
intrenched old favorites, at least in certain critical circles.
He challenged comparison with them in quite a different way than
that of Scott - more directly, perhaps, with his eccentrics, his
inns and stage-coaches, his rich humorous pictures of English
life. Indeed, this last aspect of his work was mentioned some years
later in the *Quarterly*, and in a way to show how the atmosphere
had changed since the publication of *Pickwick*. In a footnote to
Thackeray's remark about *Humphry Clinker*, the writer said: 'Smollett, however, has now been surpassed in richness of humour by
Mr. Dickens, who in this particular has never had an equal.'[27]
In this same year Scott and the older novelists were brought up
again by Bagehot, who was writing on the Waverley novels. He
distinguished between two kinds of novels, the romance, dealing
solely with the passion of love, and the other, 'which we may
call the *ubiquitous*,' which 'aims at describing the whole of
human life in all its spheres, in all its aspects, with all its
varied interests, aims, and objects. . . . Of this kind are the
novels of Cervantes and LeSage, and to a certain extent of Smollett and Fielding.' Bagehot preferred this latter class.[28]

Dickens was not, of course, the only writer of the time who
read and was influenced by Smollett. There were Bulwer[29] and
Lever,[30] in both of whom biographers have seen the effects of
their reading of Smollett; Reade, whose first literary effort
was a play based on *Peregrine Pickle,* and whose 'Terrible Temp-
tation' moved a critic to ask: 'What gentleman would read, with-

24 *Westminster Review*, XXVII (1837), 313.
25 *Edinburgh Review*, LXVIII (1838), 76.
26 *Quarterly Review*, LXIV (1839), 349.
27 *Quarterly Review*, CIII (1858), 105, n.
28 W. Bagehot, II, 199.
29 M. Sadleir, p. 286.
30 W. J. Fitzpatrick, II, 194-195.

out skipping, aloud to respectable ladies, the first chapters of
Charles Reade's new story . . . any sooner than chapters from
Fielding and Smollett';[31] Marryat, of course, whose silenc concerning Smollett we have already noticed; and Thomas Hood, who,
so far from being silent, began his preface to *Up the Rhine,*
1840, thus: 'To forestal such Critics as are fond of climbing a
Mat de Cocagne for a Mare's Nest at the top, the following work
was constructed, partly on the ground-plan of Humphrey Clinker,
but with very inferior materials, and on a much humbler scale.
I admire the old mansion too much, to think that any workmanship
of mine could erect a house fit to stand in the same row,'[32] and
who testified on more than one other occasion to his admiration
and liking for Smollett.[33]

Like Dickens and Carlyle, too, other men who made their mark
in the Victorian period had been readers of Smollett in their
boyhood. We have already referred to Macaulay's prankish letter
addressed to his father as editor of the *Christian Observer*,
indicating the he had read Smollet by the age of sixteen. That
he continued his allegiance to his youthful favorites is indicated by Morison's statement of him as a mature man that after
a hard day's journey he would 'read selections from Sterne, Smollett, or Fielding.'[34] In his essay on Fanny Burney Macaulay
spoke of *Evelina* as 'the best work of fiction that had appeared
since the death of Smollett,'[35] but, like Fanny Burney, he censured the style of Smollett's *History*.[36]

Other youthful admirers of Smollett included Robert Chambers
and his brother William.[37] William, moreover, contributes some
interesting evidence concerning the attraction Smollett had for
the common people. He got a job with a baker, who liked to read,
but had no time, so that William read to him and his two sons
while they mixed the dough. 'The baker was not particular as to
subject. All he stipulated for was something droll and laughable.
Aware of his tastes, I tried him first with the jocularities of
"Roderick Random," which was a great success, and produced shouts
of laughter.'[38]

It is doubtful whether anyone has ever written at length on
Smollett without discussing his naval scenes, but competent
analyses of this material have been all too uncommon. An exception is to be found in the *Naval Sketch Book* of William Nugent
Glascock, where a whole chapter is entitled 'Strictures on Smollett.' The comments are confined to the naval portions of the

31 M. Elwin, pp. 218–219.
32 T. Hood, VII, 1.
33 *Ibid.*, X, 21, 351, 377.
34 J. C. Morison, p. 172.
35 T. B. Macaulay, *Critical and Historical Essays*, IV, 113.
36 G. O. Trevelyan, II, 37.
37 Wm. Chambers, pp. 54–55.
38 *Ibid.*, p. 95.

novels. Glascock criticised Smollett for the extravagance of
his delineations, for his failure to make the nice distinctions of
character which mark the different grades of the navy,[39] and
for his inability to portray the 'grand aspect of nature on the
deep.'[40] The motive behind Smollett's exaggeration seems completely to have escaped Glascock. But in general he had a high
opinion of Smollett; he alluded to the 'very masterly sketch' of
Trunnion,[41] and one of his characters remarks that in the novels
'you've nature to a tee - naked to the life. That Smollett was
a d----d clever fellow.'[42]

A better known writer who must be included among Smollett's
friends is Henry Cary, who, in his *Lives of the English Poets*
(1846), wrote on the novelist at some length. Roderick Random
was Cary's favorite. 'In none of his succeeding novels has he
equalled the liveliness, force, and nature of this his first
essay.' He gave his opinion on the wide popularity of this work
by saying: 'Many of our naval heroes may probably trace the
preference which has decided them in their choice of a profession
to an early acquaintance with the pages of Roderick Random.'[43]
He conjectured that *Ferdinand Count Fathom*, or parts of it, was a
mere translation, basing his assumption on several apparently
literal translations of the French word or idiom, such as 'port'
for 'door.'[44] Of *Humphry Clinker* he stated that though it is
'abounding in portraitures of exquisite drollery, and in situations highly comical,' it 'has not the full zest and flavour of
his earlier works.'[45] He followed Scott in describing the plot
structure of the novels, though with a figure of his own: 'From
the beginning to the end, one adventure commonly rises up and
follows upon another, like so many waves of the sea, which cease
only because they have reached the shore.'[46] In summary, it can
be said that throughout his discussion Cary was surprisingly un-
prejudiced. There was practically no censure; strange to relate,
he did not even condemn Smollett's coarseness.

John Forster, in his life of Goldsmith (1848), also found much
good to say of Smollett, comparing the author with some of his
characters in a way to reflect credit on both,[47] taking Walpole
to task for calling *Humphry Clinker* a 'party novel,'[48] and writing at some length in praise of *Launcelot Greaves*.[49]

39 W. N. Glascock, *Naval Sketch Book*, pp. 124–125.
40 *Ibid.*, pp. 128–129.
41 *Ibid.*, p. 139.
42 W. N. Glascock, *Sailors and Saints*, I, 89.
43 H. F. Cary, *Lives of the English Poets*, p. 123.
44 *Ibid.*, p. 126.
45 *Ibid.*, p. 139.
46 *Ibid.*, p. 144.
47 John Forster, *Life of Oliver Goldsmith*, II, 32.
48 *Ibid.*, III, 25, n.
49 *Ibid.*, II, 34.

One of the most influential writers on the eighteenth-century
novelists during this period, or indeed at any time, was Thackeray. As Professor Blanchard has clearly shown, the picture he
drew of Fielding's life and character did great harm for several
decades, quite overshadowing the praise he bestowed on Fielding's
novels. Of Smollet's personal life, on the other hand, he had
only praise; and he had many good things to say about the novels
too. But he was the first great novelist to insist on the superiority of Fielding over Smollett, and he made his point more
emphatically, perhaps, than anyone before him. His views seem
to have carried much weight, not only because of the manner of
their expression, but also because the times were changing, a
new conception of the novel was gaining ground, and Thackeray
was an accurate prophet of the effect this trend would have on
the relative fortunes of Fielding and Smollett. If we seek a
date for this change, we could not find a more accurate time
than Thackeray's last ten years. Fielding, it is true, did not
achieve the place he holds today until scholars began to destroy
the disgraceful legends which had long formed a stock part of
his biography; but Smollett's fortunes sank rapidly. Scarcely a
single critic of prominent stature and recognized soundness since
that time has ventured to place him above Fielding. If we consider the novelists, the Brontes, Mrs. Gaskell, George Eliot,
Meredith, Hardy, how much do we find in their works which reflects
the influence of Smollett? No more, it is safe to say, than we
find them saying about him; and that is virtually nothing.

In the *English Humourists*, where we find his most important
writing on the old novelists, Thackeray gave nearly six times as
much space to Fielding as to Smollett. Much of the brief discussion of the latter is concerned with his character, which here
receives the finest eulogy that has yet been written on it, with
emphasis on Smollett's spirit and courage in struggling against
the difficulties that ever besieged him. Of the few sentences on
Smollett the writer, two are as well known as anything in the
literature of Smollett: 'He did not invent much, as I fancy, but
had the keenest perceptive faculty, and described what he saw
with wonderful relish and delightful broad humour'; and 'The novel
of *Humphry Clinker* is, I do think, the most laughable story that
has ever been written since the goodly art of novel-writing began.
The latter sentence is followed by this: 'Winifred Jenkins and
Tabitha Bramble must keep Englishmen on the grin for ages yet to
come; and in their letters and the story of their loves there is
a perpetual fount of sparkling laughter, as inexhaustible as
Bladud's well.' Besides, there was high praise of a few characters: Uncle Bowling ('as good a character as Squire Western'),
Morgan, and Lismahago.[50]

50 W. M. Thackeray, *English Humourists*, pp. 148–149.

Thackeray seems to have been the first to notice that Smollett 'did not invent much'; since his time many another critic, quite independently, without a doubt, has made the same discovery. The word 'invention,' like 'reason,' 'nature,' and 'romantic,' to mention only a few, has a past; but seemingly the argument is that because Smollett made such full use of the materials of his own life, not much originality can be claimed for him. Was it not by a similar train of thought that many writers came to deny any great merit in Boswell? After all, there was Dr. Johnson, and all one had to do was to set him down on paper. Likewise, there was the naval life of those days, with its Morgans, Oakums, and Trunnions; Strap, as we have seen, had not one original, but three or four; and models have been proposed for many of the other characters as well. But this kind of criticism, we may hope, is no longer the fashion. The novelist as well as the painter is judged by the finished portrait, and not by the presence or absence of a living model.

Thackeray had become acquainted with Smollett early in his youth, as almost everyone of that age seems to have done. Discussing his early reading in 'De Juventute,' he wrote: 'Peregrine Pickle we liked, our fathers admiring it and telling us (the sly old boys) that it was capital fun; but I think I was rather bewildered by it, though Roderick Random was and remains delightful.'[51] Elsewhere in the Humourists, while comparing history and fiction, he said: 'I take up a volume of Dr. Smollett, or a volume of The Spectator, and say the fiction carries a greater amount of truth in solution than the volume which purports to be all true.'[52] And, as stated in the preceding chapter, he had Becky Sharp reading Humphry Clinker to her young pupils at Queens Crawley.

As for his opinion on the relative merits of Fielding and Smollett, we find statements in at least three places. The account of Fielding in the English Humourists, which follows upon that of Smollett, begins with these words: 'Fielding, too, has described, though with a greater hand . . .'[53] In the Paris Sketch Book, speaking of the historical value of Pickwick Papers, he refers to Roderick Random, 'an inferior work,' and Tom Jones, 'one that is immeasurably superior.'[54] Finally, in his review of Roscoe's Fielding, he contrasted the loose workmanship of Roderick Random with the marvelous structure of Tom Jones.[55]

What seems to be a lone voice raised against Thackeray's treatment of Fielding and Smollett is that of George Gilfillan:

51 W. M. Thackeray, Roundabout Papers, p. 66.
52 W. M. Thackeray, English Humourists, p. 65.
53 Ibid., p. 149.
54 W. M. Thackeray, Paris Sketch Book, p. 80.
55 W. M. Thackeray, Critical Papers in Literature, p. 207.

'Thackeray, who is in chase of Fielding, finds nothing very new to say of Smollett, and ignores his most peculiar and powerful works.' Gilfillan himself had some very pleasant things to say about the poems and novels, but his most interesting comment is that on the *Travels:* 'We are among the very few who have read the book. It is a succession of asthmatic gasps and groans, with not a particle of the humour of "Humphry Clinker."'[56] But almost everyone else who has come after Thackeray has followed him in ranking Fielding far above Smollett. The two have only been pushed farther apart as Fielding's character has been redeemed and as later readers have found even less to admire in Smollett than did Thackeray. There seems to be no doubt that he was genuinely fond of Smollett. Roscoe, who reviewed the *Humourists,* referred to his 'enjoyment in Smollett, joined to his guarded way of speaking of him, as if he were a little cowed by his great patron, the public.'[57] Whether or not Roscoe was right, we do find something of this contradiction in the attitude of Ruskin, who on the one hand voiced *ex cathedra* diatribes against the Smollettean type of fiction and on the other retained to his latest years his fondness for reading those novels.

The first reference to Smollett by Ruskin seems to be that in a letter to a friend, written in 1840:

> As Winifred Jenkins says, 'I can't pollewt my pen' - though, by-the-bye, you may find every piece of coarseness, coined in the United Kingdom in that book. I cannot, for the life of me, understand the feelings of men of magnificent wit and intellect, like Smollett and Fielding, when I see them gloating over and licking their chops over nastiness, like hungry dogs over ordure; founding one half of the laughable matter of their volumes in innuendoes of abomination. Not that I think, as many people do, they are bad books; for I don't think these pieces of open filth are in reality injurious to the mind, or, at least, *as* injurious as corrupt sentiment and disguised immorality, such as you get sometimes in Bulwer and men of his school.[58]

As the editor points out, it was Fanny Squeers, not Winifred Jenkins, who said 'Pollewt my pen,' evidence that Ruskin was then a little rusty on his Smollett. Elsewhere Ruskin used Smollett and Le Sage as exemplars of writers who, because of their failure to appreciate natural beauty, were quite unable to conceive of nobility of character;[59] and in a letter to his father in 1863 he contrasted Smollett's humor unfavorably with that of Dickens.[60] But, we are told, in 1875 'Ruskin used to read *Humphry Clinker* aloud to the Brantwood party, missing out bits here and

56 George Gilfillan, pp. 273–274.
57 W. C. Roscoe, II, 275, n.
58 John Ruskin, I, 417–418.
59 *Ibid.,* V, 374; see also XII, 119.
60 *Ibid.,* XXXVI, 431.

there, of course.'[61] Two or three years before, he had introduced
the novel into *Fors Clavigera*, quite unnecessarily, and in a manner to show a much closer familiarity with it than he had had in
1840.[62] Finally, in *Praeterita* (1886-1889), he spoke of his
mother and father enjoying their *Humphry Clinker* while he was
still a small child, and he seemed to take pride in a certain
'Smollettesque turn' in his mother's sense of humor.[63]

This parental admiration leads us to another famous name,
Matthew Arnold. Matthew himself, it seems, failed to mention
Smollett in any of his writings; indeed, novelists altogether received very little attention from him. But his father, the aus-
tere Dr. Arnold of Rugby, was a hearty devotee and indefatigable
reader of Smollett. It is recorded that when one of his students
at Rugby in the early 1830's, the future Dean Stanley, called on
Arnold one day, Arnold

> was looking at something about Smollett, and said
> 'Humphrey Clinker' was not thought enough of generally -
> and upon my telling him I had never read it - 'Oh! you
> must read 'Humphrey Clinker'; if you have not got it, I
> will lend it to you. It is not too much to say that I
> have read it through fifty times' - and accordingly he
> jumped up and got it down for me.[64]

Two minor figures of this time stand out for rather unusual
comments on Smollett. Charles Knight, in his *London* (1842), ad-
vanced the heretical opinion that Fielding and Smollett, so far
from being muckrakers, actually exercised restraint in their descriptions of life among the city's lower classes.[65] Grace Wharton,
in 1862, criticized Smollett's novels on moral grounds (*Launcelot
Greaves* she could hardly have read, since she found it 'far worse
in its license and indelicacy' than its predecessors), but she
drew a picture of Smollett's character as attractive as any from
that age, excepting Thackeray's.[66]

But the number of Smollett's admirers thinned out rapidly during these years, even such qualified admirers as Thackerary and
Ruskin, while the ranks of his detractors were growing. Landor
praised the 'abundant humour' of *Humphry Clinker* and found some
good strokes in it, but 'I find it rather wearisome, and stuffed
with oddities of language.'[67] Harriet Martineau, urged by a
friend to read Smollett, commented: 'I cannot, it disgusts me so
utterly.'[68] Others who may be grouped here include Charles Kirkpatrick Sharpe;[69] Phillimore, the biographer of Lord Lyttelton;[70]

61 *Ibid.;* I, 417, n. 4.
62 *Ibid.*, XXVII, 619.
63 *Ibid.*, XXXV, 144.
64 R. E. Prothero and G. G. Bradley, I, 65.
65 C. Knight, *London*, II, 353-354.
66 Grace Wharton, II, 252-254.
67 John Forster, *W. S. Landor*, p. 499.
68 H. Martineau, II, 326.
69 C. K. Sharpe, II, 517-518.
70 R. Phillimore, I, 342.

Mrs. Schimmelpenninck, who never ceased to shudder at the danger she had undergone in her childhood in being exposed to the works of Fielding and Smollett;[71] and Allibone, of the *Dictionary*.[72] Two references are especially illuminating in showing how the times had changed. We have seen how many a traveler in Italy had been moved by a visit to Leghorn to pay a tribute to Smollett's memory. But Hillard, writing in 1853, just mentioned Smollett's grave and went on to speak of a 'calmer and purer spirit' also buried there, one Francis Horner, 'whose serene career of duty contrasts with the wayward course of the irritable and undisciplined Smollett.' He also devoted several pages to the *Travels*, in which he found much to criticize and nothing, apparently, to praise.[73] It is even more astonishing to find a writer in the *Athenaeum* ten years before this time referring to the *Post Captain*, published in 1802, as 'the parent of all our nautical novels.'[74] We might summarize the trend of the times with a remark from that Charles Knight already mentioned, who, as a publisher, surely knew whereof he was talking. In 1864, he wrote: 'There are some works of imagination that are almost unknown to the present race of readers. Who can avoid lamenting that Tom Jones, and Roderick Random, and Tristram Shandy are utterly gone out of the popular view.'[75]

In tracing the reputation of an early novelist, one must consider the rise of a new factor in the nineteenth century - the history of literature or of fiction. This type of work seems to have become popular about the middle of the century. One of the first of these chronicles to appear after the death of Scott was the *History of the English Language and Literature* by Robert Chambers, 1837. Here we have a comparison of Fielding and Smollett following the lines laid down by Scott. Fielding is a more skillful artist, has greater delicacy, and gives us 'pictures of the more elevated qualities of human nature.' But Smollett 'far surpasses Fielding in his humour,' which, said Chambers, writing in 1837, is 'more rich and copious than that of any other English author.' Both writers are condemned on moral grounds.[76] But it is rather surprising to find another historian, D. K. Sandford, saying in a work published ten years after *Pickwick* that 'Life is no longer picturesque enough to produce a match for Smollett in descriptive humour.'[77]

It is interesting to note in passing that up to this time histories of comparative literature, and even of comparative fiction, allotted very little space to Smollett and his contempo-

71 M. A. Schimmelpenninck, I, 12.
72 S. A. Allibone, II, 2165-2167.
73 C. S. Hillard, I, 192; II, 374-378.
74 *Athenaeum*, Dec. 9, 1843, p. 1092.
75 C. Knight, *Passages of a Working Life*, III, 12.
76 R. Chambers, *History of the English Language and Literature*, p. 164.
77 D. K. Sandford, p. 191.

raries. Scholars during the late eighteenth century often ignored them completely, perhaps because they were doubtful whether
the novel is a part of literature. Sandford's work slighted the
whole eighteenth century, with the result that the four great
novelists were dismissed with a single sentence apiece. In this
the work was more typical than unusual. Another work which gave
but little more space to Smollett was Mills' history of British
literature. This author's opinion of the novels was communicated
by the somewhat unusual method of terming the history 'certainly
the author's most important production.'[78]

One may note at least one resemblance between Smollett and
Shakespeare, in that neither found a ready acceptance in France.
Taine (1856-1859) gave four pages to the novels in his history,
devoted almost exclusively to their brutality and barbarity, of
which he offered many samples. Typical comments are that Smollett is 'mediocre,' that 'A Frenchman can hardly endure the story
of *Roderick Random,* or rather that of Smollett, when he is in a
man-of-war,' and that Roderick is 'sensual and coarse, like Fielding's heroes, but not good and jovial as these.'[79] Other aspects
of Smollett's work are almost completely ignored.

What Taine called brutality in Smollett many an English writer
has chosen to refer to as vigor. Such a one was Jeafferson, whose
work appeared in 1858, and whose discussion of Smollett mingled
praise and blame. Not only did Jeafferson emphasize Smollett's
inferiority to Fielding, possibly under the influence of Thackeray, but he claimed that Scott was equally well aware of it and
labored the comparison only because he and Smollett were compat-
riots.[80]

We have noted that from the very beginning to compare Smollett
with Fielding had been common, but these chronologically planned
histories made such an arrangement almost inevitable. The con-
temporaneity of the two men and the rough resemblances in their
works that set them so clearly apart from those of Richardson and
Sterne have probably coupled their names for all time, but the
pairing is quite different from such others as Dickens and Thackeray or Meredith and Hardy, in that the two members are held to
be very unequal in merit; Smollett's part in the combination often
seems to be that of a rather uninteresting caudal appendage, so
that it is possible to discuss Fielding without reference to Smollett, but there is little point in talking about the tail without
mentioning the body. That there are good reasons for considering
these two men together is true; that some of these reasons were
accidental and extrinsic to the nature of Smollett's work is also

78 A. Mills, II, 514–515.
79 H. A. Taine, II, 224–226.
80 J. C. Jeafferson, pp. 166–169.

true; and that the effect on his reputation has been unfortunate cannot be questioned.

It may be questioned, however, whether even those writers who extolled the relative merits of Smollett did anything to increase his popularity in the long run, for the world has not listened to them, and they have only cemented more closely the connection between Smollett's name and Fielding's. At any rate, Talfourd was one of the few who praised both men about equally. Smollett has 'more touch of romance' but 'not so profound and intuitive a knowledge of humanity's hidden treasures.' He has nothing equal to Parson Adams, but Fielding has nothing equal to Strap. And so on.[81] Masson, in his *British Novelists* (1859), also kept the balance even between the two novelists, though his discussion of them of them runs to some seventeen pages. It is possible that he was influenced by national feelings, as Jeaffreson said Scott had been; indeed he alluded to the special appeal Smollett has for Scotch readers.[82]

But such people were the exception. In Roscoe's introduction to the works of Fielding, for example, Smollett is used like a beauty patch to accentuate the graces of his rival.[83] Elwin, in 1856, printed some remarks by M. D. Hill of the same tenor. 'Peregrine Pickle is an ill-conditioned Tom Jones and more dissolute.'[84] Hannay, writing a review in the *Quarterly* in 1858 of some of Smollett's novels, felt impelled to point out in some detail the inferiority of Smollett to Fielding before he went on to discuss the subject in hand. Once the inevitable comparison was out of the way, Smollett fared well at the hands of his fellow-Scot and future biographer. Most interesting, perhaps, is the fact that Hannay was among the first to presage the modern popularity of the *Travels*. 'This is really one of Smollett's best works; more readable, as we think, and better worth reading, than his minor novels.'[85]

The comparison between the two novelists was made again by Bulwer. He wrote in *Caxtoniana:* 'It would be a waste of words to show, what no critic has disputed, viz., Fielding's superiority to Smollett (who, nevertheless, is a giant among novelists) in philosophical treatment and dignified conception of narrative art.' Both novelists showed a 'too frequent preference of conventional particulars in the selection of types of character,' with the result that neither has had 'perceptible influence on the higher forms of fiction in foreign countries.'[86] Although Bulwer preferred Fielding to Smollett, and Richardson and Sterne to either of them,

81 T. M. Talfourd, p. 7.
82 D. Masson, pp. 130. ff.
83 H. Fielding, *Tom Jones*, with a memoir . . . by Thomas Roscoe, I, xix.
84 W. Elwin, II, 146, n.
85 *Quarterly Review*, CIII (1858), pp. 95—96.
86 E. B. Lytten, *Caxtoniana*, pp. 391—392.

he liked Smollett well enough. He wrote in a letter in 1861: 'I don't pity you having to read Smollett, whose vigour is astonishing.' Speaking of high spirits in the novel, he said: 'Fielding has them, but not quite to such degree as Smollett in *Roderick Random* and *Peregrine Pickle.*' And in the same letter he expressed what many others have no doubt felt.

> Authors as they proceed in a career, become sensible of their own faults, but in getting rid of them, are apt to get rid of the merits that go along with faults . . . . Thus Smollett lost much of his 'go' in his *Humphrey Clinker*, but then he concentred his creative power on much more complete development of humourous character, as in Lismahago and Matthew Bramble.[87]

II
(1866-1890)

As we turn to the later years of the Victorian period, we find the tendencies of the preceding decades continuing and strengthening. The gulf between Fielding and Smollett widened still farther; Smollett's indecency continued to repel; and enthusiastic admirers of his, especially among the better known authors, became fewer and fewer. In this latter respect, indeed, the change is shocking. It is quite the most noticeable feature in the history of this novelist's reputation. He has, in fact, ceased to count for anything with those who make our literature. To find any enthusiastic praise of him, or to find much said about him at all, we must turn to those whose business is with literature, but whose writings hardly form part of it: the historians, essayists, critics, reviewers, biographers, among whom we find a Smollett addict now and then. But let us first see what there is from the major writers.

George Eliot seems to have but one reference to Smollett. It occurs in *Middlemarch* and though rather non-committal seems to bespeak no great admiration on her part. During Casaubon's illness Mr. Brooke advises him to get Dorothea to read to him

> light things, Smollett - 'Roderick Random,' 'Humphry Clinker'; they are a little broad, but she may read anything now she's married, you know. I remember they made me laugh uncommonly - there's a droll bit about a postilion's breeches. We have no such humour now. I have gone all through these things, but they might be rather new to you.'
>
> 'As new as eating thistles,' would have been the answer to represent Mr. Casaubon's feelings. But he only bowed resignedly, with due respect to his wife's uncle, and observed that doubtless the works he mentioned had 'served as a resource to a certain order of minds.'[88]

87 **Earl of Lytton,** *Life of Edward Bulwer,* II, 394-395.
88 George Eliot, chap. xxx, p. 281.

Very likely Casaubon's opinion was that of the author, for early in 1860 she and Lewes 'were reading aloud "Humphry Clinker" - with disappointment, despite the admiration of Thackeray and Dickens.'[89]

Trollope wrote an article on the early novelists in which he said it was unfair to bracket Fielding and Smollett. In Smollett the fault of lasciviousness 'was more conspicuous than in Fielding, - without the great redeeming gifts.'[90] Meredith contrasted the laughter of the mind, the laughter of Moliere (one of his great favorites), with passages of Rabelais, one or two in *Don Quixote*, and the supper in the manner of the ancients in *Peregrine Pickle*, sufficient evidence, perhaps, that Smollett would not rank among his most admired authors.[91] From Hardy there seems to be nothing but the information from his wife that Smollett was among the score of authors he 'dipped into' in 1890.[92] Samuel Butler has a passing reference to Smollett in *The Way of All Flesh* as one of the authors who had depicted the violent fathers of the preceding century.[93] Even Stevenson, despite his Scotch birth and the Captain Smollett in *Treasure Island* (and a narrative art which Cross suggests is analogous to that of Smollett), had nothing to say except for a lengthy reference to the scenes on the *Thunder* in his essay on 'The English Admirals.' He was probably referring to the conditions on board ship rather than to any fault of Smollett's when he commented: 'There are portions . . . over which the reader passes lightly and hurriedly, like a traveller in a malarious country.'[94] The pre-Raphaelites, too, had little to say; indeed, the only word seems to come from Swinburne, who in his essay on Dickens said it was curious that Sydney Smith preferred to Sam Weller and other finer, more original things in Dickens such matters as Miss Squeers and her letter, obviously imitated from Smollett.[95] Hall Caine recorded that he read the old masterpieces of fiction over again at Rossetti's house, including some of Smollett, but it is not indicated that Rossetti joined him. Caine's comment on the reading was: 'Perhaps it was not all pleasure, so far as I was concerned, but certainly it was all profit.'[96]

Thus the scanty record stands. The low estate of Smollett is in sharp contrast with that of Fielding, who drew high praise

89 B. C. Williams, p. 170.
90 *Nineteenth Century*, V (1879), 30.
91 G. Meredith, p. 146.
92 F. E. Hardy, *Early Life of Thomas Hardy*, p. 301.
93 S. Butler, p. 21.
94 R. L. Stevenson, p. 112.
95 A. C. Swinburne, XIV, 64.
96 H. Caine, p. 65.

from George Eliot, Swinburne, Meredith, and Hardy, among others.[97]
But in other literary circles the decline in Smollett's fortunes
was not quite so marked. One indication that he still had readers
is to be found in *Notes and Queries*, correspondents of which wrote
in fairly often during the years 1851 to 1885, usually, as it
happened, to inquire about the original of some one of the characters in the novels. His works were granted by almost everyone to
be an admissible part of a *gentleman's* library, and no doubt a considerable amount of furtive reading was done of which there could
be no record. Another indication of some continuing measure of
popularity is that one or two well known artists painted subjects
from his novels. Macready recalled a visit to Charles Robert Leslie in 1845 during which he saw a 'very charming picture of *Reading
the Will* from *Roderick Random*.'[98] Tom Taylor, in his introduction
to Leslie's autobiography, praised the same picture for its 'power
in the rendering of character and for nice discrimination of humorous expression.'[99] W. P. Frith recorded that *Roderick Random* 'suggested one of the best of my smaller productions; it was called
"A Stagecoach Adventure."'[100] We are also told that a head of
Smollett is one of several on the capitals of pilasters supporting
the roof of the monument to Scott in Edinburgh.[101]

The historical manuals continued to be produced during these
years, of course, and in such numbers that it is impossible to notice them in detail, nor is it necessary, for they seldom said
anything new. G. L. Craik (1869) was one of the exceptions by
reason of his insistence that Smollett 'is as much a writer *sui
generis* as either of his two predecessors, as completely distinguished from each of them in the general character of his genius
as they are from each other,'[102] and Morley[103] and H. J. Nicoll[104]
were more tolerant than most. But typical comments from these
works are that 'The English novel has hardly touched a lower
point than in Smollett,'[105] or that 'As a novelist, Smollett's
reputation, once very high, is growing less every year with the
best portion of the reading world, and must continue to do so as
a love of moral purity shall continue to increase.' The author of
this last remark, by the way, admitted that he had read but one of
the novels,' and such was its character that I never wish to read

97 It might be illuminating to mention here the more important authors of the nineteenth
    century of whom my investigation has yielded only negative results, and barring
    those of whom even a single word on Smollett has been recorded in this study:
    Ainsworth, Matthew Arnold, Jane Austen, Borrow, the Brontes, the Brownings,
    Clough, Wilkie Collins, Conrad, Disraeli, Fitzgerald, Mrs. Gaskell, Kingsley,
    Mill, Morris, Newman, Pater, Peacock, Rossetti, Tennyson, and Wilde.

98 *Diaries of W. C. Macready*, p. 316.
99 C. R. Leslie, I, lxv.
100 W. P. Frith, p. 146.
101 James Grant, II, 127.
102 C. L. Craik, II, 296.
103 H. Morley, pp. 832–838.
104 H. J. Nicoll, pp. 222, 224, 228.
105 J. Bascom, p. 199.

another'[106]: a telling example of how Smollett was often being criticized almost by rote, rather than by individual study of his works.

As was said at the beginning of this section, we do find among the miscellaneous writers on literature during this period some occasional praise of Smollett, but it comes from unimportant sources[107] and seems to have had no relation to the trend of Smollett's fortunes. Perhaps an exception should be made in favor of an article in *Macmillan's* entitled 'Smollett at Nice' marking another step in the renascence of the *Travels*, than which, said the writer, 'few books have ever been more heartily abused' and 'of late years few have been less read.' Smollett was praised throughout for his accuracy, truthfulness, common sense, and honesty.' 'There is not a more truthful book in the language,'[108] we are told, presumably as an antidote to the often repeated remark, having its origin in the *Sentimental Journey*, that Smollett's ill-health and irascibility made it impossible for him to view the world aright.

But most noticeable out of this body of criticism is the sharp differentiation between Fielding and Smollett which has already been mentioned, and which was by this time often magnified to produce the conclusion that Fielding is a great novelist and that Smollett counts hardly at all. This is the impression one gets from the comments of Leslie Stephen,[109] and it is the expressed opinion of L'Estrange[110] and a writer in the *Quarterly*,[111] while others made the distinction between the two almost equally clear.[112]

We have still to consider one other class of writings concerning Smollett, the biographies, of which some half dozen appeared during this period. It would have been necessary to discuss them before this point but for the fact that their influence on the course of Smollett's reputation has been negligible. The biographers are not necessarily to be condemned therefor. Smollett's personal character was pretty well fixed by his first biographers, and the paucity of materials discoverable by later investigators has meant that the early portraits remain virtually unchanged. There is nothing in the record of Smollett's fame comparable to the loss of prestige suffered by Richardson when his letters were published, or to the elevation of Fielding's stature as the old tales associated with him were proved to be unfounded in fact. Nor did the biographers of this period arrive at a new evaluation of Smollett's work calculated to startle the literary world, nor

106 C. D. Cleveland, pp. 606–607 and n.
107 See, for example, *Episodes of Fiction*, p. 73, and Wm. Stebbing, pp. 6–7.
108 *Macmillan's Magazine*, XXI (1870), 527–533.
109 L. Stephen, *Hours in a Library*, II, 177; *English Thought in the Eighteenth Century*, II, 378, 380.
110 A. G. L'Estrange, *History of English Humour*, II, 123–125.
111 *Quarterly Review*, CLXIII (1886), 48–50.
112 See *Gentleman's Magazine*, Entirely New Series, VIII (1872), 565–575, XIV (1875), 729–737; Dr. John Brown, p. 276.

did they contribute any phrases destined to become current with succeeding writers, although we find some of the earlier critics, such as Scott and Hazlitt, quoted again and again.

The life by Roscoe prefixed to his edition of Smollett's works is unimportant, being based, as he said, on the work of Moore, Anderson, and Scott. Even the critical portions consist mainly of citations from earlier writers.[113]

In an article on Smollett in the seventh edition of the *Encyclopedia Britannica*, which appeared at about the same time (1842), we find more of the old attitude than the new. The article opened with the words 'whose writings have conferred distinguished honour upon the literature of his country.' The coarseness is dismissed as being 'perfectly innocuous.' 'The solemn depravity of Rousseau is more dangerous than the ludicrous indecorum of Smollett.' *Peregrine Pickle* is an 'admirable novel,' 'an absolute mine of character and adventure.' The dinner in the manner of the ancients is perhaps 'the most irresistible piece of pleasantry that was ever devised by a ludicrous fancy.' The learning scattered through the novels reflects great credit on the author; 'neither does he ever, like Fielding, hover on the verge of pedantry.' Toward the close a very favorable picture of his character was presented.

It is interesting to turn to the article in the ninth edition (by Minto) which appeared forty-five years later. We notice first that the article is little more than half as long. Though the attitude is generally favorable, the tone is more moderate throughout. The 'fierce and distempered mood' reflected in *Roderick Random* is explained by the hardships the author had been passing through. The next three novels are commented on in terms of very qualified praise, and only *Humphry Clinker* comes off with anything better. The *Travels* are mentioned, but not a word is said about them. The chief emphasis is on Smollett's influence. The opening of *Launcelot Greaves* has been imitated 'by hundreds of novelists since Smollett's time.' 'His influence upon novel-writing was wider even than Fielding's.'

Several of the biographers, Roscoe, Herbert, and Hannay, entered their objections to the Fielding-Smollett comparison. Herbert began his biography with this point, stating that the comparison results only in confusion, that it is a weakness in our minds to find one supreme in every field.[114] Hannay, on the other hand, after conceding that he could not claim to be dealing with 'one of the very great names in literature,' closed his book with these words:

113 *Miscellaneous Works of Tobias Smollett*, ed. T. Roscoe, pp. vii ff.
114 D. Herbert, p. 2.

Attempts are sometimes made to rank men of letters, in the Madagascar fashion, into 'honours' first, second, third, and so forth to the twentieth. These arrangements look precise, but on the whole they are a trifle barbarous. There are in the main only two divisions in the business of writing: the men who are themselves form one, and the men who are the echoes of somebody else form the other. In the first class there are gradations of merit, but its members are separated by a wide gulf, over which there is no passing, from the second order. Smollett was very distinctly on the right side of the gulf.[115]

Hannay's reviewer in the *Athenaeum,* by the way, rushed headlong into the Fielding-Smollett comparison, dubbing Smollett 'a rougher Fielding, with a narrower intellect, more animal spirits, and a coarser nature.'[116]

Concerning the coarseness, Herbert wrote in a Victorianish manner of *Roderick Random:* 'It would not be easy to read this work aloud now-a-days to our wives, - utterly impossible to our sisters and daughters.' But he added that no one will 'ever suffer moral taint from *Roderick Random*. If any one does, or says he does, he tells tales about more than the book.'[117] Hannay was less concerned about any supposed immorality in the novels, but was at some pains to defend them against the charges of brutality brought by Taine and others.[118] On the *Travels,* somewhat surprisingly, Herbert, the earlier writer by more than fifteen years, was the more enthusiastic, finding them 'still readable,' 'enjoyable to some considerable extent,' 'full of rays of Smollett's soul and riots of his temper,'[119] whereas Hannay had little to say except to point out that several of Smollett's heterodox opinions on art had been vindicated by later critics.[120] On the question of Le Sage's influence on *Humphry Clinker* the two biographers seem to have been in direct contradiction. Herbert had little else to say on this work, but one of his comments is worth quoting: 'This work is the *Logos* of Tobias George Smollett purified and obedient. It is the man himself again after many evil spirits which took early possession of him were cast out.'[121]

Herbert's life of Smollett, in fact, is one of the most pleasantly written of all. Hannay's is less distinguished for its style than for its critical comments, perhaps the most detailed that had yet been written. A whole chapter is devoted to the naval scenes and characters, for example, wherein there is a summary account of earlier authors who had dealt with this

115 D. Hannay, p. 160.
116 *Athenaeum,* Dec. 8, 1888, pp. 767-769.
117 D. Herbert, p. 21-22.
118 D. Hannay, pp. 66, 80-82.
119 D. Herbert, p. 39.
120 D. Hannay, p. 149.
121 D. Hannay, p. 154; D. Herbert, p. 40.

phase of life, and evidence substantiating the truth of many of Smollett's seemingly exaggerated descriptions.

Because of the large number of cheap fugitive editions published during the nineteenth century it is hardly possible to determine how often publishers found it profitable to issue Smollett's novels. Yet it seems safe to say that, despite the great increase in population and literacy, editions were hardly as frequent as they had been in the closing decades of the eighteenth century. Certainly this is true of the two minor novels. As for collected editions of the works, we find during these sixty years a sharp contrast with the periods which preceded and followed. From the years 1796 to 1824 there were seven editions of Anderson alone, besides the collections edited by Moore, Mrs. Barbauld, Mudford, and Scott. During the years 1832 to 1890 there seem to have been no new editions of the works except for the one-volume omnibuses of Roscoe (issued later in two and in six volumes) and of Herbert. There was also a re-issue of Moore's Smollett, edited by James P. Browne, in eight volumes, in 1872. Apparently this meagre supply was sufficient to fill the demand not only of private readers but of such public institutions as the Boston Public Library, whose trustees reported in 1881: 'Every reader of English literature will require copies of the works of Fielding, Smollett, Swift, Richardson, and other classic authors of like character, as a necessary portion of a general library; but their use in this institution is limited to those of mature years.'[122] As late as 1910 Arnold Bennett noted that 'interesting information has accrued to me concerning literary censorship in the British provinces. Glasgow has about a dozen lending libraries, chiefly, I believe, of the Carnegie species. In none of these are the works of Richardson, Fielding, and Smollett allowed a place.'[123] So that publishers were probably quite justified if they were wary about embarking on any but a very modest edition of the works of Smollett.

122 *A Reading Diary*, p. 13.
123 A. Bennett, *Books and Persons*, p. 192.

CHAPTER VI

American Notes

*The popular English works of the day are reprinted in
our country - they are dispersed all over the union -
they are to be found in every body's hands - they are
made the subject of every body's conversation.*

William Cullen Bryant, 1818

*Our literature may be provincial, but we are cosmopoli-
tan in our taste for literature.*

William Allen White, 1927

In the next and last chapter of this study, covering the modern
period, British and American writers will be considered together,
simply because there is no discernible difference in the opinions
they have expressed on Smollett. Nationalities have ceased to
count in the criticism of this author; if he is no longer the dar-
ling of the Scotch, he receives now and again a tribute from the
French. When we go back to earlier times in America, it is true
that even then the prevailing attitude toward Smollett and the
opinions of individuals show little that could be called distinc-
tively American; yet it was felt that a number of earlier American
criticisms, if gathered together, would possess a certain interest
of their own, and possibly throw a tiny beam of light on our early
culture. The plan of this chapter is to run rapidly through the
eighteenth and early decades of the nineteenth centuries, and to
add the opinions of several well known figures after that time.

The first dated item that I have found relating to Smollett is
one of the most interesting of all. It is in the form of a letter
to him from Richard Smith, Recorder of the City of Burlington, New
Jersey, dated February 26, 1763, and is well worth quoting at some
length. The opening sentences are as follows:

Sir:- You will pardon the Curiosity of a Man distant
from you many Thousand Miles - who will however take it as
a very particular Favor to have that Curiosity satisfied by
a note from you sent at the first Opporty either via Philada
or New York.- The Writer of this Letter as well as many of
his Acquaintances has often been delighted with, not to say
instructed, by your works, and out of mere gratitude he cannot refrain from returning you his hearty Thanks. It is
from Truth indeed and not from Adul(ation) - That I must say
I look upon you as the First Genius in Britann and the fin-

(ished)? (mas)ter? - and I should be glad to hear his Majesty
has honored you with (recognit)ion at least equal to Johnson's
- Of the circumstances of yor life we know at this Distance
(l)ittle - but I shod be glad to be informed whether Roderick
Random or (Peregrine Pic)kle contain any Traces of your real
adventures - and at what age or under what circumstances they
were written. Count Fathom shows a Smollett in every page
but it has not all the Graces of my Favorite Pickle - as to
Lancelot Greaves many here are pleased to say that you Lent
your Name upon that Occasion to a Mercenary Bookseller.

Smith went on to express the hope that the *Continuation* would be
continued, asked for a list of Smollett's 'Genuine Works,' and
closed with this sentence: 'If I ask any Thing impertinent you will
punish (my n)eglect - but you can hardly conceive the pleasure I
should take (com)municating yo'r answer to my Friends - and in
having in Pos(session) a Letter from the Author of the Complete
Hist. of Engld and Continuation.'[1] Smith's letter possesses added
interest from the fact that Smollett's gracious and fairly long reply, giving some facts of his life and the list of his works that
Smith had requested, is one of the most valuable documents for his
biographer.

It will be noted that Smith placed stress on Smollett's historical writings. That the fame of this part of his work declined
here as rapidly as in England may be judged from the comparative
paucity of references to his histories in later notices. For example, in 1788 a letter in the *American Museum* on reading history
recommended Goldsmith, Ferguson, Robertson, Hume, and (with reservations) Gibbon, but did not mention Smollett,[2] although, as we
shall see, the histories were widely read at least for the rest of
the century; but in England, too, these volumes were freely read
long after they had lost all repute with critics. We may observe,
in passing, that the catalog of the Library Company at Burlington,
published in 1758, and listing some eight hundred titles, included
Pamela, Tom Jones, and two or three other English novels, but no
Smollett.[3] His novels were probably added before long, if we may
judge from the practice of other early libraries.

At about the same time that Smith wrote his letter, Jefferson
was a student at college, where Smollett was among his half-dozen
favorite novelists.[4] Although many years later he advised against
the reading of fiction, at least for women, it is not strange that
in his college days he should have read Smollett, who was to be
found in many of the colonial libraries in Virginia. Represented
by *Roderick Random, Peregrine Pickle,* and the *History,* he is one
of twenty-six authors who turn up often. Fielding and Sterne

1 *Notes and Queries,* CLXIV (1933), 315-316. The emendation 'finished master' appears in
        Notes and Queries. Professor Stauffer has suggested 'finest writer' as the more
        likely reading.
2 *American Museum,* III (1788), 183.
3 *Library Company of Burlington, N.J. Catalog.*
4 F. W. Hirst, pp. 28, 518.

were also popular, whereas Gray, Macpherson, Gay, Cowper, and Goldsmith are among the eighteenth-century writers who are less commonly found.[5]

A bit of evidence that Smollett was also appreciated in New England comes from the almanac of Nathaniel Ames for 1768. The editor stated that if it were not the custom to write a formal preface, he would replace it with something interesting. 'But to prevent your going asleep over it, I shall season it with some humorous Extracts from Dr. *Smollett's* Travels concerning the Absurdity of the Customs and Fashions of different Nations.'[6] Among the extracts are some racy observations on the manners of the French. And among the books listed for sale by a New Haven dealer in a newspaper advertisement in 1770 was the *Adventures of an Atom*,[7] a work which we should suppose would have little salability in America, unless it were for the name of the author.

The Pennsylvanians too were reading Smollett. Some records of the library at Hatboro have been preserved which show the number of times the books in its collection were borrowed. The figures for the four major novelists for the years 1762-1774 are as follows:

Smollett's Complete History	29	times
Continuation	14	"
Humphry Clinker	11	"
Travels through France and Italy	9	"
Tristram Shandy	15	"
Sentimental Journey	14	"
Pamela	20	"
Tom Jones	43	" [8]

Again we notice the popularity of Smollett's historical works, but considering the short time it was available during the period covered, *Humphry Clinker* makes the best showing of any of these titles.

Thus, even before the Revolution, Smollett's popularity had spread widely through the Colonies and through various classes of society. In the years after the war, his readers became even more numerous. Although the catalog of the Library Company of Philadelphia for 1789 listed *Roderick Random* as the only novel by Smollett among some twenty works of English fiction, by 1807 we find the complete works edited by Moore, as well as the *Travels* and two sets each of the *History* and of the *Continuation*.[9] An explanation may be found in a note written in 1800 which listed several novels as 'too much defaced and injured for further use,' including *Roderick Random*.[10] The large circulating libraries in New York, such as

5 *American Literature*, X (1938), 35.
6 *Essays, Humor, and Poems of Nathaniel Ames*, p. 391.
7 A. Cowie, p. 148, n.
8 *Pennsylvania Magazine of History and Biography*, LVI (1932), 289-341.
9 *Catalogue of the Books belonging to the Library Company of Philadelphia*. 1807. pp. 249-250.
10 *Modern Philology*, XXXV (1937), 159-171.

Berrian's[11] and Caritat's,[12] naturally included his works by the end
of the century, not only the histories and the major novels, but
the lesser novels as well.

This popularity was by no means confined to serving-maids and
apprentices, whom some later critics have mentioned as the chief
admirers of Smollett. In a letter by John Randolph discussing his
earliest reading (circa 1780), he said: 'I read Humphry Clinker,
also; that is, Win's and Tabby's letters, with great delight, for
I could spell, at that age, pretty correctly.'[13]   James Kent,
Chancellor of New York, wrote in 1796:

> Novels are pleasing to me in my leisure hours. I have
> purchased since you have been gone, Fielding's 'Joseph An-
> drews,' Smollett's 'Roderick Random,' 'Peregrine Pickle,'
> 'Count Faltham' (sic), and 'Lancelot Graves' (sic), Defoe's
> 'Robinson Crusoe,' and Brook's 'Fool of Quality.' These are
> works of the first impression for wit, humor, the pathetic,
> and knowledge of man. They are classical productions of the
> kind.[14]

Another eminent jurist, Thomas McKean, chief justice of Pennsylvania,
wrote to John Adams in 1813 mentioning something he had read in
Peregrine Pickle, 'for I have read and still read novels. These
fabulous histories afford me not only amusement but pleasure, because they almost universally make vice detested and punished, and
virtue triumphant, which is not the case of history of real life.'[15]
Going still higher, we learn that with the exception of McKean's
correspondent, John Adams (hence, perhaps, McKean's defence of
fiction), all of our first six presidents had Smollett in their
private libraries. The other authors so represented were Chesterfield, Goldsmith, Sterne, Dr. Johnson, and Voltaire. 'Although
" Tom Jones" was in nearly all the libraries of the Presidents,'
wrote the bibliophile Rosenbach, 'I failed to find a single volume
of Richardson's "Pamela or Virtue Rewarded."' The same authority
gives us this information about Washington's reading: 'Addison and
Goldsmith were the authors he liked best, although he delved into
Shakespeare, Swift, Smollett, Sterne, and Fielding.'[16]   Washington's copy of *Peregrine Pickle,* with his signature on the title-
pages, is still extant.[17]

With the establishment of American periodicals devoted in whole
or in part to literary interests, allusions to Smollett naturally
became much more common. They seem to have first appeared in the
1790's. Of course, the lack of originality in these magazines
acted as a bar to the free expression of native reactions to the

11 Samuel Berrian, *Catalog.* New York: 1799.
12 H. Caritat, *Catalog.* New York: 1803.
13 John Randolph, p. 191.
14 James Kent, p. 240.
15 John Adams, X, 80–81.
16 *Proceeding of the American Antiquarian Society,* new series, XLIV (1934), 337–364.
17 Boston Athenaeum *Catalog,* p. 189.

English authors; we can only infer that the editors did not wield
their shears with complete lack of discrimination, but would make
some effort to cull material likely to interest their readers. At
any rate, Smollett figured frequently in these importations, especially after 1800; I have found only two references to him in
issues of earlier date.

It was that very important publication *Portfolio* which first
carried any considerable body of material on Smollett, both original and reprinted. Letters written by or addressed to him began
to appear with the first number, and some very important ones, such
as his reply to Richard Smith and Pitt's acknowledgment of his dedication of the *History*, were here published for the first time; he
was referred to in several reviews; and discussions of his work
were often printed in its pages. Much of this attention can probably be explained by the enthusiasm of the editor, Joseph Dennie, from
one of whose letters comes the following:

> As for the Caledonian doctor, he is as facetious a blade
> as ever grinned at a merry story. His *pickle* is composed of
> excellent ingredients, and is so well adapted to the literary
> palate, that, as Horace says, 'decies repetita placebit.' Would
> to heaven you could instantaneously transport yourself to
> Groton, and halt, with a volume of Perigrine (sic) in your
> hand, at my study. What peals of laughter would arise! What
> sacrifices to Momus![18]

It might be noted that Smollett's biographer, Anderson, wrote Dennie
in 1805 commending him for having printed several previously unpublished letters of Smollett.[19] One of these was introduced in
Portfolio by this comment: 'Every line from the pen of genius should
be preserved with care, and perused with avidity.'[20]

But the editor's predilection for Smollett did not lead him to
discriminate against contributors who disparaged the novelist. A
slashing attack on the moral tendency of his works appeared in 1802
from an admirer of Richardson. Typical comments are: 'It would be
difficult to point out a more profligate and hurtful book than
"Peregrine Pickle."' '"Roderick Random" is a tissue of low adventures . . . from which the reader can derive no useful instruction.'
Launcelot Greaves, though the 'most moral and instructive,' has many
exceptional scenes. Smollett 'apparently delights in vulgar and
profligate company, and of simple and sublime virtue he knows
nothing.'[21] But another correspondent wrote during this same year:
'I have seen real life, and found pregnant instruction in the
Roderick Random of Smollett.'[22] In 1806, favorable notice was
taken of the *Nouveau Dictionnaire Historique*, but the treatment

18 *Letters of Joseph Dennie*, pp. 31–32.
19 *Ibid.*, p. 198 and n.
20 *Portfolio*, New Series, I (1808), 199.
21 *Portfolio*, II (1802), 185–186.
22 *Ibid.*, p. 138.

of Englishmen was complained of. Smollett was the example chosen. 'Zeal, for a favourite and truly original writer, urges us to inform these French critics, that their assertion that, the author of Roderick Random was but an indifferent writer is, in spite of all their assurance, destitute of a shadow of foundation.'[23] A rather lengthy discussion of Sterne, Smollett, and Fielding which appeared in 1811 contrasted Smollett very unfavorably with the other two; scarcely anything good was said about him. The only resemblance between him and Sterne 'consists in the obscenity and the impiety of their pages,' and his overloaded caricatures are very different from the perfectly natural people we meet in Fielding.[24]

Occasional criticisms appeared in other publications during these years. One contributor said that objections to novel reading are well founded if confined to 'particular works like Werter, or Peregrine Pickle,' but to condemn all novels because of them does not seem wise.[25] Elsewhere, there was a discussion 'Of Fable and Romance' which may have been reprinted, although I did not meet it in the British periodicals. Cervantes is placed first in this branch of literature, then Swift, and then Smollett. His two first works 'are remarkable for wit, humour, and pungent satire'; they are 'familiar to every one'; 'the same luminous beauties stream throughout his works, with equable felicity.' After all this high praise, the writer treated Fielding and Richardson with astonishing disrespect. Fielding, it seems, is included among those with 'inferior charms, and less captivating minds'; and as for Richardson, 'is it prejudice, or want of taste, that I have never been able to peruse two pages of this celebrated author?'[26]

In the first tender shoots of American fiction, sentiment waxed even more flourishingly than in England. The authors of these works, and their readers too, were under the spell of Richardson and Sterne. But in one of the earliest nautical novels, the *Wanderings of William* (1801), it was the more virile brace that the author mentioned in his preface.

> Smollett is the only writer of novels that has depicted the character of a sailor with any justness of colouring. But Smollett often borders in his descriptions on caricature; and the frequent repetition of his sea phrases evinces his penury of them. Fielding once designed to send his hero to sea, but his good sense made him relinquish the plan.[27]

The review of this work in *Portfolio* included one of the strongest objections to the language of Smollett's sailors that has appeared

23 *Ibid.*, New Series, I (1806), 381.
24 *Ibid.*, New Series VI (1811), 412–431.
25 *Literary Magazine and American Register*, VI (1806), 451.
26 *Portico*, I (1816), 210–211.
27 *Wanderings of William*, p. viii.

anywhere:

> It is to be deplored that . . . an author, capable of better things, should mar his pages with many a mariner's exclamation, vile, and trite as can be heard from lungs, ulcerated with blasphemy. To justify the adoption of these noisy expletives, the authority of Doctor SMOLLETT is not of more weight, than *the small dust of the balance*. In the tribunal of taste, and before an impartial jury, of the most liberal critics, the oaths of Bowling, Trunnion, Hatchway, and Pipes, have been justly condemned, as not contributing in the smallest degree, to the wit of his novels, and only serving to scandalize the serious, and disgust the well bred.[28]

But this diatribe seems unjust to the *Wanderings of William;* anything resembling the conversation of Bowling, Morgan, Trunnion, and their tribe is not to be found. It gives us, in fact, a very pale pink version of Smollett's nautical language and scenes.

A few years later, Tabitha Tenney wrote a satire on the sentimental fiction then prevalent, under the title *Female Quixotism.* The heroine, naturally, is a novel-crazed female, whose expectations concerning lovers and courtships lead her into a series of ridiculous scrapes. When in her mid-forties, she falls ill, and the first symptom of recovery 'was her calling for some of her favourite authors.' The first book the maid lays hands on is *Roderick Random.* 'As this was not so much to Dorcasina's taste, as novels of a more modern date, it had lain untouched in her closet for more than twenty years; but being now in a manner new to her, she perused it with great avidity.' Shortly after, she meets a young man named John Brown, and recalling that Roderick lived as a servant with Narcissa under this name, is favorably disposed toward him.[29]

As we pass over a decade or so, we begin to reach some authors of reputation who can be connected with Smollett in one way or another. Irving, though he owed much to Smollett, seems to have had little to say about him. In his life of Goldsmith he spoke of Smollett's 'powerful and popular pen,' and anent Goldsmith's good-natured skit in *The Bee* remarked: 'Smollett was a complete schemer and speculator in literature, and intent upon enterprises that had money rather than reputation in view.'[30] But these explicit references tell us less than Irving's writings in general. In the *Monthly Review*'s notice of *Salamagundi* it was remarked that 'the broad humour of a Smollett is here heightened into absolute caricature in too many instances.'[31] The *Westminster Review* spoke more pointedly of his *Tales of a Traveller:* 'In every attempt at pourtraying the ways of men in his adopted country, he describes the manners of other times - making feeble sketches from the finished

28 *Portfolio*, I (1801), 303.
29 T. Tenney, II, 131–132.
30 W. Irving, pp. 85–86, 189.
31 *Monthly Review*, LXV (1811), 418.

but faded pictures of Smollett and Goldsmith.[32] His writings also
reminded the *Portfolio* of Smollett, though the similarity led to
more pleasant reflections than the charge of unoriginality. The
American materials he has gathered in *The Sketch Book* are so rich
that 'could a Smollett, a Fielding, or a Le Sage, have seen America as she is, he would at once have abandoned every other field,
and blessed himself on having obtained access to the true *terra
fortunata* of the novelist.' Irving was urged to write novels, nor
be discouraged 'by the common place cant about the impossibility
of good novels being written by young men.' Smollett's youthful
authorship of *Roderick Random* was cited, 'and assuredly he had not
seen half so much of the world as Mr. Irving has done.'[33]

It is interesting to note that Irving's friend Paulding, like
a number of English authors, was not disposed to rank Scott with
novelists of the classic tradition, such as Fielding, Smollett,
and Goldsmith. Scott gives us good narratives, we are told, but
has little to offer once our curiosity in the story is satisfied.
Fielding is praised highly; 'Smollett is only second, yet a great
way off.' Of Fielding, Smollett, and Goldsmith, it is said:

> Each of these writers, without going out of the bounds
> of probability, or offending against 'the modesty of nature,'
> by extravagant and incongruous events, or boisterous, uncon-
> trolled passion, has produced works, that appeal far more
> powerfully to the heart and the imagination, than the dash-
> ing succession of characters and events, that only hang to-
> gether by a chain of improbabilities, or by the thread of
> history, exhibited in the work of the great Unknown.[34]

The first author to write about the sea with any great success
after Smollett was Cooper. He was well aware that Smollett had
almost pre-empted this field for himself. In his preface to *The
Red Rover*, which was added in 1850, Cooper wrote:

> Smollett had obtained so much success as a writer of
> nautical tales, that it probably required a new course
> should be steered in order to enable the succeeding adven-
> turer in this branch of literature to meet with any favor.
> This difficulty was fully felt when this book was origi-
> nally written, and probably has as much force to-day as it
> had then, though nearly a quarter of a century has inter-
> vened.[35]

In a preface to *The Pilot* written by Susan Fenimore Cooper we are
told of a conversation the novelist had with some friends at the
home of Charles Wilkes, nephew of that John Wilkes who was perhaps
the only man to win a clear-cut victory over Smollett in a journalistic war. We are told that Cooper said Scott's *Pirate* was not
entirely satisfactory to a nautical man because of its inexact

32 *Westminster Review*, II (1824), 345.
33 *Portfolio*, Series, 5, XI (1821), 134–135.
34 J. K. Paulding, II, 149–150.
35 J. F. Cooper, *Works*, XXII, iii.

knowledge of the sea. The others disagreed and said landsmen would read a book only if the passages of nautical matter were brief and occasional. Cooper dissented. 'He mentioned Smollett, but was told that the novels of this writer owed their success to their coarse, but vigorous wit and humor, and in spite of any connection with the sea.'[36] Out of this conversation came the idea of Cooper's *Pilot*.

While we are in Knickerbocker, we may note that on June 10, 1824, 'and subsequently' an attraction was offered at the Broadway circus entitled 'Peregrine Pickle, or, Hawser Trunnion on Horseback,' presumably the same piece shown at the Royal Amphitheatre in London in 1818; and on June 7, 1838, a benefit performance of a new piece, *Humphry Clinker*, was given.[37]

Hawthorne seems to have been fairly well versed in Smollett. He wrote to his sister in 1819 that he had read *Ferdinand Count Fathom* and *Roderick Random*,[38] and forty years later he recalled that he had first made the acquaintance of Beau Nash in the latter novel.[39] When he had reached Leghorn on his travels and wandered about the place, he recorded that 'we saw nothing in the slightest degree interesting, except the tomb of Smollett, in the burial-place attached to the English Chapel.'[40] But, as we might surmise, there were elements in Smollett's work not entirely to his taste. In one of his essays he observed that the English seem to have no regard for the 'feminine purity of the lower orders of their countrymen,' and, continuing:

> I offer it as a serious conviction, from what I have been able to observe, that the England of to-day is the unscrupulous old England of Tom Jones and Joseph Andrews, Humphry Clinker and Roderick Random; and in our refined era, just the same as at that more free-spoken epoch, this singular people has a certain contempt for any fine-strained purity, any special squeamishness, as they consider it, on the part of an ingenuous youth.[41]

Poe had even less regard for Smollett and the type of fiction he represents, if we may judge by one of his extravagant statements: 'For one Fouque there are fifty Molieres. For one Angelo there are five hundred Jan Steens. For one Dickens there are five million Smolletts, Fieldings, Marryatts (sic), Arthurs, Cocktons, Bogtons, and Frogtons.'[42] It is known that he had not read all the authors he was in the habit of alluding to, but some knowledge of Smollett on his part might be inferred from an entry in his 'Marginalia': '"Advancing briskly with a rapier, *he did*

36 J. F. Cooper, *The Pilot*, p. xiv.
37 G. C. D. Odell, III, 115; IV, 228.
38 Julian Hawthorne, I, 105.
39 N. Hawthorne, *Notes of Travel*, IV, 410.
40 *Ibid.*, III, 183.
41 N. Hawthorne, *Works*, XI, 353–354.
42 *Graham's Magazine*, IX (1842), 187.

the business for him at a blow." - *Smollett*. This vulgar collo-
quialism had its type among the Romans. *Et ferro subitus grassa-
tus, agit rem. - Juvenal.*[43]

Meanwhile, before Hawthorne and Poe had started to write, a
new type of periodical, the literary review, had made its appearance in this country, following closely the pattern of the English
reviews, sometimes to the point of taking over their articles
bodily. It may be worth while to consider a few of the references
to Smollett found in some of these publications. The *North American* seems to have been firm on two ideas: the bad moral tendency
of the early novelists, and the vast superiority of Scott and
Edgeworth, not only in this respect, but in other things too. The
two latter are declared to be above Fielding 'as much in talent as
in moral taste.' After a comparison of Fielding and Scott undertaken in support of this statement, the reviewer said: 'Of Smollett,
we should hardly speak in this connexion.' Delight is expressed
that he did not use his native land for the scene of his novels,
for then his coarse caricatures might have prevented the fine simplicity of Burns and Scott in their pictures of Scottish life.[44]
In another article, it was said that 'We hear of Smollett's sea-
pieces, Fielding's English humor,' and so forth, but Scott's genius is not confined to one compartment. 'Fielding and Smollett
have no great merit, except in direct narrative or dialogue.' But
Scott's greatest glory was in elevating the moral tone of the
novel, 'so that, instead of being obliged, as with Fielding's and
Smollett's, to devour it, like Sancho Panza's cheese-cakes, in a
corner as it were, it is now made to furnish a pure and delectable
repast for all the members of the assembled family.'[45] The same
idea was stressed in a review of *Helen*. Smollett was even a nas-
tier writer than Fielding, though his own life was finer, but both
have been 'gradually lifted to the highest shelf of the bookcase'
and can hardly be opened 'without a feeling of shame.'[46] In 1849,
however, in a review of *Dombey and Sons* by Whipple, the old novelists were praised, and Smollett's virtues were found to be great
enough to win for him a place 'side by side with Richardson and
Fielding.'[47]

The *Southern Review* looked more kindly on Smollett. He has
long been placed next to Fielding, 'with an unsettled question of
relative excellence between them,' although the reviewer has 'never
hesitated in assigning the superiority to Fielding.' *Humphry
Clinker* was highly praised; 'the reputation of this charming book
is forever established.'[48] In another article Fielding and Smol-

43 E. A. Poe, XVI, 62.
44 *North American Review*, XXXII (1831), 404–405.
45 *Ibid.*, XXXV (1832), 188–189.
46 *Ibid.*, XXXIX (1834), 171.
47 *Ibid.*, LXIX (1849), 386.
48 *Southern Review*, IV (1829), 380–381.

lett were again compared and were found about equally excellent. The reviewer for the *Southern* evidently got some of his opinions from Scott, whose discussion of the two novelists was followed pretty faithfully.[49]

The *American Quarterly Review* declared in 1834 that Fielding and Smollett 'are by universal consent, placed highest on the list' of all novelists. 'Illustrious pair! Coequal in merit and coeval in renown. Your labours raised at once your favourite art to the highest perfection, and fairly divided, with the productions of the muse, that empire over the public mind, which they had before exclusively held.' The reason for their supremacy is their realism: the 'real-life delineations' and their fidelity to 'nature and truth.' Richardson, it is observed, 'has for the last thirty years sunk into almost total neglect.'[50]

The *Knickerbocker Magazine* said, in reviewing a two-volume edition of Smollett's works published in Philadelphia in 1833: 'We are glad to see the select works of this standard author, over which so many thousands have indulged the hearty and medicinal laugh of their young days.' And we are told that Smollett's writings 'will continue the freshness of their interest, as long as the English language shall last.'[51]

The *Southern Literary Messenger* seems to offer little for our purpose. In 1839 there were printed the 'Confessions of a novel reader.' This unfortunate person came upon the works of Fielding and Smollett at college, and was taken by their good qualities, which are enumerated with remarkable enthusiasm, but which afford 'but a feeble compensation for the immoral tendency of their writings.' Under their evil influence he formed designs on his landlady's daughter, which, however, were prevented, by his illness, from having serious ends. Finally he married a wealthy but ugly and parsimonious old maid.[52] Possibly this recital was intended to be satirical, although it reads much like the usual 'moral tale.' In an article on 'Modern fiction' in this same magazine, it is stated that Bulwer has been charged with coarseness, but 'Fielding and Smollett are coarser far than Bulwer, and yet all admit the value of their works.'[53]

We shall now consider a few later references to Smollett, mostly from the pens of some of our better known authors.[54] Lowell, who had read Smollett at college,[55] went back to him some

---

49 *Ibid.*, VIII (1831), 45.
50 *American Quarterly Review*, XVI (1834), 503–504.
51 *Knickerbocker Magazine*, II (1833), 315.
52 *Southern Literary Messenger*, V (1839), 183 ff.
53 *Ibid.*, VIII (1842), 345.
54 Here, too, as in England, many names are missing; my investigation uncovered nothing from any of these: the Alcotts, Aldrich, Bierce, Charles Brockden Brown, Bryant, Crane, Dana, Joseph Rodman Drake, Franklin, Holmes, Longfellow, Norris, Stedman, Stowe, Thoreau, Whitman, and Whittier.
55 H. E. Scudder, I, 32.

thirty years later, but seemingly from a sense of duty as much as for pleasure. Writing to Norton in 1867, he said:

> I have read over 'Roderick Random' . . . but did not learn anything new from it. I found I knew Smollett well enough before.. However, I shall get 'Peregrine Pickle' for the sake of Trunnion and Pipes, who are grown very dim to me. Fielding's coarseness belongs to his time, Smollett's is of all time. But there are good sketches in him.[56]

Of Cervantes he remarked: 'Fielding assimilated and Smollett copied him.'[57] The Latin phrase of a cicerone in Italy reminded him of the 'dissolve frigus of the landlord in Roderick Random, and (I) could not help smiling.'[58] In spite of his repeated reading of Smollett, Lowell apparently had little enthusiasm for him, or else was deterred by the spirit of the times from saying much. Emerson seems to have only one reference. In his journal, he spoke of Coleridge, Southey, and Wordsworth as 'men who appreciated man and saw the nullity of circumstances'; and contrasted Smollett, Fielding, and Goldsmith, who 'treat only of the life of common sense; the Apparent.'[59] Philip Hone, the diarist, mentioned among 'several capital things' produced by the 'school of Mount, the American Wilkie,' a painting of two of Smollett's characters. He also stated that the works of Scott, Dickens, and some others, 'have created a new and better taste,' though 'at this time of day we may go back to Smollett and Fielding with some remains of our first love.' But not to Miss Burney, Mrs. Radcliffe, and Miss Porter.[60] Bayard Taylor visited the neighborhood of the Smollett family on a journey to Scotland in 1844-1845. He noted that the monument to the novelist seemed to be neglected by the inhabitants, and that a farmer showed him a house 'which he said belonged to Smollett - or Roderick Random, as he called him.'[61] In Henry Adams' autobiography we find this comment, which might refer to some time around 1845: The Madam, wife of John Quincy Adams, had a vague effect of not belonging to Boston, 'but to Washington or to Europe, like her furniture, and writing-desk with little glass doors above and little eighteenth-century volumes in old binding, labelled "Peregrine Pickle" or "Tom Jones" or "Hannah More."'[62]

Melville was reading *Roderick Random* in 1851, for in that year he borrowed the book from the New York Public Library. One of his critics has noted the influence of Smollett in his description of an amputation on shipboard.[63] The narrator of *Redburn* speaks of the 'exaggerated sailors of Smollett,'[64] but in *Omoo* there is a

56 J. R. Lowell, XV, 154.
57 *Ibid.*, VII, 164.
58 *Ibid.*, I, 161.
59 R. W. Emerson, IV, 93.
60 P. Hone, I, 353–354; II, 17.
61 Bayard Taylor, p. 45.
62 Henry Adams, p. 16.
63 C. R. Anderson, pp. 490; 402–403.
64 H. Melville, *Works*, V, 177.

passage which, if we may see the author speaking through his character, reveals considerable enthusiasm, combined with a slight
fogginess concerning the names of Smollett's people. The narrator,
telling how he and his friends passed the time on a South Sea
island, says:

> Sometimes we chatted, as well as we could, with the na-
> tives; and, one day - joy to us! - Po-Po brought in three
> volumes of Smollett's novels, which had been found in the
> chest of a sailor, who some time previous had died on the
> island.
>
> Amelia! - Peregrine! - you hero of rogues, Count Fathom!
> - what a debt do we owe you![65]

And in *White Jacket*, giving advice to men who have lonely profes-
sions, Melville recommends certain objects to be placed about the
room; 'perhaps best of all is a shelf of merrily bound books, containing comedies, farces, songs, and humorous novels. You need
never open them; only have the titles in plain sight. For this
purpose, *Peregrine Pickle* is a good book.'[66] Bret Harte told his
biographer that Smollett was one of the authors in his father's
library, and that an avidity to read these books was present, but
no further comment seems to have appeared.[67] Nathaniel Parker
Willis, who read *Tristram Shandy* every year, apparently thought of
Smollett, as well as Fielding, as reading for boys, for in listing
the stages in the development of our reading tastes, he said a
'forward boy' will read them at fourteen.[68]

An article by W. S. Sargent in the *Atlantic Monthly* for 1859
included some high praise of Smollett, and Fielding too, though
the article is on the former. The 'passage of time serves but to
confirm' these men in their merited honors. Their great merits
quite outweigh their coarseness and grossness, 'which were often
less their own fault than that of the age.' But though men will
always read their works, and though the most refined portion of
society read them in the latter part of the eighteenth century,
'So great is the change in the habit of thought and expression in
less than half a century, that we believe there is not in all
America a gentleman who would now venture to read either of these
works (*Roderick Random, Peregrine Pickle*) aloud to a fireside
group.'[69] In 1877, the following lines, inscribed to Oliver Wen-
dell Holmes, appeared in *Scribner's Monthly*:

> Tom Jones disports himself through Fielding's pages
> To show the natural man to future ages;
> The characters in Peregrinus Pickle
> All teach us wisdom, while our sides they tickle;
> They argue not from what their acts ensue,
> But tell us what they are from what they do.[70]

65 H. Melville, *Ibid.*, II, 347.
66 H. Melville, *Ibid.*, VI, 57-58.
67 T. E. Pemberton, p. 5.
68 N. P. Willis, pp. 31-32.
69 *Atlantic Monthly*, III (1859), 693-703.
70 *Scribner's Monthly*, XIV (1877), 446.

An astonishing situation with regard to Smollett is found in Lanier's *English Novel*. He heaped harsh criticisms on Richardson, Fielding, and Sterne; referring to the eighteenth-century novelists *in toto* he said that 'if I had my way with these classic books I would blot them from the face of the earth'; and he introduced Smollett as the 'third so-called classic writer.' But his actual discussion of Smollett is favorable. Not only is *Humphry Clinker* highly praised, with emphasis on the character of Mrs. Jenkins, but *Peregrine Pickle,* which we should think would have been anathema to him, was described as 'famous for its bright fun and the caricature it contains of Akenside.'[71] Is it barely possible that Lanier had not read the book?

Howells wrote an interesting passage on Smollett in connection with his visit to Leghorn. Having spoken of several people buried in the English cemetery, he said:

> Most important of all is the tomb of that strenuous spirit, more potent for good and ill in the English fiction of his time than any other novelist of his time, and second only to Richardson in the wide influence of his literary method, Tobias Smollett, namely, who here ended his long fight with consumption and the indifference of his country to his claims upon her official recognition.

The *Travels* and *Humphry Clinker* are called, respectively, 'the truest monument' and 'the best effect' of Smollett's stay in Italy. Howells' knowledge and appreciation of the man's character appear in the next remark:

> It is a very simple shaft which rises over his grave, with the brief record, 'Memoriae Tobiae Smollett, qui Liburni animam efflevit, 16 Sept., 1773,' but it is imaginable with what wrath he would have disputed the record, if it is true, according to all the other authorities, that he exhaled his spirit two years earlier, and how he would have had it out with those 'friends and fellow-country-men' who had the error perpetuated above his helpless dust.'[72]

The Connecticut Yankee mentioned his reading of Smollett in a passage which we wish was more revealing of the attitude of the author. Remarking that the ladies and gentlemen of Camelot used language that 'would have made a Comanche blush,' the narrator continued:

> Indelicacy is too mild a term to convey the idea. However, I had read 'Tom Jones' and 'Roderick Random' and other books of that kind, and knew that the highest and first ladies and gentlemen in England had remained little or no cleaner in their talk, and in the morals and conduct which such talk implies, clear up to a hundred years ago.'[73]

---

71 S. Lanier, pp. 185–188.
72 W. D. Howells, pp. 257–258.
73 Mark Twain, XVI, 38.

Finally, we meet another president who read Smollett, though his memory of it had become rusty when he wrote to Ted Junior in 1906, from on board the USS Louisiana: 'Have you ever read Smollett's novel, I think "Roderick Random" or "Humphry Clinker," in which the hero goes to sea? It gives me an awful idea of what a floating hell of filth, disease, tyranny, and cruelty a warship was in those days.'[74]

Rapidly summarizing the findings of this chapter, we note that Smollett seems to have been as popular here as in England, over a period that began surprisingly early and continued about as long as in England. The evidence of this seems clear, though it is necessarily limited, particularly since literary reviews and men of letters did not appear until a later date. Among our first major literary coterie, the Knickerbocker School, several people knew and liked his novels, and two of the important figures, Irving and Cooper, had them well in mind in creating their own works. There seem to have been no such enthusiastic devotees of Smollett as Dickens and Carlyle, but, as we have seen, several authors were at least appreciative admirers. Objections to the immorality of the novels began to be voiced at about the same time as in England, and increased similarly. In fact, as the century waxed older, the situations in the two countries grew more and more analogous, until any distinctions observable at an earlier time completely disappeared.

74 T. Roosevelt, XIX, 515.

CHAPTER VII
A Classic Novelist
1891-1940

*A good book once added to the treasury of literature
is safe, in spite of vicissitudes of fortune.*

A. T. Sheppard

In the first two decades of the nineteenth century Smollett's
fortunes reached their highest peak; by 1890 they were at their
nadir. It was in the 1820's, I judge, that Smollett began to lose
favor with the reading public. Susan Ferrier in 1824 and Sir
Egerton Brydges in 1825 referred with satisfaction to the dwind-
ling number of his readers. The tons of Waverley novels printed
during these years caused a vast change in reading habits. The
barometric periodicals whooped up Scott, forgot Fielding and Smollett. As early as 1815, indeed, the renegade *Critical Review* had
deserted its first editor and fifty-year favorite for the new idol.
Anderson's edition of Smollett was last reprinted in 1824, and we
have seen what a meagre supply thereafter trickled off the presses.
We have seen that even large libraries either banned Smollett entirely or restricted the circulation of his works. In 1864 the
London publisher Charles Knight lamented 'that Tom Jones, and Roderick Random, and Tristram Shandy, are utterly gone out of the popular
view.' Knight's observation was often repeated, not with laments,
but with purring and a rubbing of hands. Meanwhile, even Smollett's
great friends, though less fickle than the vulgar, were thinning out,
and as they dropped off one by one, no others took their places.
Finally, they were all gone. Victorianism had buried Smollett deep
in oblivion, seemingly for all time; and in 1890, surveying a job
well done, the Earl of Carnarvon exclaimed: 'Smollett's day and influence are of the past.'[1]

But the reverberations of his lordship's nunc dimittis were
shattered by a trumpeting rebuke from John Churton Collins.[2] The
corpse stirred; through its veins surged two of those powerful
forces known as currents of literary thought; and though the body,
like the reanimations of Poe, may not really be alive, it does
move about, it is still with us. The first of those two forces
was the growing interest in the history of literature. For many
years, as we have seen, the historical manuals had been appearing

1 Earl of Carnarvon, p. xxxviii, N.
2 J. C. Collins, p. 210.

132

in large numbers, but it was not until the latter part of the century that the historico-scientific approach to literature began to prevail. The second force was the rise of realistic and naturalistic fiction, which by this time was making it ridiculous to call Smollett immoral. As if to signalize the changed state of affairs, three new editions of Smollett's works, each in twelve volumes, appeared within seven years, beginning in 1895.

At the same time, two magazine articles alluded to the new tendencies working in Smollett's favor. In a review of Henley's edition (1902), Richard Burton noted Wilkie Collins' statement that no publisher would dare risk a complete edition of Smollett or Sterne. Burton went on to say that the realistic novel was accustoming readers to coarser fare, and that the study of fiction in the colleges was causing more attention to be paid to the eighteenth-century novels. He declared that Smollett possessed more than historical interest, and spoke of Smollett's gift for straight story-telling and for making his characters exhibit themselves through dialogue. But the travels, as well as the miscellanies, he found to be 'only of value to the student who would trace the novelist's growth and decadence and have a fuller understanding of the man.' He also expressed the belief that Henley had dealt rather savagely with Smollett.[3]

The other article, written by J. A. Nicklin for the *Gentleman's Magazine* in 1896, entitled 'An eighteenth century saga,' began with these words: 'If ever there was an opportune time for magnifying the reputation of Tobias Smollett, it is surely the present. His merits, until now, have been steadily depreciated on the score of overwhelming coarseness, but a generation which glorifies the author of "Jude the Obscure" ought not to find "Peregrine Pickle" too rank for its taste. Though Smollett's heroes have the disadvantage in point of language and bearing, in their sentiments and character they are no such ruffians as some recent popular heroes.' Impressed, perhaps, by the storm of criticism which had greeted Hardy's late novels, Nicklin said that realism seemed already on the wane, and that Smollett should share in its brilliance before it was too late. 'By virtue alike of energy and knowledge, he is a very king among the realists.' The title of the article refers to *Roderick Random*, which is praised as 'certainly the most complete embodiment of the spirit of enterprise of the eighteenth century as the whole of Smollett's novels are the best documents for the study of the century's social life,' and as possessing a greater wealth of material than Tom Jones.[4]

The three editions referred to were all accompanied by critical introductions, each of which merits some consideration. The first

3 *Dial*, XXXII (1902), 81-83.
4 *Gentleman's Magazine*, CCLXXX (1896), 453-458.

editor (1895), and one who has probably written more about Smollett over a period of years than anyone else, was the omniscient George Saintsbury. After giving a rather well balanced picture of Smollett's character, he wrote that Smollett is an utter stranger to delicacy in any of its forms, 'admittedly one of the nastiest writers in English.'[5] 'His virtue, like that of some very great writers besides himself, lay in working on established lines in a fresh and striking manner.'[6] The rougher features of Smollett's books are not chargeable upon him, but upon his times. It was not in his nature nor was it his business to 'prettify' English life.[7] After a discussion of *Roderick Random*, which contains nothing very unusual except a defence of Roderick's character, *Peregrine Pickle* is taken up, the work on which there has been most difference of opinion, we are told. The fame of this book suffers, as does all of Smollett's work, from his journalistic proclivities; he sticks so close to his own times that his books inevitably suffer from the passage of time. Trunnion's death, however, is 'unquestionably one of the great deathbeds of English fiction'; 'there is no snivel or sensibility by Commodore Trunnion's bed as there is by some other celebrated pieces of funeral furniture.[8] Saintsbury envies those who read *Peregrine Pickle* for the first time; one finds disappointment very often when reading it on later occasions.[9] *Ferdinand Fathom* 'may be considered Smollett's least good novel';[10] *Launcelot Greaves*, therefore, is praised more than commonly. The effective opening is pointed out, and several characters are listed who have a life about them to which hardly a character in *Fathom* can pretend.[11] One's opinion of *Launcelot Greaves* hinges on this point: if we can once accept the main conception of Smollett, preposterous though it is, we can find much that is enjoyable in the book; if not, the whole thing is ruined for us. Saintsbury said he liked it better the more he read it; the author's advance in good-nature and softened feeling gives it a marked advantage over the earlier works.[12] Of *Humphry Clinker* it is difficult to say anything hard. It has four great characters, especially Matthew. His benevolence is superb; Dickens, who played at this type of man constantly from Pickwick to Jarndyce, never could get near him.[13]

In another criticism of Smollett written by Saintsbury at about this same time, we find some other opinions of interest. 'It is probable,' he writes, 'that in that vague reflection of critical opinion in general judgment which rarely goes very far wrong, Smol-

5 G. Saintsbury, *Prefaces and Essays*, p. 74.
6 *Ibid.*, p. 76.
7 *Ibid.*, pp. 87–88.
8 *Ibid.*, pp. 92–96.
9 *Ibid.*, p. 100.
10 *Ibid.*, p. 109.
11 *Ibid.*, p. 112.
12 *Ibid.*, p. 117.
13 *Ibid.*, p. 118; pp. 122–124.

lett takes on the whole the lowest place among the four great novelists of the mid-eighteenth century in England.' Smollett's lack of
invention, the ill-temper in some of his works, and his total lack
of construction explain why he 'has not on the whole been a favourite with critics, and why he pleases far more at a first, especially
an early and unfastidious reading, than at nicer perusal in later
years.' The cudgels are again taken up for *Launcelot Greaves*, 'that
rather unjustly depreciated book,' and Roderick and Peregrine are
called 'two of the most unmitigated young ruffians who ever escaped
condign punishment.'[14]

It is more interesting, however, to skip over some years to observe what changes of opinion are to be found. In his history of
the English novel, there is this comment by Saintsbury: 'In passing
to the third of this great quartette, we make a little descent, but
not much of a one, while the new peak to which we come is well de-
fined and separated, with characters and outlines all its own. It
may be doubted whether any competent critic, not, like Scott, bribed
by compatriotism, ever put Smollett above Fielding, or even on a
level with him.' This last statement, as we have seen, is quite
inaccurate. *Peregrine Pickle* still seems to be a favorite and
Ferdinand Count Fathom a dull book, but *Launcelot Greaves* is
praised less warmly than in the earlier accounts except for its
opening, to which Cross meanwhile had called attention. The historical importance of Smollett's novels is emphasized - their use
of setting and the foreign scenes and characters, especially.[15]

A few years later, in his *Peace of the Augustans*, Saintsbury
seems to have written his last discussion of Smollett. There is
just one point here that deserves special attention. The writer
said he had been 'very familiar' with Smollett in his youth, up
to twenty-five or so; then he rather lost him for another twenty-
five years, when he read and re-read him for the edition of his
works; and then again, 'practically in old age,' he read Smollett
once more, both for literary purposes and for pastime. Although
his opinions have naturally varied somewhat, he has always found
Smollett amusing, especially for his 'pre-eminence of narrative
faculty.' One's various objections to Smollett do not affect
'the delight in the unfailing spring of narrative power which almost all the books, the first and last especially, show; and you
may even feel inclined to admit that as a *mere* tale-teller Smollett really does deserve the title of best of this great bunch of
four.'[16] This passage is noteworthy because Saintsbury was one
of the many who had said that Smollett pleases us chiefly in our
youth, and also because of the one quality in the novels which
seems to have impressed him most after all this reading - not the

14 Henry Craik, IV, 257–259.
15 G. Saintsbury, *The English Novel*, pp. 115–126.
16 G. Saintsbury, *Peace of the Augustans*, pp. 137–138.

frequently praised broad humor or the oddities of character, not
the coarseness, but the storytelling ability. Several other modern
critics have also thought this to be Smollett's greatest attraction.

The next editor was Henley, who did so much to help the cause of
Fielding. For Smollett he did much less. His discussion of the
novels is a mixture of praise and censure, but it is the censure
which stands out. He spoke of Smollett 'writing angrily and trucu-
lently where Le Sage had written with an urbane and intelligent
smile; writing, too, with an utter contempt for the good taste,
the good breeding, the reticence, the ironical and far-reaching
amenity, which, as being essentials in the great tradition of
French Literature, were so to say inherent in Le Sage.[17] Concerning Smollett the man, one of his typical comments is: 'He was the
vainest of mankind, in truth; and - for many years at least -
whatever he did was made eminent and admirable to him by the mere
circumstance that he had done it.'[18] Of *Roderick Random* he wrote:

> The book was hard, coarse, cruel - a rough-and-tumble
> hurly-burly of impudent, squalid, and unedifying adventure;
> but it was novel, it was brilliant, it had touches of ten-
> derness, it teemed with vividly seen and instantly presented
> character, it abounded in life and spirit and fun.[19]

Counting over the diverse merits of *Peregrine Pickle,* which, like
many another, Henley found to be a combination of great excellences
and great faults, he was moved to the reflection the 'the half of
Smollett was not told unto him, so that he never guessed, so contemptuous of everything but farce was he, how good a humorist, in
the sense that Shakespeare and Fielding and Dickens are humorists,
he might have been.' *Ferdinand Count Fathom* proves that he never
guessed, says Henley, for aside from the first chapter, 'There is
not much to praise.' Although it is a book of such a kind that
'the sole care of him that reads is to get his reading done as soon as
ever he can, and then forget what he has read as soon as ever he
may,' Smollett liked it, 'and to me, at least, it is not incredible
that, his vanity being what it was, he wrote this story of a villain
to show how Fielding should have written that of Jonathan Wild.'[20]
The comment on Smollett's next novel is as follows: 'I have said
nothing of *Sir Lancelot Greaves* for the simple reason that I find
so little merit in it that I have no more than that to say.'[21] The
Travels is dismissed with even less. *Humphry Clinker,* finally, is
rewarded by some appreciative if not extravagant praise, but in a
scant page.[22] A summary at the end begins with a tirade against
Smollett's indecency, which is best characterized by Henley's own

17 *The Works of Tobias Smollett*, ed. W. E. Henley, I, xvii.
18 *Ibid.*, xix.
19 *Ibid.*, p. xvii.
20 *Ibid.*, xxv-xxvi.
21 *Ibid.*, xliii.
22 *Ibid.*, xliii-xliv.

comment: 'I have said what I believe to be the worst that can be said of Smollett.'[23] Then he is praised - for his power of, realizing a character out of his own mouth, for his narrative ability, and for his humor. And last, we are told that 'literature is not all great,' and that somewhere beyond the pale 'there is honourable room for Smollett.'[24]

Henley's work on Smollett was obviously not a labor of love. Indeed, it is difficult to see why he undertook to edit the works, since he lacked what is surely one requisite for a successful editor, some degree of enthusiasm for his subject, or, at least, sympathy with his aims. His introduction included most of the good and bad things that had been said about Smollett, but, as I have suggested, the bad predominate, and very distinctly. It is not likely that anyone who approached Smollett through this criticism would be inclined to go on to the novels themselves. Two of the reviewers of Henley's edition, indeed, referred to his lack of sympathy with his subject. Richard Burton, as was said, declared that Henley had been savage enough with Smollett, whom, as a man, he exposed in all his weakness. The other, a writer in *Blackwood's*, approved of Henley's work in general, but quarreled with him because he insisted 'more strongly than is necessary upon Smollett's coarseness.' The reviewer reminds us, something that Henley seems to have forgotten, that Smollett was describing coarse men in a coarse age. In spite of this material, we are told, the novels have an essential wholesomeness. The rogues in them 'are neither held up for our imitation nor dissected after the manner of obscene psychology'; he would never hesitate to put one of the novels in the hands of a boy; 'his books are honest and free, at full liberty to come and go in all hands, clean companions of that manhood and valiance that is Britain's boast and Britain's solace.'[25]

The third editor, Maynadier, was more favorably disposed than Henley, but as his criticisms have probably been of less influence than those of the other two editors, they need not be noticed at great length. *Roderick Random* is defended rather vigorously against the charges of lack of structure, indecency, and even the unattractive character of the hero, on the grounds that the type Smollett was working in, and the kind of life he was describing, necessitated most of those faults which have been charged to the novel. Prophetically enough, Maynadier commented: 'If our contemporary novelists were as realistic as their eighteenth-century predecessors, some of their pages . . . would be as unsavoury as any of Smollett's.'[26] This editor deserves credit for observing that the 'Memoirs' of Lady Vane are not the 'raciest part of *Pere-*

23 *Ibid.*, p. xlvi.
24 *Ibid.*, xlvii.
25 *Blackwood's Edinburgh Magazine*, CLXVII (1900), 697-699.
26 *The Works of Tobias Smollett*, Dalquhurn edition, I, xxi-xxiii.

grine Pickle'; they are 'quite without Smollett's vivacious humor.'[27]
The spininess and daring of this intruded story had been remarked
on ever since the day of their publication, when they may actually
have seemed wicked, but to anyone who has taken the trouble to read
them in the last one hundred years they must have seemed the dullest
pages by far in any of Smollett's novels. To be commended, too, in
Maynadier's denial of the hoary dictum that Bramble is only an older
Roderick or Peregrine,[28] one of those plausible and satisfying remarks which are repeated incessantly without anyone's taking the
trouble to think about them. Saintsbury, in one of his later
books, also denied that Roderick or Peregrine ever could have
grown into Matthew.[29]   Maynadier has another interesting comment
on *Humphry Clinker.* The mellow humanity of this work has usually
been ascribed to a change in Smollett's character, and possibly to
the influence of Sterne, but the suggestion is made here that the
change may have been due to a change in the English people themselves, who had become less brutal in the twenty years since *Peregrine Pickle.*[30]

But though the appearance of the new editions reflected a change
in the attitude toward Smollett, conditions remain very different
from what they were in the early nineteenth century, as becomes
clear when we turn to consider modern authors. So far as there
has been any 'revival' of Smollett, it has been brought about
through the far-reaching influence of the schools and not by our
novelists and other creative writers of today. Blanchard has noticed this same phenomenon with respect to Fielding,[31] although
the dichotomy there is not so strongly marked. Indeed, Somerset
Maugham has somewhere said that literary immortality is confined
chiefly to the class-room, but the statement is much truer of
some authors than of others, and perhaps truer of few others than
of Smollett. The examination of the opinions of recent authors
yields only negative results, with but a few exceptions.

F. Marion Crawford referred to the 'undeniable fact that women
who blush scarlet, and men who feel an odd sensation of repulsion
in reading some pages of "Tom Jones" or "Peregrine Pickle," are
not conscious of any particular shock when their sensibilities are
attacked in French,'[32] but Crawford's own opinion of Smollett does
not seem to be on record. Henry James, we are told, 'knew the
kind of fiction which held him - Scott's, Reade's, Mérimée's,
Balzac's - and the kind which repelled - Richardson's, rather surprisingly, Fielding's, Smollett's - and it was from these likes

27 *Ibid.,* IV, xxiii.
28 *Ibid.,* XI, xii-xiii.
29 G. Saintsbury, *Peace of the Augustans,* p. 134.
30 *The Works of Tobias Smollett,* Dalquhurn edition, XI, xviii-xix.
31 F. Blanchard, p. 535.
32 F. M. Crawford, p. 38.

and dislikes that his first reviews got under way.'[33]   James wrote
that Scott was the first pure story-teller among the English;
Richardson, Fielding, and Smollett are all moralists. 'Even Smollett - who at first sight appears to recount his heroes' adventures very much as Leporello in the opera rehearses the exploits
of Don Juan - aims to instruct and to edify.'[34] Succeeding remarks indicate that James placed Fielding well above Smollett.
There is one sympathetic reference, however, in 'A Passionate Pil-
grim,' wherein James said that while walking to Worcester 'I felt
like one of Smollett's pedestrian heroes, faring tavernward for a
night of adventures.'[35] We learn that Kipling read Smollett in
his schooldays, - but nothing more than that.[36] W. H. Hudson distinguished the *Atom* as 'the beastliest classic in the English
language' and on another occasion, speaking of this work and
Roderick Random, 'remarked on Smollett's love and knowledge of
dirt and smells.'[37] Conan Doyle, after stating that Richardson,
Fielding, and Smollett are the only eighteenth-century novelists
who count, went on to discuss Smollett as follows:

> It is not a subject to be dogmatic upon, for I can
> imagine that these three writers would appeal quite dif-
> ferently to every temperament. . . Yet I cannot think that
> any large section of the critical public could maintain
> that Smollett was on the same level as the other two.
> Ethically he is gross, though his grossness is accompanied
> by a full-blooded humour which is more mirth-compelling
> than the more polished wit of his rivals. I can remember
> in callow boyhood - *puris omnia pura* - reading 'Peregrine
> Pickle,' and laughing until I cried over the Banquet in
> the Fashion of the Ancients. I read it again in my man-
> hood with the same effect, though with a greater apprecia-
> tion of its inherent bestiality. That merit, a gross
> primitive merit, he has in a high degree, but in no other
> respect can he challenge comparison with either Fielding
> or Richardson. His view of life is far more limited, his
> characters less varied, his incidents less distinctive,
> and his thoughts less deep. Assuredly I, for one, should
> award him the third place in the trio.[38]

In that part of George Moore's *Avowals* represented as a conversation between him and Gosse, he asks for information on Smollett, who 'is one of whom I know little, only some passages.' It
would be untrue to say he had or had not read Smollett; 'my memory of him is gusto, and plenty of it, and an outlook on life in
strict conformity with his style.' Gosse urges him to consider
Smollett more carefully, 'in view of the influence he exercised
and still exercises on the English novel.'[39] But Moore, as we
have seen, is only one of a large number of novelists of the last

33 C. P. Kelley, p. 27.
34 H. James, p. 10.
35 *Atlantic Monthly*, XXVII (1871), 365.
36 G. C. Beresford, p. 244.
37 Morley Roberts, pp. 221, 244.
38 A. C. Doyle, pp. 137–138.
39 G. Moore, p. 33.

seventy-five or one hundred years who might be cited in refutation of the latter part of Gosse's statement. Arnold Bennett likewise seems to have had nothing to say about the novels, but he is to be numbered among those readers of modern times who have 'discovered' the *Travels*. The following entries from his journal are both dated September, 1907. 'The latter (the *Travels)* is very good and very like Fielding's "Lisbon."' And again, with reference to the *Travels:*

> A fine *splenetic* book, thoroughly interesting. The kind of book that a few men might, and probably do, cherish as a masterpiece too special in its flavour to please the crowd. It gives the impression of a sound, sincere personality, not very cultured in the arts, but immensely well informed, and breathing a hard, comfortable common sense at every pore. A doctor's personality, and yet still more the personality of a police magistrate; slightly less *doux*, and more downright, than that of Fielding. One leaves this book in thankfulness that one is not an eighteenth-century traveller.[40]

Shaw has also had a word to say on Smollett. It concerns the element of brutality or insensitivity in his works, the quality which seems most objectionable today as the indecency did to an earlier generation. Significantly (and for good reason, as well be seen shortly), it is not the early novels, but the more humane *Humphry Clinker* that Shaw refers to. Speaking of pre-Dickensian fiction, he says:

> Poverty in rags is a joke, yellow fever is a joke, drunkenness is a joke, . . . humiliations and painful accidents of all sorts are jokes. Hen-pecked husbands and termagant mothers-in-law are prime jokes. The infirmities of age and shyness of youth are jokes; and it is first-rate fun to insult and torment those that suffer from them.
>
> We take some of these jokes seriously enough now. Humphrey Clinker may not have become absolutely unreadable (I have not tried him for more than forty years); but there is certainly a good deal in this book that is now simply disgusting to the class of readers that in its own day found it uproariously amusing.[41]

The exact extent of Shaw's reading in Smollett was brought out in 1926, when E. S. Noyes wrote him to ask whether the similarity in plot between *Pygmalion* and the 'nymph of the road' incident in *Peregrine Pickle* had been intentional. Shaw's secretary replied that the resemblance had repeatedly been called to Shaw's attention. The letter continued: 'This is interesting as showing that people still read Smollett. He (Shaw) never read P.P.: Humphrey Clinker was his sole boyish excursion into Smollett.'[42]

Thus among our major authors the attitude remains about the same as in the latter nineteenth century, an attitude mainly of

40 *Journals of Arnold Bennett*, pp. 255, 257.
41 G. B. Shaw, pp. 200-201.
42 *Modern Language Notes*, XLI (1926), 327-330.

indifference. Most of these people seem to have nothing whatever to say about him. Others, like Kipling, may have read him in boyhood, but evidently they retained none of those fond recollections of the experience which earlier writers recounted so enthusiastically. The conversation between Moore and Gosse fairly well represents the modern situation - the author pretty indifferent, the scholar, the professional writer about writers, more concerned. Of all our major authors since 1860, I have found not one who has expressed warm admiration for the novels of Smollett. Once again, we must look in other directions for more fruitful fields.

There have been three biographies of Smollett of some length to appear within the last fifty years. The first, Seccombe's article for the *Dictionary of National Biography*, which, in fact, appeared shortly before 1890, is undoubtedly the most important, being based on a fair amount of original research; but since the article is almost purely biographical, there is nothing of interest for us, except, perhaps, the following remark:

> Of the five great eighteenth-century novelists, Defoe, Richardson, Fielding, Smollett, and Sterne, Smollett is now valued the least; yet in the influence he has exercised upon successors he is approached by Sterne alone of his contemporaries. The tide of subsequent fictitious literature is strewn on every hand with the *disjecta membra* of 'Peregrine Pickle,' of 'Count Fathom,' and 'Humphry Clinker.'[43]

The first part of this statement seems open to question; though Smollett was in low estate when this article was written, so were most of the others mentioned. Probably each had adherents here and there, but only Fielding was consistently placed above Smollett.

It may be noted, incidentally, that the article on Smollett in the eleventh edition of the *Encyclopedia Britannica* was also by Seccombe, while the fourteenth edition (typically) carried only a condensed and unsatisfactory version of what had appeared in the eleventh; for example, although Buck's *Study in Smollett* was listed in the later bibliography, Seccombe's statement about the 'resounding success' of *Peregrine Pickle* was carried over verbatim.

Smeaton's biography, which appeared in 1897, is of little importance. Written in a simple, popular style, with attempts at higher flights here and there, it is generally favorable in tone, but it is also superficial, gives no evidence of original research, and in places is purely fictitious, as in the description of Mrs. Smollett's feelings at sundry times. Reviews in the *Nation* and the *Literary World* both objected to the style of the work. The critical chapters, where they seek to be original, are unconvincing, as when we are told that Smollett looked over the previous accomplishments in English fiction, saw where there was room for something

---

43 *Dictionary of National Biography*, article 'Smollett.'

new, and proceeded to fill the gap;[44] or where a progression in psychological subtlety is traced through the succeeding novels.[45] Evidently this work caused hardly a ripple in the currents of the Smollett tradition.

The most recent life is that by Lewis Melville, published in 1927. The critical portions of this work, which are of some length, are composed mostly of quotations, paraphrases, and echoes from many preceding writers: Scott, Hazlitt, Thackeray, Seccombe, Saintsbury, and Cross are among those drawn upon. There is the statement that Smollett 'could not invent: he could only exaggerate';[46] the women in *Roderick Random* are criticized;[47] we are told that Peregrine is a great cad;[48] the practical jokes are condemned and Trunnion's death-bed scene highly praised;[49] there is an attempt to defend *Ferdinand Count Fathom;* Scott is quoted on the terror scenes;[50] the plan of *Launcelot Greaves* is deplored and the opening pages are admired;[51] Seccombe is quoted in praise of the *Travels;* [52] and *Humphry Clinker* is given an excellent rating, with help from Hazlitt, Thackeray, and Saintsbury.[53] As a biographer Melville seems to have added little or nothing to our knowledge of Smollett.

Reviews of Melville's work differed sharply, as reviews have a way of doing, and very possibly praise was bestowed in inverse proportion to the reviewer's knowledge of Smollett. Thus, the *Nation and Athenaeum* found it to be a scholarly and readable book: Melville's few generalizations upon Smollett are not to be missed;[54] whereas the *Times Literary Supplement* found nothing at all to say in favor of the work. It is 'out of date before it is fairly published,' seems to contain not a single piece of original research, is made up mostly of quotations linked together by 'lame and colourless narrative,' and is full of inaccuracies, as an example of which nine verbal errors were pointed out in a single letter.[55]

Thus the last half century has brought us no good biography of Smollett; he alone of the greater early novelists has been so neglected. Another reviewer of Melville's work, writing in the *New York Times,* said: 'Research has cleared the field, and now a Strachey is needed to do justice to the life of a fiery spirit, a generous man on the whole, and as courageous a figure as can be found in English letters.'[56] If there is a Strachey around, it is doubtful whether

44 O. Smeaton, pp. 123-124.
45 *Ibid.*, p. 127.
46 L. Melville, p. 39.
47 *Ibid.*, p. 44.
48 *Ibid.*, p. 61.
49 *Ibid.*, pp. 62—63.
50 *Ibid.*, pp. 103 ff.
51 *Ibid.*, pp. 183—184.
52 *Ibid.*, p. 217.
53 *Ibid.*, pp. 258 ff.
54 *Nation and Athenaeum*, XL (1926), 394.
55 *Times Literary Supplement*, Dec. 9, 1926.
56 *New York Times*, Nov. 13, 1927, IV, 24.

Smollett would be the subject to tempt him, but a **Professor Cross** could improve the situation tremendously.

As the same reviewer suggested, there have been important contributions to our knowledge of Smollett's life, principally these: Noyes's edition of the letters, Buck's *A Study in Smollett,* and a number of articles in the journals. Although the biographical material remains scanty, enough has been turned up to make possible a re-interpretation of the man's character.

When we turn to the writers about writers, the critics, essayists, historians, and biographers, we find a sizable amount of material dealing with Smollett. Some of it, to be sure, consists only of brief allusions, but besides the discussion in historical works, there have also been a number of essays and magazine articles devoted wholly to him. It cannot be affirmed that these writings present any generally accepted verdicts on Smollett's work as a whole; in fact, the variety of opinions is sometimes bewildering. Nevertheless, a few phenomena emerge clearly enough.

The most apparent change in modern times concerns the *Travels through France and Italy,* which is not the most highly praised, perhaps, but is now the most consistently praised of Smollett's works. *Humphry Clinker* still has its detractors; everyone seems to speak well of the *Travels.* Going back to the beginning of this period, we have an article in *All the Year Round* devoted to the *Travels* and saying: 'Considering what the discomforts of the voyage must have been, it is wonderful that Smollett should have kept so well the even temper which, with a few slight exceptions, characterizes his remarks';[57] a complete about-face from earlier opinions. In 1901 the book was favorably discussed in a chapter of Schuyler's *Italian Influences.*[58] In 1907 the *Travels* was recognized by its inclusion in the World's Classics series, with a lengthy introduction by Seccombe. Seccombe opened with some general remarks occasioned by a consideration of the wide celebration of the second centenary of Fielding, and doubts (which the event proved to be well founded) whether Smollett would get such attention in 1921. 'Smollett's fame, indeed, seems to have fallen upon an unprosperous curve. The coarseness of his fortunate rival is condoned, while his is condemned without appeal. Smollett's value is assessed without discrimination at that of his least worthy productions, and the historical value of his work as a prime modeller of all kinds of new literary material is overlooked.' Concerning the *Travels* themselves, Seccombe referred to them as 'that one of Smollett's books which has sunk farthest in popular disesteem'; the book is 'in many respects one of Smollett's best,' containing an 'unrivalled key' to his personality, being the work of a schol-

57 *All the Year Round,* LXVIII (1891), 420-424.
58 E. Schuyler, pp. 220-245.

ar, an observer of human nature, and a 'satirist of no mean order.'[59]
As we have seen, the *Travels* had already attracted considerable
though scattered attention before 1907, but this edition seems to
have established the claim of the work to recognition in a definitive manner. It will be remembered that Arnold Bennett was reading
it and praising it highly in this same year, probably in Seccombe's
edition. Ten years later J. H. B. Browne, a prominent Scotch lawyer, said he probably liked the *Travels* the best of all of Smollett's
works, better than Fielding's last journey too.[60] In 1919[61] and
1920[62] there were magazine articles devoted to this one book of
Smollett's; the *Cambridge History of English Literature* termed it
'one of the most entertaining books of travel extant';[63] and just
a few years ago Bloor wrote; 'what a delightful book it is . . .
bad temper has never worked quite such a wonder anywhere.'[64]

Another marked change is to be seen in the attitude towards
Smollett's indecency. Fifty years ago he was a dangerous and immoral writer; today he is at worst an unpleasant one. In 1894 a
writer spoke of 'the prurient incidents in Smollett's career';[65]
in 1905 the editor of Benjamin Franklin, speaking of the coarseness of many of his lesser writings, said: 'He out-Smolletts
Smollett in his letters to young women at home and experienced ma-
trons abroad';[66] in 1908 we are told that his coarseness still
goes far 'towards keeping Smollett out of the modern home or con-
fining him to the locked cabinet.'[67] This is the last time I have
found Smollett relegated to the locked cabinet. References of
this kind are not infrequent during these years, but in more recent times they are rare exceptions. Even the charge of brutality
in his works is often held to be unwarranted.

This leads to another point, the endeavors of a number of critics to find in Smollett a more serious purpose than had hitherto
been seen. Seccombe in 1907 referred to Smollett as a scholar, an
observer of human nature, and a 'satirist of no mean order.'[68] The
Times Literary Supplement in 1921[69] and Frederic Harrison in 1922[70]
compared him with Juvenal for his satiric intent and force. Muir,
in 1929, suggested that the exigencies of the picaresque type, the
necessity for getting the hero in and out of so many places and
scrapes, 'perhaps explains partly the cold-blooded manner in which
Smollett puts his heroes through their paces, and his extreme in-

59 Tobias Smollett, *Travels through France and Italy*. ed. Thomas Seccombe, pp. vi, xviii.
60 J. H. B. Browne, pp. 52–53.
61 *Anglo Italian Review*, IV (1919), 31–45.
62 *National Review*, LXXV (1920), 344–353.
63 *Cambridge History of English Literature*, X, 46.
64 R. H. U. Bloor, p. 163.
65 *Scottish Review*, XXIII (1894), 227.
66 *The Writings of Benjamin Franklin*, ea. A. H. Smyth, I, 171.
67 H. Jackson, p. 95.
68 Tobias Smollett, *Travels through France and Italy*, ed. Thomas Seccombe, p. xviii.
69 *Times Literary Supplement*, March 17, 1921, p. 165.
70 F. Harrison, p. 155.

sensitiveness to them.[71]   Green, in 1935, again emphasized Smollett's satirical intent, remarking that 'none of our eighteenth-century novelists has shown up the rottenness of contemporary English social and political conditions with more truth and contempt of accepted opinion. Smollett has been reproached for his lack of good taste; but that is sheer cant.'[72]

A fourth note of prominence in modern times is rather marked - and uniformly favorable - attention to Smollett's style. Burton, in 1909, was speaking about his 'gift of forthright phrase,' and saying: 'A page or so of Smollett, after a course in present-day popular fiction, reads very much like a piece of literature. In this respect, he seems full of flavor, distinctly of the major breed.'[73]   In later years, praise of Smollett's style has become more common. Biron wrote in 1920: 'His style, if not in the least literary, is certainly literature, direct, pointed, and economic.'[74] The next year a writer in the *Times Literary Supplement* said: 'As a rhetorician and word master he is second to none we have in the satiric line.'[75]   Cazamian wrote in 1924 that 'his language, often vivid and concrete, has at times a force of expressive eloquence; the tremor of an overstrung sensibility raises it in places to a sort of harsh, short-lived lyricism.'[76] Elton also praised his style, especially in comparison with Richardson's;[77] E. A. Baker wrote: 'Smollett is a prince among story-tellers. In sheer narrative force he has never been beaten';[78] and in 1935 Bloor also stated that Smollett 'has never been surpassed in sheer power of narration.'[79]

When we consider the modern period chronologically, we are struck by the vogue Smollett enjoyed during the 1920's. 'The world is suddenly being flooded with Smollett,' said one writer in 1926. Indeed, this decade was more productive of publications written by and relating to Smollett than any other ten years we have yet passed through. During this period five books about him appeared, his works were reprinted two or three times, *Humphry Clinker* was included in the Modern Library and World's Classics series, *Roderick Random* in Everyman's Library, and an unusually large number of articles were published in the literary periodicals, including two leading articles in the *Times Literary Supplement*. What was the cause of all this activity? Very little of it had any connection with the bicentennial of his birth. Did Smollett's hard realism accord with the disillusioned pessimism of the post-war years? Whatever the reason, the activity subsided in the succeeding decade, unaccount-

71 E. Muir, pp. 29–30.
72 F. C. Green, p. 364.
73 R. Burton, p. 78.
74 *National Review*, LXXV (1920), 353.
75 *Times Literary Supplement*, March 17, 1921, p. 165.
76 E. Legouis and L. Cazamian, p. 895.
77 O. Elton, I, 204.
78 E. A. Baker, IV, 207.
79 R. H. U. Bloor, p. 161.

ably and completely. Except for the continued contributions to the scholarly periodicals, signs of interest in Smollett have well-nigh vanished.

In the historical works since 1930, however, Smollett has several times been lauded: extravagantly by Ford Madox Ford, who put him ahead of Fielding or Dickens;[80] more discriminatingly by Osgood;[81] by Green, in his *Minuet*, with the emphasis on his serious purpose of reform that we have already noticed;[82] and by Elizabeth Cook, who placed *Roderick Random* among the ten great novels of the world, though tenth, with the comment on her list: 'Lacking balance and proportion in some respects, these would be admitted by all critics into the front rank of the great novels of the world. Why? Because they convey characters with a superb, epic range.'[83]

But this resume of modern criticism of Smollett has up to this point presented his fortunes in a far more favorable light than is warranted. If one plods conscientiously through most of the hundreds of pages that have been written about him in the past half century, one finishes with the strong impression that this is not a respected or beloved author. The impression is affirmed by turning over the dozens of manuals that have appeared in modern times. From Raleigh and some of his contemporaries[84] down through such writers as Lafcadio Hearn,[85] Andrew Lang,[86] Garnett and Gosse,[87] Harold Williams,[88] and John Buchan,[89] to more recent years, with Grant C. Knight,[90] Norman Collins,[91] and David Garnett,[92] one finds Smollett being treated with varying degrees of harshness, dislike, or, at best, marked indifference. Even in the best known histories, those of Cross,[93] Legouis and Cazamian,[94] and E. A. Baker,[95] for example, criticisms of Smollett include more than a little censure, so that the general impression derived from all these works, as was said, is pretty uncomplimentary. An apologist for Smollett might advance several explanations for his poor showing in the historical manuals: that some of the authors had only superficial acquaintance with him, and that his faults, as a number of writers have said, lie on the surface; or that many of the manuals stem not so much from the author's mind as from the pages of preceding compilations; or that

80 F. M. Ford, pp. 76–77.
81 C. G. Osgood, pp. 338–340.
82 F. C. Green, pp. 349–364.
83 E. Cook, p. 168.
84 W. Raleigh, pp. 186–190; P. Russell, pp. 6, 60–61.
85 L. Hearn, I, 418–425.
86 A. Lang, *History of English Literature*, pp. 467–468; *Adventures among Books*, pp. 175–210.
87 R. Garnett and E. Gosse, III, 322–323.
88 H. Williams, p. 83.
89 J. Buchan, pp. 346–347.
90 G. C. Knight, pp. 53–59.
91 N. Collins, pp. 56–69.
92 D. Verschoyle, pp. 80–82.
93 W. L. Cross, *Development of the English Novel*, pp. 63–69.
94 E. Legouis and L. Cazamian, pp. 894–898.
95 E. A. Baker, IV, 197–239.

Smollett is not one of the names which must be praised if the work is to be pronounced a safe guide for students; or that the historical arrangement which throws him into juxtaposition with Fielding often leads not so much to an analysis of his own work as a demonstration that he lacked the particular qualities which make Fielding a great novelist. But the fact remains that the opinions prevailing through the majority of these books probably reflect the attitude of the age as accurately as does any other indicator.

But if the general tendency of all this academic writing on Smollett has been to fix certain opinions about him, and perhaps predominantly unfavorable ones, we must consider, on the other hand, that his survival today is to be credited in large part to the same influence. After the middle of the nineteenth century, there was a possibility of his dropping utterly out of sight, and we need only recall what a large proportion of modern writing about him has come from teachers and scholars to appreciate the part these people have played in keeping him before the world. But to say that Smollett lives mainly in and because of academic circles is hardly to distinguish him from many other writers of his century. When we look for his place in these circles, we find that it is not a high one. Several people have commented on the neglect he has met with in modern times. Seccombe remarked: 'The estimate formed of Smollett's work during the past generation has probably been a diminishing one, as we may infer in part from the fact that there is no standard Life and no definitive edition of the works,'[96] and although this was written in 1911, the two desiderata he mentioned have not yet been supplied. There was Herbert Read saying in 1935: 'It has long been a commonplace of criticism that Smollett is the most neglected of our eighteenth-century authors.'[97] As a result of the activity which was just then getting under way, a more hopeful attitude was revealed in several comments written in 1927. Thus, a writer in the *New York Times* saying: 'Tobias Smollett, one of the few great writers of English fiction, is slowly emerging from the oblivion to which the smugness of Victorian taboos consigned him.'[98] And Sherburn, noticing two scholarly contributions, commenting: 'These two books . . . will do much to further interest in a man of letters who has hardly got his deserts at the hands of the historians or critics of literature.'[99] Professor Cross, too, observing: 'Not long ago Smollett seemed to be down and out, but the satirist is now getting on his feet once more, though he has been rather slow about it.' The following remark, which succeeds the one just quoted, is especially illuminating: 'Our knowledge of him is just where our knowledge of Fielding was when Dobson and Lowell took him

96 *Encyclopedia Britannica*, 11th edition, article 'Smollett.'
97 H. Read, p. 187.
98 *New York Times*, Jan. 2, 1927, III, 15.
99 *Modern Philology*, XXIV (1927), 380.

in hand.'[100] But this activity, as we have seen, ceased at just about this time.

Yet several general trends in the modern criticism of Smollett have been pointed out in this chapter, and these, it is to be noted, are all complimentary to him. Here is one sign that another decade or two may bring a more favorable re-appraisal of his work. Those writers of modern times who have criticized him most severely have pretty much repeated one another's ideas, ideas which were current long before modern times. These ideas may represent their honest opinions, but the opinions probably are not based on individual analysis and reflection. If they say anything in praise of Smollett, as they often do, that too is likely to be unoriginal. On the other hand, several of Smollett's admirers in more recent years have made a fresh appraisal of him and got away from the traditional opinions. The praise which Scott, Hazlitt, and Thackeray bestowed on him is no longer potent to convince us; as often as not, it only calls forth dissent. The broad humor, the droll caricatures, the Gothic descriptions will not serve to keep him in high estate. A better opinion of him, if it emerges at all, will come when critics can convince their readers that Smollett possesses high integrity. a profound satirical intent, and a style of unusual merit,

Meanwhile he continues to be a fixture in our literature, not of major stature, perhaps, but in no immediate danger of being lost sight of. He is frequently referred to by name, rather widely studied in the schools, now and then read for his own sake. In short, he is a classic - a pure, unalloyed classic, not a pinchbeck, like Defoe or Gray or Keats, cheapened by a measure of popular affection. Because Smollett is no longer widely known, it has become respectable to know him. Even a superficial knowledge of this sometime most popular of novelists is evidently a sign of merit. John Middleton Murry, applying for a scholarship, was asked if he could give the titles of any books by Smollett.[101] In *Of Human Bondage*, Philip Carey, while at the house of Dr. South, picks up a book. The testy doctor, whose character is not unlike that of Smollett, enters and says:

> What's that you're reading?
> *Peregrine Pickle*. Smollett.
> I happen to know that Smollett wrote *Peregrine Pickle*.[102]

This evidently implies that Dr. South is a man of learning, and knows it; the incident would have been pointless a century before. In 1933 a woman writing in *Harpers* of her homemade theory of education told how she tried to show her daughters 'that a young woman might have a fine taste in ski clothes and cocktails and still

---

100 *Yale Review*, XVI (1927), p. 799.
101 J. M. Murry, p. 41.
102 W. S. Maugham, p. 615.

be on speaking terms with Smollett or Cicero.'[103]   And there we
take leave of Tobias Smollett, for who can deny that in this match
he has completely refurbished his erstwhile shoddy reputation and
made himself eminently respectable?   'But it never occurred to
them,' said Agnes Repplier of our great-grandfathers, 'to make a
merit of reading "Tom Jones" or "Humphry Clinker."'[104]

103 *Harpers*, CLXXII (1936), 660.
104 A. Repplier, pp. 109-110.

BIBLIOGRAPHY

The following bibliography is selective. A large amount of material considered to be of only minor importance for the purposes of this study has been omitted.

The date of the first edition of certain publications is shown in parentheses at the end of the entry. Usually this information has not been given for authors whose chronological position will be readily known to persons consulting this work.

Abel, Clarke, *Narrative of a Journey in the Interior of China.* London: 1818.

Adams, Henry, *The Education of Henry Adams.* Modern Library. New York: 1931.

Adams, John, *The Works of John Adams.* Edited by Charles Francis Adams. 10 volumes. Boston: 1856.

(Adolphus, J. L.), *Letters to Richard Heber, Esq.* Boston: 1822.

Aikin, John, and William Johnston, *General Biography.* 10 volumes. London: 1814.

Alison, Archibald, *Essays Political, Historical, and Miscellaneous.* 3 volumes. Edinburg and London: 1850.

All the Year Round. London. Volume LXVIII.

Allibone, S. Austin, *A Critical Dictionary of English Literature.* 3 volumes. Philadelphia: 1899. (1859-1891)

Allingham, William, *A Diary.* London: 1907.

Allsop, Thomas, *Letters, Conversations and Recollections of S. T. Coleridge.* Third edition. London: 1864.

American Antiquarian Society, *Proceedings.* Worcester, Mass. Volume XLIV, New Series.

American Literature. Durham, N. C. Volume X.

The American Museum. Philadelphia. Volume III.

The American Quarterly Review. Philadelphia. Volume XVI.

Ames, Nathaniel, *Essays, Humor, and Poems of Nathaniel Ames.* Edited by Sam. Briggs. Cleveland: 1891.

Anderson, Charles Roberts, *Melville in the South Seas.* New York: 1939.

The Anglo-Italian Review. London. Volume IV.

The Anti-Jacobin Review and Magazine. London. Volume XXI.

Arblay, d', Fanny, *Diary and Letters.* Edited by her niece.
7 volumes. London: 1854.
Early Diary of Frances Burney. Edited by Annie Raine Ellis.
2 volumes. London: 1889.
Evelina. New York: 1906.

The Athenaeum. London. Dec. 9, 1843; Dec. 8, 1888.

The Atlantic Monthly. Boston. Volumes III, XXVII.

The Authoress. London: 1819.

Bagehot, Walter, *Works.* 5 volumes. Hartford: 1889.

(Baker, David Erskine), *The Companion to the Play-House.*
2 volumes. London: 1764.

Baker, Ernest A., *The History of the English Novel.* Volume 4.
London: 1930.

Barbauld, Mrs., *The British Novelists.* Volume XXX. London: 1810.

(Barrett, Eaton Stannard), *Six Weeks at Long's.* 3 volumes.
London: 1817.

Barstow, Marjorie Latta, *Wordsworth's Theory of Poetic Diction.*
Yale Studies in English. No. LVII. New Haven: 1917.

Bascom, John, *Philosophy of English Literature.* New York: 1876.

Beattie, James, *Dissertations Moral and Critical.* 2 volumes.
Dublin: 1783.
Essays. Third edition. London: 1779.

Beattie, William, *Life and Letters of Thomas Campbell.*
3 volumes. London: 1850.

The Bee, or Literary Weekly Intelligencer. Edinburgh. Volumes
III, VIII.

Bennett, Arnold, *Books and Persons.* London: 1917.
The Journals of Arnold Bennett. Edited by Newman Flower.
Volume 1. London: 1932.

Beresford, G. C., *Schooldays with Kipling.* London: 1936.

Berrian, Samuel, *Catalog.* New York: 1803.

Bewick, Thomas, *Memoir of Thomas Bewick Written by Himself.*
London: 1924. (1862)

The Biographical Magazine. London. Volume I.

Bisset, Robert, *The Historical, Biographical, Literary, and
Scientific Magazine.* London. Volume I.
Modern Literature. 3 volumes. London: 1804.

Blackie, John Stuart, *Notes of a Life.* Edinburgh and London:
1910.

Blackwood's Edinburgh Magazine. Edinburgh. Volumes XV, CLXVII.

Blanchard, Frederic T., *Fielding the Novelist.* New Haven: 1927.

Bloor, Robert H. U., *The English Novel from Chaucer to Galsworthy.* London: 1935.

Boston Athenaeum, *Catalog of the Washington Collection.* Boston: 1897.

Boswell, James, *Boswell's Journal of a Tour to the Hebrides.* Edited by Frederick A. Pottle and Charles H. Bennett. New York: 1936.
    The Life of Samuel Johnson, LL.D. 3 volumes. Dublin: 1792.
    Boswell's Life of Johnson. Edited by George Birkbeck Hill. 6 volumes. Oxford: 1887.
    Private Papers of James Boswell from Malahide Castle. 22 volumes. Privately Printed: 1931.

The British Critic. London. Volume XII.

British Magazine. London. 1751.

The British Review, and *London Critical Journal.* London. Volume XI.

Brown, Dr. John, *Letters.* London: 1907.

Browne, J. H. Balfour, *Recollections Literary and Political.* London: 1917.

Brunton, Mary, *Works.* 7 volumes. Edinburgh: 1820.

Brydges, Samuel Egerton, *Censura Literaria.* 10 volumes. London: 1805-1809.
    Recollections of Foreign Travel. 2 volumes. London: 1825.

Buchan, John, *A History of English Literature.* London and New York: 1933.

Buck, Howard Swazey, *A Study in Smollett.* New Haven: 1925.

Burney, Fanny. See Arblay, d', Fanny.

Burns, Robert, *The Letters of Robert Burns.* Edited by J. De Lancey Ferguson. 2 volumes. Oxford: 1931.

Burton, Richard, *Masters of the English Novel.* New York: 1932.

Butler, Samuel, *The Way of All Flesh.* Modern Library. New York: n.d.

Butler, William, *Chronological, Biographical, Historical, and Miscellaneous Exercises.* Ninth edition. London: 1830. (1799)

Byron, George Gordon, *The Works of Lord Byron. Letters and Journals.* Edited by Rowland E. Prothero. 6 volumes. London and New York: 1922-1924.
    Poetry. Edited by Ernest Hartley Coleridge. 7 volumes. London and New York: 1918-1924.

Caine, Hall. See *My First Book.*

Cambridge History of English Literature. Volume X. Cambridge
and New York: 1933.

Campbell, Thomas, *Specimens of the British Poets.* 7 volumes.
London: 1819.

Caritat, H., *Catalog.* New York: (1802).

Carlyle, Rev. Dr. Alexander, *Autobiography.* Edited by J. H.
Burton. Boston: 1861.

Carlyle, Thomas, *Early Letters.* Edited by Charles Eliot Norton.
2 volumes. London and New York: 1886.
History of Friedrich II of Prussia. 8 volumes. London: 1898.
Letters of Thomas Carlyle to John Stuart Mill. Edited by
Alexander Carlyle. London: 1923.
Sartor Resartus. Everyman's Library. London and New York:
1934.

Carter, Elizabeth, *A Series of Letters between Mrs. Elizabeth
Carter and Miss Catherine Talbot from the Year 1741 to
1770.* 4 volumes in 3. London: 1819.

Cary, Henry Francis, *Lives of English Poets from Johnson to
Kirke White.* London: 1846.

Chalmers, Alexander, *Works of the English Poets.* 21 volumes.
London: 1810.

Chambers, Robert, *History of the English Language and Literature.*
Hartford: 1837.

Chambers, William, *Memoir of Robert Chambers.* New York: 1872.

The Christian Observer. London. Volume XVI.

Churchill, Charles, *The Author.* London: 1763.

Clayden, P. W., *Rogers and His Contemporaries.* 2 volumes.
London: 1889.

Clemens, Samuel L., *A Connecticut Yankee in King Arthur's Court.*
Author's National Edition. Volume XVI. New York and London: n.d.

Cleveland, Charles D., *A Compendium of English Literature.* New
York and Chicago: 1872. (1850?)

Climenson, Emily J., *Elizabeth Montagu The Queen of the Blue-
stockings.* 2 volumes. London: 1906.

Coleridge, Samuel Taylor, *Complete Works.* Edited by W. G. T.
Shedd. 7 volumes. New York: 1853.
Coleridge's Miscellaneous Criticism. Edited by Thomas M.
Raysor. London: 1936.
Table Talk. 2 volumes. New York: 1835.

Collins, Norman, *The Facts of Fiction.* London: 1932.

Collison-Morley, Lacy, *Giuseppe Baretti.* London: 1909.

Colman, George (The elder), *Dramatick Works.* 4 volumes.
London: 1777.

Conway, Moncure D., *Thomas Carlyle.* New York: 1881.

Cook, Elizabeth Christine, *Reading the Novel.* Boston: 1933.

Cooper, James Fenimore, *Works.* Mohawk edition. **33 volumes.**
New York and London: n.d.
The Pilot. Boston and New York: 1884.

Court and City Magazine. London. Volume II.

The Court Magazine; or, Royal Chronicle. London. Volume I.

Cowie, Alexander, *John Trumbull.* Chapel Hill: 1936.

Cowper, William, *The Correspondence of William Cowper.* Edited
by Thomas Wright. 4 volumes. New York and London: 1904.
Letters of William Cowper. Edited by J. G. Frazer.
2 volumes. London: 1912.

Crabbe, George, *Poetical Works, with . . . Life by His Son.*
8 volumes. London: 1834.

Craik, George L., *Compendious History of English Literature and
of the English Language.* 2 volumes. New York: 1869.

Craik, Henry, ed., *English Prose Selections.* 5 volumes. New
York: 1903. (1893-1896)

Crawford, F. Marion, *The Novel What It Is.* New York: 1893.

Creech, William, *Edinburgh Fugitive Pieces.* Edinburgh: 1815.
(1791)

The Critical Review: or, Annals of Literature. London. Volumes
III, XIII, XVI, XXI, XXV, XXVII, XXXI, XXXII, XLIII, LX,
LXV, LXVII, LXIX: 2nd series I, II, X, XXII, XXIII, XXX,
XXXII, XXXIV, XXXVII, XXXIX, XL: 3rd series II: 4th series
V; 5th series II, III.

Cross, Wilbur L., *Development of the English Novel.* New York:
1928.
The History of Henry Fielding. 3 volumes. New Haven: 1918.

(Cumberland, Richard), *Henry.* 4 volumes. London: 1798.

Cumberland's Minor Theatre. Volume IV. London: (183-).

Davies, Thomas, *Memoirs of the Life of David Garrick, Esq.*
2 volumes. London: 1780.

Delany, Mary Granville, *Autobiography and Correspondence.* Edited
by Lady Llanover. 6 volumes. London: 1861-1862.

Dennie, Joseph, *Letters of Joseph Dennie 1768-1812.* Edited by
Laura Green Pedder. University of Maine Studies, Second
Series, No. 36. Orono, Maine: 1936.

De Quincey, Thomas, *Works.* Riverside edition. 12 volumes.
New York and Boston: 1876-1877.

Dermody, Thomas, *The Harp of Erin.* 2 volumes. London: 1807.

The Dial. Chicago. Volume XXXII.

Dibdin, Charles, *A Complete History of the Stage.* 5 volumes. London: (1795).

Dickens, Charles, *Works.* Roxburgh edition. 48 volumes. Boston: 1892.
　American Notes　Pictures from Italy. Everyman's Library. London and New York: 1934.
　Christmas Stories. Everyman's Library. London and New York: 1933.
　Letters of Charles Dickens. Edited by his sister-in-law and his eldest daughter. 2 volumes. New York: 1879.

Dictionary of National Biography. London.

D'Israeli, I., *Calamities of Authors.* 2 volumes. New York: 1812.
　Essay on the Manners and Genius of the Literary Character. London: 1795.

Doran, Dr. (John) *'Mann' and Manners at the Court of Florence, 1740-1786.* 2 volumes. London: 1876.

Douglas, Sir George, *The 'Blackwood' Group.* New York: n.d.

Doyle, Arthur Conan, *Through the Magic Door.* London: 1907.

Drake, Nathan, *Literary Hours: or Sketches, Critical, Narrative, and Poetical.* Fourth edition. 3 volumes. London: 1820. (1798)

Dunlop, John, *History of Fiction.* 2 volumes. Philadelphia: 1842. (This is 'From the second London edition' of 1816. Date of first edition is 1814.)

Edgeworth, Maria, *Chosen Letters.* Edited by F. V. Barry. Boston and New York: n.d.
　Life and Letters of Maria Edgeworth. Edited by Augustus J. C. Hare. 2 volumes. Boston and New York: 1895.

Edinburgh Magazine; or, Literary Miscellany. Edinburgh. Volume IV.

The Edinburgh Review. Edinburgh. Volumes XXV, LXVIII.

Egan, Pierce, *Life in London.* London: 1822.
　The Life of an Actor. London: 1904. (1825)

Eliot, George, *Middlemarch.* Modern Readers' Series. New York: 1929.

Elton, Oliver, *Survey of English Literature 1730-1780.* 2 volumes. New York: 1928.

Elwin, Malcolm, *Charles Reade.* London: 1931.

Elwin, Whitwell, *Some XVIII Century Men of Letters.* 2 volumes. London: 1902.

Emerson, Ralph Waldo, *Journals.* Edited by Edward Waldo Emerson and Waldo Emerson Forbes. Volume IV. Boston and New York: 1910-1913.

Encyclopaedia Britannica. Third edition. Edinburgh: 1797.
Seventh edition. Edinburgh: 1842.
Ninth edition. Edinburgh: 1887.
Eleventh edition. Cambridge and New York: 1911.
Fourteenth edition. London, New York and Chicago,
Toronto: 1929.

*The English Review. or, an Abstract of English and Foreign
Literature.* London. Volumes I, II, XVII.

Episodes of Fiction. New York: (1889).

Espinasse, Francis, *Literary Recollections and Sketches.* New
York: 1893.

An Essay on the New Species of Writing Founded by Mr. Fielding.
London: 1751.

European Magazine and London Review. London. Volumes XIX,
XXXIII, LVIII, LXXVI.

Everett, Charles Warren, *Education of Jeremy Bentham.* New York:
1931.

Faulkner, Thomas, *An Historical and topographical description of
Chelsea and its environs.* London: 1810.

Ferrier, Susan, *The Inheritance.* London: 1929. (1824)

Fielding, Henry, *Amelia.* Edited by George Saintsbury. London:
1893.
The Covent-Garden Journal. Edited by Gerard Edward Jensen.
2 volumes. New Haven: 1915.
Jacobites' Journal. London.
Tom Jones. With a Memoir of the Author by Thomas Roscoe.
2 volumes. London: 1831.

Fields, James T., *Yesterdays with Authors.* Boston and New York:
1900.

Fitzpatrick, W. J., *Life of Charles Lever.* 2 volumes.
London: 1879.

Fletcher, Charles, *The Naval Guardian.* 2 volumes. London: 1805.

Forbes, Sir William, *An Account of the Life and Writings of James
Beattie, LL. D.* London: 1824.

Ford, Ford Madox, *The English Novel.* London: 1930.

Forster, John, *Life and Times of Oliver Goldsmith.* 4 volumes.
Boston and New York: n.d.
The Life of Charles Dickens. 2 volumes. London: 1904.
Walter Savage Landor. London: 1874.

Franklin, Benjamin, *The Writings of Benjamin Franklin.* Edited
by Albert Henry Smyth. 10 volumes. New York: 1905.

Frith, W. P., *My Autobiography.* New York: 1888.

Garden, Francis, Lord Gardenstone, *Miscellanies in Prose and
Verse.* Second edition. Edinburgh: 1792.

Garnett, Richard, and Edmund Gosse, *English Literature an Illustrated Record*. 4 volumes. New York: 1905.

Garrick, David, *The Private Correspondence of David Garrick with the Most Celebrated Persons of His Times*. 2 volumes. London: 1831.

   Some Unpublished Correspondence of David Garrick. Edited by George P. Baker. Boston: 1907.

The General Magazine and Impartial Review. London. Volumes II, III, IV.

The Gentleman's Magazine. London. Volumes XIX, XXXIX, XLI, LXXXVIII, XCVI, CCLXXX; Entirely New Series, VIII, XIV.

Gilchrist, Anne, *Her Life and Writings*. Edited by H. H. Gilchrist. Second edition. London: 1887.

Gilfillan, George, *Third Gallery of Portraits*. Edinburgh: 1854.

Glascock, William Nugent, *Naval Sketch Book*. 2 volumes. London: 1834.
   Sailors and Saints. 3 volumes. London: 1829.

Godwin, William, *The Enquirer*. London: 1797.

Goldsmith, Oliver, *The Works of Oliver Goldsmith*. Edited by Peter Cunningham. 12 volumes. New York and London: 1900.

(Goodall, W. ?), *Adventures of Captain Greenland*. London: 1752.

Graham's Lady's and Gentleman's Magazine. Philadelphia. Volume XX.

(Grant, Mrs. Anne), *Letters from the Mountains*. 2 volumes. Boston: 1809.

Grant, James, *Cassell's Old and New Edinburgh*. 3 volumes. London: 1882.

Granville, A. B., *Autobiography of A. B. Granville*. Edited by P. B. Granville. Second edition. 2 volumes. London: 1874.

Gray, Thomas, *The Letters of Thomas Gray*. Edited by Duncan C. Tovey. 3 volumes. London: 1900.

Green, F. C., *Minuet*. London: 1935.

Greig, J. Y. T., *David Hume*. London: n.d.

Grolier Club, *One Hundred Books Famous in English Literature*. Introduction by George F. Woodberry. New York: 1902.

(Hamilton, Lady Anne), *The Epics of the Ton*. London: 1807.

Hannay, David, *Life of Tobias George Smollett*. London: 1887.

Hardy, Florence Emily, *The Early Life of Thomas Hardy 1840-1891*. New York: 1928.

Hare, Augustus J. C. See Edgeworth, Maria.

Harper's Monthly Magazine. New York. Volume CLXXII.

Harrison, Frederic, *De Senectute*. London: 1923.

Hawkins, Sir John, *The Life of Samuel Johnson*. Second edition.
     London: 1787.

Hawthorne, Julian, *Nathaniel Hawthorne and His Wife*. 2 volumes.
     Boston: 1884.

Hawthorne, Nathaniel, *Notes of Travel*. 4 volumes. Boston and
     New York: 1900.

Hazlitt, William, *Complete Works of William Hazlitt*. Edited by
     P. P. Howe. 21 volumes. London and Toronto: 1933.

Hearn, Lafcadio, *A History of English Literature*. Tokyo: 1927.

Heilman, Robert Bechtold, *America in English Fiction 1760-1800*.
     Baton Rouge: 1937.

Henderson, Arthur, *A Second Letter to Dr. Samuel Johnson . . .
     with an Impartial Character of Dr. Smollet*. London: (1775)
The Hibernian Magazine. Dublin. Volume I.

Hildyard, M. C. See Lockhart, John Gibson.

(Hill, John), *The Inspector*. London: 1751.

Hillard, George Stillman, *Six Months in Italy*. 2 volumes.
     Boston: 1853.

Hirst, Francis W., *Life and Letters of Thomas Jefferson*.
     New York: 1926.

Hone, Philip, *Diary*. Edited by Bayard Tuckerman. 2 volumes.
     New York: 1889.

Hood, Thomas, *Works*. Edited by his son and daughter. 11 volumes.
     London and New York: n.d.

Howells, W. D., *Roman Holidays and Others*. New York and London:
     1908.

Hume, David, *The Letters of David Hume*. Edited by J. Y. T. Greig.
     2 volumes. Oxford: 1932.

Hunt, Leigh, *Autobiography of Leigh Hunt*. Edited by Roger Ingpen.
     2 volumes. New York: 1903.
   Correspondence. Edited by his eldest son. 2 volumes.
        London: 1862.
   The Examiner. London: 1820.
   The Indicator. New York: 1845.
   Lord Byron and Some of His Contemporaries. Second edition.
        2 volumes. London: 1828.
   Men, Women, and Books. London: 1876.
   Table-Talk. London: 1882.

Imperial Magazine. *London*. Volume I.

Irving, J., *Some Account of the Family of Smollett of Bonhill*.
     Dumbarton: 1859.

Irving, Washington, *Oliver Goldsmith*. New York: 1849.

Jackson, Holbrook, *Great English Novelists*. London: (1908).

Jacobites' Journal. See Fielding, Henry.

James, Henry, *Notes and Reviews*. Cambridge, Mass.: 1921.

Jeaffreson, J. Cordy, *Novels and Novelists*. 2 volumes.
  London: 1858.

(Jenner, Charles), *The Placid Man: or, Memoirs of Sir Charles
  Beville*. 2 volumes. London: 1770.

Jerrold, Walter, *Douglas Jerrold*. 2 volumes. London: (1914).

Joliat, Eugene, *Smollett et la France*. Paris: 1935.

Johnson, Samuel, *Letters of Samuel Johnson, LL. D.* Edited by
  George Birkbeck Hill. 2 volumes. New York: 1892.

Keats, John, *Letters*. Edited by Maurice B. Forman. Oxford: 1931.

Kelley, Cornelia Pulsifer, *The Early Development of Henry James*.
  University of Illinois Studies in Language and Literature.
  Volume XV. Urbana, Illinois: 1930.

Kenrick, William, *Fun A Satire*. London: 1752.

Kent, James, *Memoirs and Letters of James Kent, LL. D.* Edited by
  William Kent. Boston: 1898.

(Kidgell, John), *The Card*. 2 volumes. London: 1755.

The Knickerbocker; or, New York Monthly Magazine. New York.
  Volume II.

Knight, Charles, *London*. 6 volumes. London: 1842.
  Passages of a Working Life. 3 volumes. London: 1864.

Knight, Grant C., *The Novel in English*. New York: 1931.

Knox, Vicesimus, *Essays Moral and Literary*. Sixth edition.
  2 volumes. London: 1785.

Lackington, James, *Memoirs of the Forty-Five First Years of the
  Life of James Lackington*. London: (1793).

Lamb, Charles and Mary, *Works*. Edited by E. V. Lucas. 7 volumes.
  New York and London: 1903.

Lang, Andrew, *Adventures among Books*. London: 1905.
  A History of English Literature. London: 1933.
  Life and Letters of John Gibson Lockhart. 2 volumes. New York
  and London: 1897.

Lanier, Sidney, *The English Novel*. New York: 1900.

Legouis, Emile, and Louis Cazamian, *History of English Literature*.
  New York: 1931.

Leslie, Charles Robert, *Autobiographical Recollections*. Edited by
  Tom Taylor. 2 volumes. London: 1860,

L'Estrange, A. G., *The Friendships of Mary Russell Mitford.*
New York: 1882.

History of English Humour. 2 volumes. London: (1877).

Letters concerning the Present State of England. London: 1772.

Letters from a Late Eminent Prelate. See Warburton, William.

The Library. Oxford. Volume XIII.

The Library: or, Moral and Critical Magazine. London. Volume II.

Library Company of Burlington, New Jersey. *Catalog.* Philadelphia: 1758.

Library Company of Philadelphia. *Catalog.* Philadelphia: 1789.
Catalog. Philadelphia: 1807.

The Life and Real Adventures of Hamilton Murray. Written by Himself. 3 volumes. London: 1759.

The Literary Gazette, and Journal of Belles Lettres, Arts, Sciences, etc. London. Volumes V, LXXXVI. Nos. 160, 235, 283.

The Literary Magazine and American Register. Philadelphia. Volume VI.

Lockhart, John Gibson, *Life of Robert Burns.* Everyman's Library. London and New York: n.d.
Lockhart's Literary Criticism. Edited by M. Clive Hildyard. Oxford: 1931.
Memoirs of the Life of Sir Walter Scott. 5 volumes. Boston and New York: 1901.

The London Magazine. London. Volume V.

The London Magazine: or, Gentleman's Monthly Intelligencer. London. Volumes XX, XXXV, XL, XLII.

The London Review of English and Foreign Literature. London. Volume V.

Lowell, James Russell, *Complete Writings.* 16 volumes. Boston and New York: n.d.

Luxborough, Lady, *Letters Written by the Late Right Honourable Lady Luxborough to William Shenstone.* London: 1775.

Lytton, Edward Bulwer, *Caxtoniana,* New York: 1864.

Lytton, Earl of, *Life of Edward Bulwer First Lord Lytton.* 2 vols. London: 1913.

Macaulay, Lord, *Critical and Historical Essays.* 4 volumes. London: 1885.

Mackenzie, Henry, *Account of the Life and Writings of John Home.* Edinburgh: 1822.

Mackintosh, Sir James, *Memoirs.* Edited by Robert James Mackintosh. 2 volumes. London: 1835.

Macmillan's Magazine. London. Volume XXI.

Macready, William, *Macready's Reminiscenses*. Edited by Sir Frederick Pollack. New York: 1875.

Magazine of Magazines. Limerick. Volume I.

Mangin, Edward, *An Essay on Light Reading*. London: 1808.

Marryat, Frederick, *The Dog Fiend or Snarley Yow*. Boston: (1904).

Martin, Theodore, *Memoir of William Edmondstoune Aytoun*. Edinburgh and London: n.d.

Martineau, Harriet, *Harriet Martineau's Autobiography*. Edited by Maria Weston Chapman. 2 volumes: Boston: 1877.

Massingham, H. J., *The Friend of Shelley*. London: 1930.

Masson, David, *British Novelists and Their Styles*, Cambridge: 1859.

(Mathias, T. J.), *The Pursuits of Literature*. Ninth edition. London: 1799.

Maugham, W. Somerset, *Of Human Bondage*. Garden City: 1915.

McKillop, Alan Dugald, *Samuel Richardson*. Chapel Hill: 1936.

Medwin, Thomas, *Life of Percy Bysshe Shelley*. Oxford: 1913.

Melville, Herman, *Works*. Standard edition. 16 volumes. London: 1922.

Melville, Lewis, *The Life and Letters of Tobias Smollett*. Boston and New York: 1927.

Meredith, George, *An Essay on Comedy*. Edited by Lane Cooper. New York: n.d.

Mills, Abraham, *The Literature and the Literary Men of Great Britain and Ireland*, 2 volumes, New York: 1851.

The Mirror. Edinburgh. Number 83.

Mitford, Mary Russell, *Recollections of a Literary Life*. 3 vols. London: 1852.

Modern Language Association of America, *Publications*. Menasha, Wisconsin. Volume XLV.

Modern Language Notes. Baltimore. Volume XLI.

Modern Philology. Chicago. Volumes XXIV, XXXV.

Montagu, Lady Mary Wortley, *Works*. Edited by J. Dallaway. 5 volumes. London: 1803.
   Letters and Works. Edited by W. May Thomas. 2 volumes. London: 1887.

The Monthly Chronicle. London. Volume I.

The Monthly Ledger, or Literary Repository. London. Volume I.

The Monthly Magazine; or, British Register. London. Volumes IV, XI, XXII, XLIII.

Monthly Mirror. London. Volumes I, II.

The Monthly Review; or, Literary Journal. London. Volumes I, IV,
V, VII, VIII, XVI, XXII, XXIII, XXIV, XXV, XXVI, XXVIII,
XXIX, XXXIII, XXXIV, XXXVII, XXXVIII, XXXIX, XL, XLII, XLV,
XLVIII, LI, LVII, LXIV, LXV, LXXIII, LXXVI.

Moore, George, *Avowals.* New York: 1926.

Moore, Oliver, *The Staff Officer.* 2 volumes. Philadelphia and
Baltimore: 1833.

Moore, Thomas, *Memoirs, Journal, and Correspondence of Thomas
Moore.* Edited by Lord John Russell. 8 volumes. London:
1853.

Morison, J. Cotter, *Macaulay.* New York: 1883.

Morley, Henry, *A First Sketch of English Literature.* London: 1873.

Mudford, William, *The British Novelists.* 5 volumes. London:
1810-1816.
*A Critical Examination of the Writings of Richard Cumberland,
Esq.* 2 volumes. London: 1812.

Muir, Edwin, *Structure of the Novel.* New York: 1929.

Murphy, Arthur, *The Life of David Garrick, Esq.* Dublin: 1801.

Murray, Hugh, *Morality of Fiction.* London: 1817.

Murry, John Middleton. *Between Two Worlds,* London: 1935.

My First Book. Introduction by Jerome K. Jerome. London: 1897.

Nangle, Benjamin Christie, *The Monthly Review First Series
1749-1789. Indexes of Contributors and Articles.* Oxford:
1934.

The Nation and Athenaeum. London. Volume XL.

The National Review. London. Volume LXXV.

New Novelist's Magazine. London. Volume I.

(Newman, Jeremiah Whitaker), *The Lounger's Common Place Book.*
Third edition. 3 volumes. London: 1805.

Nicoll, Allardyce, *History of Early Nineteenth Century Drama.*
2 volumes. Cambridge: 1930.

Nicoll, Henry J., *Landmarks of English Literature.* New York:
1883.

The Nineteenth Century. London. Volume V.

The North American Review. Boston. Volumes XXXII, XXXV, XXXIX,
LXIX.

The Northumberland and Newcastle Monthly Magazine. Newcastle.
Volume I.

Norton, Charles Eliot, *Letters.* 2 volumes. Boston and New York:
1913.

Notes and Queries. London. Volume IX, Seventh Series; IX, Tenth Series; CLXIV.

Odell, George C. D., *Annals of the New York Stage.* Volumes III, IV. New York: 1928.

Ogilvie, John, *Philosophical and Critical Observations on . . . Composition.* 2 volumes. London: 1774.

The Orrery Papers. Edited by Countess of Cork and Orrery. 2 volumes. London: 1903.

Osgood, Charles Grosvenor, *The Voice of England.* New York: 1935.

(Paulding, James K.), *A Sketch of Old England.* 2 volumes. New York: 1822.

(Pegge, S.), *Anonymia; or, Ten Centuries of Observations on Various Authors and Subjects.* London: 1809.

Pemberton, T. Edgar, *Life of Bret Harte.* New York: 1903.

The Pennsylvania Magazine of History and Biography. Philadelphia. Volume LVI.

The Peregrinations of Jeremiah Grant. London: 1763.

Perth Magazine of Knowledge and Pleasure. Perth. Volume I.

Phillimore, Robert, ed., *Memoirs and Correspondence of George, Lord Lyttelton.* 2 volumes. London: 1845.

Pilkington, Mrs. Laetitia, *Memoirs.* New York: (1928). (1748-1754)

Piozzi, Hester L., *Autobiography Letters and Literary Remains of Mrs. Piozzi.* Edited by A. Hayward. 2 volumes. London: 1861.

Poe, Edgar Allen, *Complete Works.* Edited by James A. Harrison. New York: 1902.

Poetzsche, Erich, *Samuel Richardsons Belesenheit.* Kiel: 1908.

The Port Folio, by Oliver Oldschool, Esq. Philadelphia. Volumes I, II; New Series I, VI; Series 5, XI.

The Portico A Repository of Science & Literature. Baltimore. Volume I.

Prior, James, *Memoir of the Life and Character of the Right Hon. Edmund Burke.* London: 1824.

Prothero, Rowland E. and G. G. Bradley, *Life and Correspondence of Arthur Penrhyn Stanley, D. D.* Third edition. 2 vols. London: 1894.

The Quarterly Review. London. Volumes I, VII, XI, XXXIV, XLIX, LIX, LXIV, CIII, CLXIII.

Rae, W. Fraser, *Sheridan.* 2 volumes. London: 1896.

Raleigh, Walter, *The English Novel.* Fifth edition. New York: 1908. (1894)

Randolph, John, *Letters of John Randolph to a Young Relative.* Philadelphia: 1834.

Raysor, T. M.   See Coleridge, Samuel Taylor.

Read, Herbert, *Reason and Romanticism.*   London: (1926).

A Reading Diary of Modern Fiction.   New York: 1881.

Reeve, Clara, *The Progress of Romance.*   Facsimile Text Society. New York: 1930.   (1785)

Repplier, Agnes, *Points of View.*   Boston and New York: 1892.

Richardson, Samuel, *Correspondence of Samuel Richardson.*   Edited by Anna L. Barbauld.   6 volumes.   London: 1804.

Roberts, Kenneth, *Northwest Passage.*   Garden City: 1937.

Roberts, Morley, *W. H. Hudson.*   New York: 1924.

Robinson, Henry Crabb, *Henry Crabb Robinson on Books and Their Writers.*   Edited by Edith J. Morley.   3 volumes. London: 1938.

Roosevelt, Theodore, *Works.*   National edition.   New York: 1926.

Roscoe, William Caldwell, *Poems and Essays.*   2 volumes. London: 1860.

Royal Magazine, or *Quarterly Bee.*   London.   Volumes II, XIV, XV, XXV.

Ruskin, John, *Works.*   Library edition.   Edited by E. T. Cook and Alexander Wedderburn.   39 volumes.   London: 1903-1912.

Sadleir, Michael, *Bulwer: a panorama.*   Boston: 1931.

Saintsbury, George, *The English Novel.*   London and New York: 1913. *The Peace of the Augustans.*   London: 1916. *Prefaces and Essays.*   London: 1933.

Sanders, Gerald De Witt, *Elizabeth Gaskell.*   New Haven: 1929.

Sandford, Daniel K., *On the Rise and Progress of Literature.* Glasgow, Edinburgh, and London: 1847.

Schimmelpenninck, Mary Anne, *Life of Mary Anne Schimmelpenninck.* Edited by her relation Christiana C. Hankin.   2 volumes. London: 1858.

Schuyler, Eugene, *Italian Influences.*   London: 1901.

The Scots Magazine; or, *General Repository of Literature, History, and Politics.*   Edinburgh.   Volumes XXXIII, LVIII.

Scott, Michael, *Tom Cringle's Log.*   Everyman's Library. London and New York: n.d. (1829)

Scott, Sir Walter, *The Fortunes of Nigel.*   3 volumes. Edinburgh: 1822. *Lives of the Novelists.*   Everyman's Library.   London and New York: n.d.

The Monastery. 2 volumes. Westminster: 1895.

The Scottish Review. London. Volume XXIII.

Scribner's Monthly. New York. Volume XIV.

Scudder, Horace E., *James Russell Lowell.* 2 volumes. Boston and
    New York: 1901.

Seward, Anne, *Letters of Anne Seward.* 6 volumes. Edinburgh: 1811.

Sharpe, Charles Kirkpatrick, *Letters from and to Charles Kirkpat-*
    rick Sharpe. Edited by Alexander Allardyce. 2 volumes.
    Edinburgh and London: 1888.

Shaw, Bernard, *The Quintessence of Ibsenism.* New York: 1925.

Sheridan, Richard Brinsley, *The Works of Richard Brinsley Sheridan.*
    Edited by F. Stainforth. London: 1897.

Smeaton, Oliphant, *Tobias Smollett.* New York: n.d.

Smith, James, *Memoirs, Letters, and Comic Miscellanies.* 2 volumes.
    London: 1840.

Smith, William James, *The Grenville Papers.* 4 volumes.
    London: 1852.

Smollett, Tobias George, *The Miscellaneous Works of Tobias Smol-*
    lett, M. D. with Memoirs of His Life and Writings, by
    Robert Anderson, M.D. Sixth edition. 6 volumes.
    Edinburgh: 1820.
    The Works of Tobias Smollett, M.D. with Memoirs of His Life;
        to which is prefixed a view of the commencement and
        progress of romance, by John Moore, M.D. 8 volumes.
        London: 1797.
    Miscellaneous Works of Tobias Smollett, complete in one
        volume, with memoir of the author, by Thomas Roscoe.
        London: 1851.
    The Works of Tobias Smollett. Edited by David Herbert.
        Edinburgh: 1883.
    Works. Edited by W. E. Henley. 12 volumes. Westminster and
        New York: 1899.
    The Works of Tobias Smollett. Dalquhurn edition. Edited by
        G. H. Maynadier. 12 volumes. New York: 1908.
    The Letters of Tobias Smollett, M.D. Edited by Edward Noyes.
        Cambridge, Mass.: 1926.
    Plays and Poems. With Memoirs. London: 1777.
    Travels through France and Italy. With an introduction by
        Thomas Seccombe. World's Classics. Oxford: 1907.

Snyder, Franklyn Bliss, *The Life of Robert Burns.* New York:
    1932.

Southern Literary Messenger. Richmond. Volumes V, VIII.

The Southern Review. Charleston. Volumes IV, VIII.

Southey, Robert, *The Doctor.* London: 1862.
    Journal of a Tour in Scotland in 1819. Edited by C. H. Herford.
        London: 1929.

Stebbing, William, *Some Verdicts of History Reviewed.* London: 1887.

Stephen, Leslie, *History of English Thought in the Eighteenth Century.* 2 volumes. London: 1876.
Hours in a Library. 3 volumes. London: 1892.

Sterne, Laurence, *A Sentimental Journey through France and Italy.* Edited by George Saintsbury. London: 1900.

(Stevenson, John Hall), *Makarony Fables.* Dublin: 1772.

Stevenson, Robert Louis, *Travels and Essays.* New York: 1895.

Stuart, Lady Louisa, *Letters of Lady Louisa Stuart to Miss Louisa Clinton.* Edited by James A. Home. Edinburgh: 1901.

Sussex Archaeological Collections. Volume XI. London: 1859.

Swinburne, Algernon Charles, *Complete Works.* 20 volumes. Edited by Edmund Gosse and Thomas James Wise. New York and London: 1926.

Taine, H. A., *History of English Literature.* Translated by H. Van Laun. 2 volumes. New York and Chicago: n.d.

Talfourd, R. Noon, *Critical and Miscellaneous Writings.* Third American edition. Boston: 1856.

Taylor, Bayard, *Views a-foot.* New York: 1890.

Taylor, John, *Records of My Life.* New York: 1833.

(Tenney, Tabitha), *Female Quixotism.* 2 volumes. Boston: 1825. (1808)

Thackeray, William Makepeace, *Critical Papers in Literature.* London: 1904.
The English Humourists of the Eighteenth Century. London: 1904.
Paris Sketch Book. London: 1902.
Roundabout Papers. London: 1907.
Vanity Fair. Modern Library. New York: 1933.

Thicknesse, Philip, *Observations on the Customs and Manners of the French Nation, in a Series of Letters.* London: 1766.
Useful Hints to Those Who Make the Tour of France. London: 1770.
Year's Journey through France and Part of Spain. 2 volumes. Dublin: 1777.

(Thornton, Bonnell), *Have At You All: or, the Drury-Lane Journal.* By Madam Roxana Termagant. London: 1752.

The Times Literary Supplement. London. Mar. 17, 1921; Dec. 19, 1926.

Times, The New York. Jan. 2 and Nov. 13, 1927.

(**Topham**, Edward), *Letters from Edinburgh.* Written in the Years 1774 and 1775. 2 volumes. Dublin: 1778.

Town and Country Magazine. London. Volumes I, III, XVII.

Trevelyan, G. Otto, *Life and Letters of Lord Macaulay.*
2 volumes. New York: 1877.

Twain, Mark. See Clemens, Samuel L.

Universal Magazine of Knowledge and Pleasure. London. Volumes
XLIX, XCIIII.

Verschoyle, Derek, ed., *The English Novelists.* New York: 1936.

Walpole, Horace, *The Letters of Horace Walpole.* Edited by Mrs.
Paget Toynbee. 16 volumes. Oxford: 1904.

  *Memoirs of the Last Ten Years of the Reign of George the
  Second.* 2.volumes. London: 1822.
  Memoirs of the Reign of King George the Third. Edited by
  Sir Denis Le Marchant. 4 volumes. London: 1845.

The Wanderings of William. Philadelphia: 1801.

(Warburton, William), *Letters from a Late Eminent Prelate to One
of His Friends.* New York: 1809.

Warner, Richard, *Literary Recollections.* 2 volumes. London:
1830.

West, Mrs. (Jane), *Letters to a Young Lady.* Troy and New York:
1806.

The Westminster Magazine, or the Pantheon of Taste. London.
Volumes III, IV, V, XIII.

The Westminster Review. London. Volumes II, VII, XX, XXVII.

Wharton, Grace, *The Literature of Society.* 2 volumes. London:
1862.

Whitridge, Arnold, *Tobias Smollett A Study of His Miscellaneous
Works.* Published by the author: 1925.

Wilkes, John, *The Correspondence of the Late John Wilkes.* Edited
by John Almon. 5 volumes. London: 1805.

Williams, Blanche Colton, *George Eliot.* New York: 1936.

Williams, Harold, *Two Centuries of the English Novel.* London:
1911.

Willis, Nathaniel Parker, *Prose Writings.* New York: 1885.

Wilson, David Alec, *Carlyle to Threescore-and-ten (1853-1865).*
London and New York: 1929.

Wilson, John, *Noctes Ambrosianae.* Edited by R. Shelton Mackenzie.
5 volumes. New York: 1863.

(Woodhouselee, Lord), *Essay on the Principles of Translation.*
Third edition. Edinburgh: 1813. (1791)
  *Memoirs of the Life and Writings of the Honourable Henry Home
  of Kames.* 2 volumes. Edinburgh: 1807.

Wordsworth, Christopher, *Memoirs of William Wordsworth*. 2 vols.
    London: 1851.

Wordsworth, Dorothy, *Journals of Dorothy Wordsworth*. Edited by
    William Knight. 2 volumes. London: 1897.

Wordsworth, William and Dorothy, *Letters of William and Dorothy
    Wordsworth The Later Years*. Edited by Ernest de Selincourt.
    3 volumes. Oxford: 1939.

Wraxall, Sir Nathaniel William, *Historical and Posthumous Memoirs
    of Sir Nathaniel William Wraxall*. Edited by Henry B.
    Wheatley. 5 volumes. New York and London: 1884.

The Yale Review. New Series. New Haven. Volume XVI.

The Yorkshire Magazine. York. Volume I.

Young, Arthur, *Travels during the Years 1787, 1788, and 1789*.
    2 volumes. Dublin: 1793.

Campbell, Thomas, 50, 67, 79, 87
Canning, George, 17
Caritat, H., 120
Carlyle, Alexander, 1, 4, 37, 61, 67
Carlyle, Thomas, 79, 94, 95-97, 131
Carnarvon, Earl of, 132
Carter, Elizabeth, 3
Cary, Henry, 102
Cazamian, Louis, 145, 146
Cervantes, 23, 24, 34, 39, 49, 54, 58, 65, 70, 92, 97, 100, 111, 122, 126, 128
Chalmers, Alexander, 76-77
Chambers, Robert, 101, 107
Chambers, William, 101
Chapone, Hester, 7
Chateaubriand, F., 67
Chesterfield, Lord, 80, 120
Christian Observer, The, 70-71
Churchill, Charles, 16
Cicero, 149
Clemens, Samuel L., 130
Cleveland, C. D., 95, 112-113
Clough, A. H., 112n.
Coleridge, S. T., 79, 81-83, 87, 93, 95, 128
Collier, Jane, 5
Collins, John Churton, 132
Collins, Norman, 146
Collins, Wilkie, 112n., 133
Colman, George, 35
Conrad, Joseph, 112n.
Conway, Moncure, 96
Cook, Elizabeth, 146
Cooper, James F., 77, 124-125, 131
Cooper, Susan F., 124
Court and City Magazine, 29
Court Magazine, The, 34
Coventry, Francis, 34
Cowper, William, 54, 63, 68, 119
Crabbe, George, 50, 79
Craik, G. L., 112
Crane, Stephen, 127n.
Crawford, F. Marion, 138
Creech, William, 62-63

Critical Review, The, 16, 17, 18, 23, 25, 27, 28, 29, 33, 49, 58-59, 71-72, 132
Croker, J. W., 71
Cross, Wilbur L., 2n, 5, 11 and n., 111, 135, 142, 143, 146, 147
Cumberland, Richard, 36, 60-61, 64

Dana, R. H., 127n.
Dante, 96
Davies, Thomas, 61
Defoe, Daniel, 27, 58, 85, 97, 120, 141, 148
Delany, Mary G., 5, 8, 15-16
Dennie, Joseph, 121
De Quincey, Thomas, 81
Dermody, Thomas, 61, 63
Dibdin, Charles, 73
Dickens, Charles, 6, 46, 69, 77, 79, 97-99, 100, 105, 107, 108, 111, 125, 126, 128, 131, 134, 136, 140, 146
Dictionary of National Biography, 141
Disraeli, Benjamin, 112n.
D'Israeli, Isaac, 60
Dobson, Austin, 147
Doyle, Conan, 139
Drake, Joseph R., 127n.
Drake, Nathan, 61
Duck, Stephen, 51
Dunlop, John, 75

Edgeworth, Maria, 72, 77, 80, 126
Edinburgh Magazine: or Literary Miscellany, 51n.
Edinburgh Review, The, 70, 100
Egan, Pierce, 77-78
Eliot, George, 103, 110-111, 112
Elton, Oliver, 145
Elwin, Whitwell, 109
Emerson, Ralph W., 128
Encyclopedia Britannica, 52, 75, 114, 141
English Review, The, 49n., 51

Jackson, H., 144
James, Henry, 138-139
Jeaffreson, J. C., 109
Jefferson, Thomas, 118
Jeffrey, Francis, 71
Jenner, Charles, 36
Jerrold, Douglas, 79
Johnson, Samuel, 14n., 16, 17, 38, 39, 40-41, 42, 50, 54, 56, 57, 63, 71, 80, 104, 120
Johnston, William, 75
Joliat, Eugene, 26
Juvenal, 126, 144

Kames, Henry Home, Lord, 40, 56, 63
Keats, John, 87-88, 93, 95, 148
Kenrick, William, 12
Kent, James, 120
Kidgell, John, 35, 89
Kingsley, Charles, 112n.
Kipling, Rudyard, 139, 141
Knapp, Lewis M., 2, 3, 47
Knickerbocker Magazine, 127
Knight, Charles, 106, 107, 132
Knight, Grant C., 146
Knox, Vicesimus, 57

Lackington, James, 63, 67
Ladies Magazine, 8
Lamb, Charles, 50, 79, 83, 85-86, 93
Landor, W. S., 106
Lang, Andrew, 67, 146
Lanier, Sidney, 130
Lantier, E. F., 70
Lennox, Charlotte, 24
Le Sage, 10, 34, 49, 50, 53, 57, 58, 65, 70, 81, 92, 97, 100,, 105, 115, 124, 136
Leslie, C. R., 112
L'Estrange, A. G., 113
Lever, Charles, 100
Lewes, G. H., 111
Lewis, M. G., 85
Library, The, 24
Literary Gazette, 70, 73, 78, 92

Literary World, The, 141
Lockhart, J. G., 71, 81, 92
London Magazine, 74
London Magazine, or Gentleman's Monthly Intelligencer, 9, 21, 25, 28, 30-31
London Review, 46
Longfellow, H. W., 127n.
Lowell, J. R., 127-128, 147
Luxborough, Lady, 8
Lyttelton, George Lord, 1, 7, 21, 106
Lytton, Edward Bulwer, 100, 109-110, 127
Lytton, Edward Robert Bulwer, 1

Macaulay, T. B., 71, 79, 101
Macdonald, Andrew, 47
McKean, Thomas, 120
McKillop, A. D., 32-33
Mackintosh, Sir James, 75
Macmillan's Magazine, 113
Macpherson, James, 119
Macready, W. C., 112
Magazine of Magazines, 9
Mallet, David, 39
Mangin, Edward, 78
Mann, Horace, 20, 42n.
Marivaux, P. C. de, 34, 54, 65
Marryat, Frederick, 83, 101, 125
Martineau, Harriet, 106
Masson, David, 109
Mathias, T. J., 61
Maturin, Charles, 78
Maugham, W. S., 138, 148
Maynadier, G. H., 137-138
Medwin, Thomas, 87
Melville, Herman, 128-129
Melville, Lewis, 142
Meredith, George, 108, 111, 112
Merimee, P., 139
Mill, J. S., 97, 112n.
Millar, Andrew, 19
Mills, Abraham, 108
Minto, William, 114
Mirror, The, 51n.
Mitford, M. R., 77
Moliere, 92, 111, 125